T0368273

History of the Muslims of Regina, Saskatchewan, and Their Organizations

Islamic Association of Saskatchewan
Canadian Council of Muslim Women
Muslims for Peace & Justice

"A Cultural Integration"

Naiyer Habib & Mahlaqa Naushaba Habib

Order this book online at www.trafford.com
or email orders@trafford.com

Most Trafford titles are also available at major online book retailers.

Print information available on the last page.

ISBN: 978-1-4907-5201-3 (sc)
ISBN: 978-1-4907-5203-7 (hc)
ISBN: 978-1-4907-5202-0 (e)

Library of Congress Control Number: 2015900981

Trafford rev. 02/17/2017

North America & international
toll-free: 1 888 232 4444 (USA & Canada)
fax: 812 355 4082

OUR FLAG

Contents

Foreword

On July 28, 2014, an estimated four thousand Muslims gathered in Saskatoon to celebrate the Eid al-Fitr (the festival of the breaking of the fast of Ramadan) and the sense of being Muslim in Saskatchewan. Other gatherings of Muslims met for Eid in Regina, Moose Jaw, Swift Current, and Prince Albert. Despite this robust presence of Muslims in the province, there has been no sustained study by academics and little data available to enable understanding and analysis. Indeed, much of the work on Canadian Muslims or on Islam in Canada passes over western Canada with an assumption that Islam is constructed elsewhere. Even recent studies of the television program *Little Mosque on the Prairie* have more concern with its role in the representation of Islam in Canada than in its reflection of the concerns of Muslims in Mercy, Saskatchewan. Thus, we are left with little understanding of the history, composition, and structure of this important community of Muslims. Does the prairie environment matter in the history and experience of its Muslims? Does the early presence in Swift Current of Lebanese Muslim farmers pattern subsequent expressions of Islam? Is the ethnic mosaic of the Saskatchewan ummah different than that in Ontario, Alberta, or British Columbia? What are the achievements and complexities of realizing Islam in the physical, cultural, and religious environment of Saskatchewan?

Given this gap in data and analysis, it is a pleasure to welcome the publication of this important collection of essays, *The History of the Muslims of Regina, Saskatchewan, and Their Organizations.* The book is written by Dr. Naiyer Habib and Mahlaqa Naushaba Habib, pioneers of the community, and features the research and reflections of members of the Regina community of Muslims. While containing a history and general demographic of Saskatchewan, the book focuses its attention on providing data on three major Islamic associations in Regina: the Islamic Association of Saskatchewan, the Canadian Council of Muslim Women, and Muslims for Peace

& Justice. The assembly of data and live analysis is a welcome source for our reading of the history and structure of Islam in Saskatchewan, especially questions of gendered space, leadership, and political action, and it contains data that will advance our further understanding of the realization of Islam both regionally and nationally.

Derryl N. MacLean, Ph.D,
Associate Professor
Department of History, Simon Fraser University
September 3, 2014

Acknowledgments

I would like to thank my wife, who is also the co-author of this book for asking me to write this book with the objective as noted in the introduction.

I express my sincere thanks to all members of the Muslim community and people of other faiths or no faith, for their love and respect to us, and for allowing us to serve the community. I am grateful to the late Dr. M. Anwarul Haque, who provided the important content of the book. This is the history of the early Muslims and he gave me the documents of registration of the Islamic Association of Saskatchewan, which he established along with other founding members of the association listed in the book. I greatly miss him in my life. My individual thanks to Riazuddin Ahmed, Abdul Qayyum, Mohammad Afsar, Zia Afsar for their consultation and for confirming information included in the book; also Akram Din for various suggestions in this write-up.

I acknowledge and appreciate all the help from Akram Din when he was on the board of the association. He forced me, in a way, to join the Islamic Association of Saskatchewan, Regina in 1977. He also participated and encouraged me to bring the association to a recognizable level in the community at large. It was a pleasure working with Abdul Jalil in the last years of my presidency. His cooperation and enlightening thoughts were of great help.

We offer our great appreciation to the following news media and publications for allowing us to print the various important information without which the book would have been incomplete:

- Canadian Broadcasting Corporation for the news, interviews, and pictures. It was with the help of Darren Yearsley of CBC who made it possible.
- *Briarpatch Magazine* for the article, *When Cultures Differ.*

- *Leader-Post* of Regina, Marion Marshall, Managing Editor for allowing me to publish many letters, articles, and news items in this newspaper.
- The *Toronto Star,* TorStar Syndication Services, Joane MacDonald for the write-up, *Nod to Ramadan.*
- *Prairie Messenger* for the article, *Muslims Reach Out to Larger Community,* by Frank Flegel, who interviewed me.
- Access Communication Co-operative Ltd, Katherine Wilson and Tami Mitchell, for allowing me to publish important aspects of *Muslims in Focus* with pictures. It includes all pictures and inserts for the conferences of 2002, 2003, and 2004 of Muslims for Peace & Justice.
- Global TV formerly CKCK, STV, Lyndon Bray, Marketing Manager and Cynthia Waite, Executive Assistant for allowing me to publish the news, interviews, and pictures.
- We are grateful to Alia Hogben, Executive Director of Canadian Council of Muslim Women for allowing me to publish information related to this national organization.
- I would like to express my thanks to Homa Hoodfar and Sajida Sultana Alvi for allowing us to include the write-ups of Mahlaqa Naushaba Habib and Zia Afsar from their book, *Muslim Veil in North America (Issues and Debates).*
- I would like to thank Riazuddin Ahmed, Kashif Ahmed, to Mohammad Afsar, and Zia Afsar for their permission to include their write-up in our book and Ahmed Aboudheir for the content on him.

We thank M. Tassaddukh Ali for our photograph on the back cover of the book.

We are grateful to Lisa Kenney of Eagle Eye Editing, and Shabnam Siddiqui for reproofing the book and being part of the editing team toward its final completion.

We highly appreciate the suggestions of Adnan Naiyer Habib and Norlela Aziz for the improvement in the publication of this book.

Very importantly, we express our thanks and gratitude to Dr. Derryl MacLean, Ph.D. (McGill), Professor at Simon Fraser University, Department of History (Middle East, Africa, and Asia) with research interests in South Asia, Central Asia, and Middle East, for obliging us by writing the Foreword for the book.

Introduction

Islamic Association of Saskatchewan: History 1903 to 1998

We migrated to Canada in 1973 to make Canada our home. It was during the Trudeau era when we were welcomed. There were no resources in English available about Islam or Muslim culture. Now, a click on the Internet brings voluminous literature on Islam and no doubt also on anti-Islam. It is respectable to note that many other faiths, in particular Christians, respond to anti-Islamic slur defensively and scholarly.

During this period in world history, there were two world super powers, which created some balance in world politics. International status was balanced. We passed through this memorable period. We were a component of that, and that of today. We felt that we should pen down facts showing what we went through to leave it for future generations to ponder over.

This book reflects the efforts of an immigrant family and of immigrant families along with members of the community of similar views and thinking to maintain our culture and religion, while integrating with society at large. This was a two-way-street of accommodation and respect.

We did not want our generation to be lost in the wilderness of confusion. Today our children are just, non-biased, non-discriminatory, and non-racial with respect for all. Our grandchildren now are also walking on that path.

Most of us had come from a background where we were surrounded by large Muslim communities. We saw how Muslims were striving to make their ends meet. Some amalgamated themselves into Western culture, and some isolated themselves from the society that was so different to them.

An example of extreme amalgamation was that of a Muslim family who was invited by us on Eid day and brought a bottle of wine (prohibited in Islam) for us as an Eid gift. It was in 1968 or 1969 in the city of Orlando, Florida. We were the only two Muslim families and one Hindu family in the entire city of Orlando, a beautiful city with orange blossoms. It has changed entirely today. Isolation from or amalgamation into the Western society was not an option. The Westerners were never compelling us to do so. Rather, they were very helpful.

A respected lady who was no less than a mother to us, learned that we ate Halal (slaughtered according to the Muslim law) meat and that we were not eating any meat, but only fish and vegetables. She, on her own, went to a farm to bring chicken for us. Not only that, she took leave from work to look after my wife, who was pregnant, and also when our son, who was only four weeks old, got sick. She attended to them at their bedside in the hospital, and at home. Thus, these are the examples that we always remember.

Depending on the priority chosen by individuals or families, they were either ruined or they flourished, based on criteria that they felt to be successful. We adopted the path of integration while maintaining our religious priorities and culture based on Islam. We were flexible and accommodative. We mingled with the society at large and provided them opportunities to mingle with us. We and the Westerners had mutual respect for each other.

This was an effort to understand one another. Our community in Regina with people like us, whatever we were, is a living example of our efforts that we longed for. These efforts are reflected in this book.

Population started to grow. The newly arriving immigrants became participants in decision-making. Initially, it looked acceptable to us. With time and increase in their number, the demand of Islamization on their criteria and not ours started to increase with drastic changes in the lives of the Muslims and their community. We, the pioneers of the 1960s and 1970s, not coping with the change by the larger number of such view keepers, were either gradually eliminated or left in active participation. Things started to change and the Westerners started to look at Muslims from different angles.

We are not hesitant to indicate that during our leadership from 1977 onward with our limited resources, we covered all aspects of our community life at various levels, be it religious, political (local, provincial, national, international), media and social from the beginning. These are reflected in this book according to dates. It is now, since 9/11, that a majority of the Muslim leaderships and communities have embarked on those projects. Our invitation to them at the time of the First Gulf War fell on deaf ears. Things might have been different for Muslims in this MOSAIC of our country. This book is our effort to present important points for reflection that a casual reader or glancer may miss.

God bless us all in our new home and bless our new home Canada.

The quality of some images is not high, as they were extracted from old video recordings and were optimized. They were inserted because of their historic importance.

Most individuals in the picture on the book cover can be identified in pictures with their names in the interior of the book at various places.

About the Authors

Mrs. Mahlaqa Naushaba Habib & Dr. Naiyer |Habib
Contributors to Canada and the Muslim Community

Family

Dr. Naiyer Habib was born in India during the Partition of India and Pakistan. The majority of the maternal side of the family had to move to Pakistan as refugees while his father's side of the family stayed in India in the district of Purnea, Bihar. Dr. Habib was married to his cousin, Mahlaqa Naushaba (Khanam).

Mrs. Habib has an MA in Political Science from the University of Karachi. Her father, Dr. Fazl ur Rahman Khan was a medical doctor. Mrs. Habib was born in India, but her family moved as refugees to Pakistan at the Partition of India.

Now they have two sons, one a lawyer in Abbotsford, British Columbia, Canada and the other one, a medical doctor practicing as a kidney specialist in Salt Lake City, Utah, USA.

EDUCATION AND PROFESSIONAL CAREER

India

Dr. Habib was educated by his mother, Madina Khanam while living in a rural area up to fifth grade. Subsequently, he completed middle school in Kanharia Middle School and high school in Zila School, Purnea. He completed intermediate science at Aligarh Muslim University in India. He completed his Bachelor of Medicine and Bachelor of Surgery degrees from the Prince of Wales Medical College, Patna, and Doctorate in Medicine, Patna University, Bihar India.

Mrs. Habib completed her Master of Political Science at the University of Karachi, Sindh, Pakistan. She had a hard life from childhood after the passing away of her father during that time.

United States

They came to the United States for higher learning in 1967. Dr. Habib received his training and education in internal medicine and cardiology, completing his residency and fellowship at Watts Hospital, Duke University, Durham, North Carolina; Orange Memorial Hospital, University of South Florida, Orlando; and in Mount Carmel Hospital, Ohio State University, Columbus. He was Chief Resident at Orange Memorial Hospital. He earned respect and received awards in these institutions during his training period.

Mrs. Habib looked after the family.

Immigration to Canada

They decided to return to their native countries. Unfortunately because of communal and political problems as a result of the Partition of India, they felt very disappointed and left their native countries with sadness. They came to Canada on July 14, 1973.

They were in Saskatoon from 1973 to 1976. Then they moved to Regina because of Dr. Habib's appointment by the University of Saskatchewan to be stationed at the Plains Health Centre.

Mrs. Habib taught Islam to children on Sundays in Saskatoon.

Pioneering Cardiology in Regina

Dr. Habib was appointed by the University of Saskatchewan on August 14, 1976 as Assistant Professor at the Plains Health Centre, Regina to initiate and establish a cardiology program for southern Saskatchewan. He started the cardiology program from scratch, which became Interventional Cardiology at the Plains Health Centre. He headed Cardiology from 1976 to 2001.

As head of the section of Cardiology, Dr. Habib was an active member on numerous committees designed to improve quality and utilization of services. He was elected and served as the president of the medical staff.

He was in the media on various issues in the health care system and did not hesitate in criticizing the system, including the government, with facts and offering advice to improve health care and defend patient's rights as well as the rights of physicians.

Academic Career

Dr. Habib was Clinical Professor of Cardiology at the University of Saskatchewan and actively involved himself in teaching and ensuring evidence-based practice. Dr. Habib was a member of numerous local, provincial, national, and international medical associations. He is a Fellow of the Royal College of Physicians and Surgeons of Canada, the American College of Cardiology, the American College of Physicians, and College of Chest Physicians. He is a member of the Canadian Medical Association, British Columbia Medical Association, and Canadian Cardiovascular Society. He was a member of the Canadian Association of Interventional Cardiology, Canadian Medical Protective Association, American Heart Association, Saskatchewan Heart Foundation, and Saskatchewan Medical Association.

Dr. Habib was a founder and past-president of the Regina Cardiac Society, serving on committees of the Saskatchewan Medical Association, Saskatchewan Heart Foundation, and College of Physicians and Surgeons of Saskatchewan.

Dr. Habib was involved in numerous research trials. His studies earned the reputation for being quite productive. He has considerable experience in research methods. In addition to his many clinical and administrative duties, Dr. Habib remained an active contributor to the scientific literature having published in peer reviewed journals.

He lectured as guest speaker on various topics regarding cardiology over the years. He organized and chaired many continuing medical education conferences and seminars in Saskatchewan.

Mrs. Habib managed his practice all along with additional nursing and clerical staff. She was his right hand in his medical research administrative work and in other work of his academic career, while raising the family.

Recognition of Service

Dr. Habib served as head of Cardiology from 1976 to 2001 when he stepped down, considering the bureaucracy that had entered the medical system. He continued his practice of cardiology as an interventional cardiologist with continued academic involvement. Since stepping down as head of Cardiology and subsequently leaving Regina, he has led a semi-retired life near his son in Abbotsford. The head of the Department of Medicine, Dr. James D. McHattie, wrote to Dr. Habib, "The Region and the Province owe you a tremendous debt of gratitude for your service and your leadership. Your dedication has been one of the single most important reasons for the quality of the services that are being provided." Similar feelings were expressed by the administrative heads of the Regina Health District and media.

He was appointed as Assistant Professor of Medicine - Cardiology on tenured position by the University of Saskatchewan in 1976 and progressed to the status of Clinical Professor of Cardiology till his retirement in 2014. Dr. Habib's academic, administrative, and overall talent was recognized by the then Head of Medicine, Dr. Marvin Balla of the University of Saskatchewan who wrote to him, "The Department of Medicine wishes to acknowledge and express its most sincere gratitude to you for your commitment and dedication to development of excellence within the Department of Medicine, particularly as related to teaching and patient care at the Plains Health Centre in Regina. The Department of Medicine recognizes your major accomplishments in establishing an excellent cardiology facility and service at the Plains Health Centre in Regina." Similarly, Dr. Gerald Sinclair, Head of the Department of Medicine at the Plains Health Centre, affiliated with the University of Saskatchewan, recognized his services. He was praised as a pioneer of cardiology for southern Saskatchewan by the cardiology staff of the Regina General Hospital and by the Regina Cardiac Society during his departure in October 2004 from Regina.

In answer to the question, why he did not receive the Order of Saskatchewan award for such services and achievements whereas others far inferior to him did? Habib smilingly answered, "He is happy to do what he could, for which people loved and respected him. Someone neither thought of me nor did I initiate it myself which many do!"

He was very much respected by his patients and medical staff. The cardiology medical staff along with others of Regina Health District of Southern Saskatchewan gave him an overwhelming and emotional farewell in October 2004, which he considered to be very memorable.

He practiced cardiology as a semi-retired physician in Abbotsford, Surrey and Hope, British Columbia, Canada, retiring completely in December 2011.

From CHSRF RESEARCH APPLICATION, L. Pointe, Assistant Researcher, Regina Health District. Updated by Naiyer Habib.

COMMUNITY SERVICE

Dr. Habib and Mrs. Habib have been serving the Muslim Community since soon after their arrival to Canada, dating back to 1975. They have continued to do so till this day. Their service was recognized in the farewell given to them by the Regina Muslim Community and Muslims for Peace & Justice in October 2004.

The Islamic Association of Saskatchewan, led by the then president, Dr. Ahmed Aboudheir, recognized Dr. Habib for 27 years of community service in Regina as a pioneer, cofounder and president of the Islamic Association of Saskatchewan, Regina. The Canadian Islamic Congress recognized Dr. and Mrs. Habib with an award for lifelong service to the Muslim community, in the year 2005. Dr. Habib was recognized by Dr. Ayman Aboguddah, President and founder of the Huda School of Regina, as a supporter of the Huda School, which started after Dr. Habib's term of office in the Muslim community.

Saskatoon

In 1975–1976, Dr. Habib was the vice-president of the Islamic Association of Saskatchewan, Saskatoon. Mrs. Habib taught and took over the charge of Sunday Islamic School there when the first teacher departed for his home country.

Regina

Mrs. Habib and Dr. Habib initiated once a week evening Islamic School at their residence in Regina. Mrs. Habib taught and managed the school at their residence for eight years from 1976 to 1984 at 308 Habkirk Drive until it was moved to a building that had been acquired by the Association, located at 240 College Avenue, naming it Islamic Centre and Mosque.

When in Regina, Dr. Habib was elected as president of the Islamic Association of Saskatchewan, Regina in 1977. He served as president for several terms: 1977–1981, 1984–1986, 1989–1992, and 1996–1998.

Mrs. Habib served as a director on the board of the Islamic Association of Saskatchewan, Regina.

During his term of presidency and serving the community, Dr. Habib never gave priority to his family need over the community need without neglecting either of them. He kept emphasizing during his leadership to others to do the same. He believed that the family unit, including children, must be involved in community work and community leadership. He used to escort children from the playground to attend Islamic lectures and functions. During his term, he initiated and maintained various programs for the Muslim community including a youth program and initiation of Friday Prayer for the community in 1977 when he became the president. He defended Islam and Muslims in the media, as well as politically. He was quoted in *Maclean's Magazine* and *Time*. He appeared on local TV stations and in local newspapers numerous times. He was instrumental in initiating a local TV program on Islam. He was deeply involved with Interfaith, along with Riazuddin Ahmed, the latter initiating the program. He was invited to be a guest speaker on Islamic topics by various organizations.

He regularly attended meetings of the Council of Muslim Communities of Canada, when that organization was active, representing the Islamic Association of Saskatchewan, Regina. He sent two youth representatives to Toronto to attend the first National Conference on Youth. There were 3 youths for two positions: Adnan Habib, Andaleeb Qayyum, and Samiul Haque. He could only choose two, and it was decided according to alphabetical order, which meant that his son was to be first. He changed the selection to date of birth to avoid any conflict of interest. So Andaleeb Qayyum and Samiul Haque were selected. Samiul Haque went for Haj with his parents. So Andaleeb Qayyum and Adnan Habib were sent. This led to the organization of the first youth camp in 1985 for boys and girls at Camp Monihan in the Regina area - for Regina, Saskatoon, Swift Current and Winnipeg under the supervision of parents and arranged by Regina youths, Andaleeb Qayyum, Adnan Habib, Adnan Qayyum, Shahla Qayyum, Saba Qayyum, Samiul Haque, Sabreena Haque, Munirul Haque, Usra Siddiqui, Arsalan Habib, Natasha Malik, and Ziad Malik.

Gulf War 1991 and Bosnian Crisis

During the first Iraq war and Bosnian crisis, Dr. Habib, along with Riazuddin Ahmed, played a critical and active role on behalf of the Islamic Association of Saskatchewan. There were multiple rallies and news media interviews. During the 1991 Iraq War, realizing what was happening to Muslims, Dr. Habib communicated with all major Muslim organizations across the United States and Canada to form a Muslim confederation. Unfortunately, no organization responded to his call. He addressed the Muslim community of a Richmond, British Columbia Masjid in a Friday Prayer, asking them to unite together and attempt to form a Muslim confederation. He continues to remind major Muslim organizations in Canada to unite on one platform to take a stand on Muslim issues together, if they cannot form one national organization, which is the need. Riazuddin Ahmed was instrumental in initiating the Interfaith-Intergroup Peace Committee during this crisis. The Interfaith-Intergroup in Regina played a critical role during the Gulf War. The group has remained active in Regina, and is now called the Regina Multi-Faith Forum.

Muslims for Peace & Justice (MPJ)

In the year 2001, while not in the leadership of the Muslim community in Regina, Dr. Habib met with Dr. Ejaz Ahmed, and Dr. Abdul Jaleel the day after the 9/11 crisis. This led to the formation of Muslims for Peace & Justice, initially coordinated by Dr. Ejaz Ahmed. Dr. Habib was elected first president of the Muslims for Peace & Justice in 2002 and served till the year 2004 when he departed for British Columbia. MPJ acquired its constitution and was to be incorporated by the elected board for 2005 in the province of Saskatchewan. This organization is the active advocacy group on behalf of Muslims in Saskatchewan.

Mrs. Habib was trustee and was always with her husband advising and working without fail.

Canadian Islamic Congress

Dr. Habib is a life member of the Canadian Islamic Congress, serving as a director on the national board, after serving as a regional director in Regina. He remained active in British Columbia on behalf of the Canadian Islamic Congress till March, 2011, working with local supporters to establish this organization in British Columbia. He held multiple conferences on relevant topics related to Islam and Muslims, and was instrumental in initiating Islamic History Month in British Columbia with the central organization. It was the idea of the past president and founding president of the Canadian Islamic Congress, Dr. Mohamed Elmasry. Since the resignation of Dr. Habib, the Canadian Islamic Congress, which had flourished during his tenure, no longer exists in B.C. The Islamic History Month is still observed by some local organizations in the province.

Canadian Council of Muslim Women (CCMW)

Mrs. Habib, while in Regina, was visited by Dr. Lila Fahlman, the founder of Canadian Council of Muslim Women, in fall of 1981. This led to the formation of a core group of ladies in Regina, leading to the formation of a chapter of the Canadian Council of Muslim Women. Mrs. Habib was the founding president. She served as president of the Canadian Council of Muslim Women for several terms. She, along with others, primarily led by Sister Zia Afsar, took a leading role in the support of women in Bosnia during the Bosnian massacre. She represented the Canadian Council of Muslim Women, Regina, at various women's organizations in Regina, and nationally at the council.

During her last term in office, she initiated a scholarship for Muslim girls at the University of Regina in 2004. Mrs. Samina Ahmed filled the vacancy.

Mrs. Habib remained active in community work with her husband, Dr. Habib.

Knowing his wife, Dr. Habib has formed an opinion that the majority of women are more mature, considerate and tolerant than their husbands.

Muslims of Swift Current (Saskatchewan)

In the late 1980s, while in Regina, Dr. Habib learned about a large Muslim community in Swift Current, primarily of Lebanese origin. They were in the third or fourth generation. There were mixed marriages, and the children and young people had moved away from Islam. A previous attempt by Dr. M. Anwarul

Haque some years before to establish an Islamic environment had failed. Dr. Habib made a trip to Swift Current with Abdul Qayyum (serving as past-president of the Islamic Association of Saskatchewan, Regina), Mohammed Sadeque, and Zubair Akhtar (active devoted members of the Muslim Community of Regina). They met at the residence of Abdullah Gader with Dr. Bhaba, a Christian from Lebanon who had invited senior Abdul Zaineadin and a couple of other Muslims. A subsequent Muslim community gathering was held in a community hall where Dr. Habib arranged for Salim Ganem, the brother of Sister Lila Fahlman and active member of the then Council of Muslim Communities of Canada and the Vice-President, David Russell, of the Council of Muslim Communities of Canada. Dr. Zahir Alvi, a longtime server of the Muslim community in Saskatoon, also joined. Dr. Alvi had also served as president of the Islamic Association of Saskatchewan, Saskatoon. This led to the formation of a Muslim community group in Swift Current. Mohammed Afsar meanwhile had moved from Hamilton, Ontario. He was a very active member of the Muslim community there. He showed the guidance needed and got involved with the Muslim community of Swift Current where there now exists an Islamic Centre.

Interfaith

Riazuddin Ahmed was a founding member of the Interfaith-Intergroup Peace Committee in Regina. He initiated this group.

Dr. Habib believes all religions should be respected. He says the followers of all religions may preach their religion without any comment on religions of others because they do not know about the religion of others. If asked what is the view of your religion about another religion, it should be responded to politely if known, otherwise not. He believes that adverse or biased comments about other religions without proper knowledge is the main cause of conflicts that prevail in the world all over.

Epilogue

Dr. Habib's view is to support women in Islam and keep their status as it used to be at the time of the Prophet. He believes that we should part away from belonging to different sects and groups and go back to Islam to the time of the Prophet. He strongly feels that the Muslim community is a part of the Canadian Mosaic, maintaining Islamic identity while integrating with society at large.

He states that Canada is best because of the contribution of all Canadians. He is very much disturbed to see how Muslims, belonging to a nation of high morality and character, mostly devoid of the ills of society at large, such as alcoholism, rape, gambling, teenage or unwanted pregnancy, divorce, etc. are viewed and treated in Canada and elsewhere. He remains apprehensive that some of these elements are infiltrating the Muslim society.

He salutes the people and members of other faiths for defending Muslims and Islam in these regions. The Muslim youth, boys and girls, are facing increasing pressure of discrimination despite efforts to avoid it. The youth ought to pray and make an effort to see Canada as a country that is expected to be for all, irrespective of color, race or religion. They should ask others to get involved and be active in this. If difficulty is faced, we should pray to God to make it easier. He will. This was the advice from a Muslim to an audience. (Akram Din).

Akram Din
Former secretary, Islamic Association of Saskatchewan, Regina

Our Province and Cities

(Muslim Connection)

A brief account of Saskatchewan and its cities - Regina, Saskatoon, Swift Current, and Davidson - are given because these locations are connected to the Islamic Association of Saskatchewan, Regina. Details are available on the Internet.

Saskatchewan

Saskatchewan is a western province of Canada. It is bordered on the west by the province of Alberta, on the north by the Northwest Territories, on the east by the province of Manitoba, and on the south by the United States—Montana and North Dakota.

Its total area is 681,900 square kilometers, with a land area of 592,534 square kilometers, and water area of 59,366 square kilometers.

Its name was derived from the Saskatchewan River, named by the Cree, meaning swift flowing river. Its main economy is based on agriculture (wheat, canola) and mining such as uranium and potash. It has energy resources of crude oil and electricity.

This province has more sunshine than any other province of Canada. It has very cold winters with heavy snow, but bright sunshine. The temperature may drop to –40°C at times. Summer temperatures may be up to 37°C. It is the second province in Canada for tornados. It also gets flooded because of the melting of the large amount of snow that collects in the winter. Winter may last up to six months.

Its population in 1930, when the first association was formed, was 921,785 (Wikipedia) and when the Islamic Association of Saskatchewan, Regina was formed (in the year 1970–1971), its population was 926,242. When we are closing our history in 1998, the population was 976,615, and in 2011, it was 1,053,960. It is the first time that it exceeded a million in population. According to the 2001 census, Muslims were 2230 out of the total Saskatchewan population of 978,935 in that year.

Regina is the capital city of Saskatchewan and Saskatoon is regarded as an academic centre.

Regina

Downtown Regina in winter

Regina is the southernmost city of Saskatchewan. It is the capital of Saskatchewan. It was named Regina in 1882 after Queen Victoria Regina. It was designated the capital of Saskatchewan in 1906. The city has its own richness and history. These can be found on the Internet.

This is also the Centre of the Islamic Association of Saskatchewan, Regina. In 1883, the population of the city of Regina was 1000, and buildings were 400 in number. It had a population

3

of 53,209 in 1931 when the first association under A. K. Haymore was founded. It swelled to 139,469 when the Islamic Association of Saskatchewan, Regina was founded in 1970–1971. In 1996, nearest to the conclusion of this history in 1998, it had a population of 80,404. For interest, and from available data on *Wikipedia,* and according to the 2006 census, the total population was 179,246. Out of this, Islam, Hinduism, Buddhism and Judaism were 2.9 percent.

Saskatoon

Saskatoon is in the northern part of the province. It is about 256 kilometers from Regina going north on Highway 11. It has a land area that has extended from 148.34 square kilometers in 2001 to 209.56 square kilometers in 2011. Its population of 1931 grew from 43,291, to 126,449 in 1971. Its population in 1996 was 193,653. Out of the population of 190,120, according to the census of 2001, Judaism, Sikh, and Islam composed 0.6 percent. This city's richness, heritage, culture, and resources are detailed on the Internet.

Swift Current

Swift Current is situated in the southwest of Saskatchewan along the Trans Canada Highway. It was established in 1883 and was incorporated as a town in 1907, from village status. According to statistics, the 2001 population was 14,821. It has a land area of 24.03 square kilometers. The history and resources can be found on the Internet.

Davidson

Davidson is located in the south central part of Saskatchewan, between Regina and Saskatoon on Highway 11. It was originally named Midway Town because of its central location between Saskatoon and Regina, and declared a town on November 15, 1906. The heritage, resources, and other information are available on the Internet.

Dr. Al-Katib was a founding member of the Islamic Association of Saskatchewan, Regina in 1970–1971. He was a resident of Davidson and his wife was a mayor of Davidson.

Early Muslims of Regina

Dr. M. Anwarul Haque
Edited by Dr. Naiyer Habib
Addendum Dana Turgeon*
*Dana Turgeon—Historical Information and
Preservation Supervisor, Office of the City Clerk

Mohammad Ta Haynee was the first Muslim in Regina. His name was Muhammad Ali Ta Haynee according to Dr. Haque's information. According to his granddaughter's husband, Rod McDonald, it was Mamouth Ali T'Haynee. In the archive of the City of Regina provided by Dana Turgeon, his name was listed as Michael Alley Haynee. He was having trouble with his name when he came to Regina. He changed his last name to just Haynee before the 1905 census according to Dr. Haque. In conclusion, his name is Mohammad Ali Ta Haynee.

He was a captain in the army of the Ottoman Empire (see Al-Katib) in 1885. He was injured three times and two of his horses were killed while he was in the army.

To Dr. Haque's knowledge, the first Muslim to come to Regina was Mohammad Ali Ta Haynee (See addendum by Dr. Al-Katib). He came to North Dakota in 1889 from Lebanon. From North Dakota, he moved to Regina in 1903.

He established Alley's Fancy Wholesale and Retail Dry Goods firm, from which he supplied pushcart peddlers working throughout southern Saskatchewan (Dana Turgeon) at the corner of Winnipeg Street and 12th Avenue (Rod McDonald). It was almost like a department store of today (Haque).

Proficient in several languages, Mr. Haynee acted as an interpreter for immigrants coming to the city, as well as for the North West Mounted Police (Dana Turgeon).

Addendum from Dr. Al-Katib of Davidson, Saskatchewan about Mohammad Ta Haynee in the opening ceremony of ICM, Montague Street:

"I wanted to mention further information about Mr. Mohammad Ta Haynee, the first Muslim in Regina. Actually for Regina, we should be very proud to have a person like him to be the first Muslim in Regina. I have had the pleasure to meet him. I talked to him, being partly of Turkish origin. I would like to share with you some information that will please you. In 1885, he was a captain in the Ottoman Army. He was wounded in his right knee. He was a Mujahid. Now to have a Mujahid in Regina to meet to little people like us from the war of 1895 when Turks in the Ottomans were defending the foundation of Islam in Europe meant to us something. Furthermore, after he was wounded, I have seen documentary evidence that Mohammad Ta Haynee became a Yawer. A Yawer means special camp—the persons of which walk with some followers. A Turkish field marshal, Ghazi Osman Pasha was an interesting military personality in Turkish history. Now to have a follower like Mohammad Ta Haynee as his Yawer is a further blessing for us in Regina. I would like to mention about Ghazi Osman Pasha. Ghazi Osman Pasha was a colonel in the Turkish Army in the 1876 war. The Russian Army was attacking the Balkans. Ghazi Osman Pasha was able to hold half a million Russian soldiers for six months in a town in Yugoslavia called Plevna. At the end, they did not surrender and they had to give him an honorable retreat. Anyhow, I thought I should share this view with you and I thought that you would be interested in the historical fact of Mohammad Ta Haynee. The other thing I wanted to say briefly that...a note was just sent to tell me to get moving, but I am going to say my words...I think I deserve it. I am a founding member.

"When I was here, you know, I do not think any of you were here. I would like to share with you my thinking what made us people involved in the organization. In my case, I will share two verses from the Qur'an. One of them was 'Fee bidaai sineena lillahi alamru min qablu wamin baAAdu wayawmaithin yafrahu almuminoona' (30:4). It means 'To God belongs the command before and after and that day the believers shall rejoice with the help of God,' and I thought that as a Muslim, it is my duty to help form an Islamic association. The other thing, I was moved by a small sentence, which I would like to share with you, 'Waman yabtaghi ghayra alislami deenan falan yuqbala minhu wahuwa fee alakhirati mina alkhasireena' (Whoever seeks a religion other than Islam, on the Day of Judgment, it will not be accepted from him and he will be one of the losers)' (3:85). These two sentences from the Qur'an made me a founding member of the Islamic Association and I am very, very proud to be here with you to share this blessing, which only can come from God. God is Great. Allahu Akbar."

Dr. Haque continues...

He was born in the Middle East in August, 1864. Shortly after him, his friend Saeed Ganem moved to Regina in 1903. When he came to Regina, he was unmarried. So he returned to Lebanon in 1911 and married Irene Ganem (vs Rebecca Gangon—as per McDonald), the sister of Saeed Ganem. She was born in Lebanon in October 1892. Mr. Haynee was married at the age of 47 and had 17 children—10 girls and 7 boys. One of his sons, Zack Haynee was one of our founding members of this association. Mohammad Ali Haynee (Ta Haynee) died on May 26, 1982. At the time of his death, he was108 years old, probably the oldest man in Regina or possibly in the province of Saskatchewan. His wife Irene Haynee died on September 05, 1982. She was 90 years of age then.

As he was a pioneer in opening the general store, which was probably at that time some sort of department store of today, and was the oldest man in the province, the city honored him by naming a street after him in the Glencairn area, which is the east of Regina, as Haynee Street, and declared his store as a heritage store. The government and the city were preserving the store. (It does not exist now.)

After Mr. Haynee, in 1910 Alex Guttaney and his brother Sam Guttaney moved to Regina from Cleveland Ohio. Siv Saeed and his brother Alex Saeed moved to Regina from Lebanon in 1912, and then moved to Dilke, northeast of Regina. A few other Muslims from Lebanon followed.

Frank Abdul came to Regina and opened a food store in Craven. Suleiman Kibeth, a Turkish Family came to Regina and started to work for the CPR. Then Mr. Joe Sibly Hatim and Sam Hatim and his brother Alex Hatim came to Regina and subsequently moved to Swift Current. In 1912, John Satin Sesin and Sam Satin, originally from Czechoslovakia, moved to Regina with his daughter Annie Sesin Satin and his son John Sesin Satin Jr. He came to Regina from Detroit, Michigan. In 1912, Abdul Qadir Haymore at age 16, moved to Regina with his family. He was a young man. He did a lot of odd jobs like working for the CPR and watching the store. He went to school at night, and qualified himself to be a teacher. So he was the first Muslim teacher in the public school system in Regina. He taught in several schools, not just one school. In 1901, Abdul Kadir Haymore married Annie Satin. They had a son and a daughter. The son is still living in Regina but their daughter has moved to Edmonton. (The spelling of the names of anyone here is not certain.)

Before 1911, the census was taken according to religion. So in 1911, there were 75 Muslims in Saskatchewan, almost all of them in the southern part of the province. After 1911, the census was not done according to religion, so we do not know how many Muslims were there at that time. I believe that all of them came from the Middle East because in the census of 1911, there were no Hindus in Saskatchewan, as far as I could research. Before the first world war, a few other Muslims came to Regina, like Ali Hassan, and later on moved to Swift Current.

The Muslim population coming to Regina grew bigger and most of them settled in southern Saskatchewan. As the Muslim community gradually got larger, the need for a community organization was felt. In the 1930s, the first association was formed in Regina with Abdul Qadir Haymore as the Imam (leader), and Salim Ganem, who is the son of Saeed Ganem, as the secretary. Both were educated people. Mr. Haymore was a teacher. This was the first Muslim organization in Saskatchewan and perhaps in all of Canada. Abdul Qadir Haymore was the first president of the newly formed Muslim organization. Salim Ganem then moved to Edmonton in 1941. He organized religious activities like prayers, reading of the scriptures and explaining them to the Muslims and to the non-Muslims at that time, telling them what Islam is. However, nothing was known to have been done in terms of teaching the children.

The association continued to function under the leadership of Abdul Qadir Haymore. When Brother Haymore died on July 20, 1967, the association stopped functioning. His wife Annie Haymore is still living in Regina. She is 82 years old.

After the second world war, more Muslims came from Muslim and non-Muslim countries, to Regina and Saskatoon. These were mostly physicians, teachers and students. The majority of them were from the Indian subcontinent. Because of the university setup in Saskatoon, with more students and teachers, there are more Muslims in Saskatoon than in Regina.

Most of the professional people came to the southern part of the province, and Regina.

Thank you for your attention.
Dr. M. Anwarul Haque, Founding President.

Muslim Associations of Saskatchewan

Islamic Association of Saskatchewan, Saskatoon

In September of 1970 - or in the summer of 1970, the second association was formed in Saskatoon as the Islamic Association of Saskatchewan with Dr. Ma, a Chinese-Muslim as the president. Dr. Naiyer Habib served as the vice-president of this association in 1976, and Adnan Habib of Regina, as secretary of the association in 1989.

Islamic Association of Saskatchewan, Regina (IAOSR) History from1903–1998 (The period ends as we left the association in 1998)

As the Muslim community started growing in Regina, and because of Saskatoon and Regina being far apart distance-wise, the decision to form an association in Regina was taken in late 1969 and formalized in early 1970.

At that time, there were eleven families present at the meeting to form an association. It was also decided then to have a Mosque in Regina as soon as possible. Noticing that the name of this association was almost the same as the Saskatoon association, the association of Regina was identified as the Regina Chapter. It was later incorporated as Islamic Association of Saskatchewan, Regina.

These associations were formed with the basic idea of uniting all the Muslims of Saskatchewan under one single association known as the Islamic Association of Saskatchewan with chapters in Regina, Saskatoon, and Swift Current. The central association was to have one voice in the province to deal with the governments on behalf of the Muslims of Saskatchewan and hold seminars and conferences. The local chapters were to focus on religion and local education. With this idea in mind, and on approval from the board of directors of the Islamic Association of Saskatchewan, Regina Chapter, Dr. Haque travelled to Swift Current in the summer of 1971 to make arrangements to form an association in Swift Current. At that time, the Muslims of Swift Current were not interested in forming an Islamic association because they were happy with their Arab association.

On November 7, 1970, after the Eid al-Fitr prayer in the morning at the university cafeteria in Regina, the association was formed, and it was named Islamic Association of Saskatchewan, Regina Chapter. An application was submitted to the incorporation branch for registration on December 16, 1970, and the association was incorporated on January 11, 1971. Dr. Haque was elected as the founding president with others on the board as founding executives, for the association.

Following are copies of the documents related to the establishment of the association, courtesy of Dr. M. Anwarul Haque:

PROVINCE OF SASKATCHEWAN

PROVINCE OF SASKATCHEWAN REGISTERED

JAN 11 1971

REGISTRAR OF COMPANIES

THE SOCIETIES ACT

APPLICATION FOR INCORPORATION

1. **Full names of applicants:** (Please print)

Names:	Places of Residence:	Occupations:
1. M. Anwarul Haque	129 Westfield Drive Regina, Saskatchewan	Physician
2. F. M. W. Al-Katib	Davidson, Saskatchewan	Physician
3. Mrs. Sultana J. T. Rafay	#305 - 4555 Rae Street Regina, Saskatchewan	Consultant Nutritionist
4. Mrs. Farida Sethi	#19-2 Spence Street Regina, Saskatchewan	Teacher
5. Mr. Zackary Haynee	3308 College Avenue Regina, Saskatchewan	Realtor
6. Mr. Basil Ramadan	#202-4725 Albert Street Regina, Saskatchewan	Administrative Assistant University of Sask. Regina Campus

2. **The name of the Society is:**

The Islamic Association of Saskatchewan, Regina Chapter

3. **The objects of the Society are:**

1. The Association shall carry on religious, charitable, educational, civic, social, literary, athletic, scientific and any other matter pertaining to the objectives and principles of Islam as way of life.

2. To promote co-operation and fellowship among members and similar organizations in Canada, the United States and elsewhere.

3. To contribute to better understanding between Moslems and non-Moslems through educational and cultural activities.

(2)

4. The place in Saskatchewan where the operations of the Society are to be chiefly carried on is: Regina

5. The registered office of the Society to which communications and notices may be sent and at which process may be served will be situated at:

Post Office Box 3294, Regina, Saskatchewan

6. The names of the applicants who are to be the first directors of the Society are:

President	-	Dr. M. Anwarul Haque
Vice - President		Dr. F. M. W. Al-Katib
Secretary	-	Mrs. Sultana J. T. Rafay
Treasurer	-	Mrs. Farida Sethi
Members	-	Mr. Zackary Haynee
		Mr. Basil Ramadan
		~~Mrs. Alex H. Karout~~

Dated at......Regina...............this......16th..............day of......December......, 19..70

Signatures of applicants:

M. Anwarul Haque

F. M. W. Al-Katib

Sultana Rafay

Farida Sethi

Zackary Haynee

Basil Ramadan

14

Fee: $10
No. 13471

№ 1187

Certificate

The Societies Act

Canada
Province of Saskatchewan

I Hereby Certify that

THE ISLAMIC ASSOCIATION OF SASKATCHEWAN, REGINA CHAPTER

is this day incorporated under the provisions of The Societies Act.

Given under my hand and Seal at Regina this ELEVENTH day of JANUARY one thousand nine hundred and SEVENTY-ONE

GOVERNMENT OF THE PROVINCE OF SASKATCHEWAN

CANADA

I, ················· LEO JOSEPH BEAUDRY ·························
REGISTRAR OF COMPANIES

Do Hereby Certify that

in accordance with the provisions of The Societies Act, the

Special Resolution of THE ISLAMIC ASSOCIATION OF SASKATCHEWAN,

REGINA CHAPTER passed on September 26, 1971 changing its objects

is approved and the change in objects has been registered.

Given under my hand and seal at Regina this ············ day

Management of the Association

Leadership 1931–1967:

- Abdul Qadir Haymore, first president and founder of Islamic Association in Regina (1931–1967)
- Salim Ganem, secretary (1931–1941), moved from Regina

1967–1998

The following were the presidents of IAOSR with the boards of directors. Unfortunately, names of all the directors are not available. It was found that all papers of the association disappeared from the board office sometime after 1998, when Dr. Habib gave his Charge to the President in writing of all documents with his signature, and that of the elected president. Refer to *Charge of Documents 1998* in Table of Contents.

Names with period noted in parentheses:

❖ Dr. M. Anwarul Haque, Founding President (1971–1977)

❖ Founding Board of Directors:
❖ Dr. F. M. W. Al-Katib
❖ Sutana J. T. Rafay
❖ Fareda Sethi
❖ Zackary Haynee
❖ Basil Ramadan

➢ Dr. Naiyer Habib, President (1977–1981)

➢ Members of the Board of Directors:
➢ Anwar Qureshi, Vice-President
➢ Akram Din, Secretary
➢ Riffat Hussain, Board Member
➢ Aftab Ghani, Board Member
➢ Sajjad Malik, Board Member
➢ Mrs. Anwar Sultan, Board Member

> ➤ Mehdi Zahidi, Student Representative

- Dr. M. Anwarul Haque, President (1981–1982)
- Abdul Qayyum, President (1982–1984)
- Dr. Naiyer Habib, President (1984–1986)
- Sajjad Malik, President (1986–1989)
- Nasir Butt
- Anwarul Haque
- Mahlaqa Naushaba Habib
- Hazem Raafat
- Dr. Naiyer Habib, President (1989–1992)
- Abdul Qayyum, President (1992–1994)
- Dr. Ejaz Ahmed, President (1994–1996)
- Dr. Naiyer Habib, President (1996–1998)
- Abdul Jalil
- Alam Qureshi
- Ayman Aboguddah

Others who served on the board of directors at one time or the other were: Abdul Jalil, Riazuddin Ahmed (1991), Khalilur Rahman, Alam Qureshi, Mrs. Mahlaqa Naushaba Habib, Arif Sethi, Fareda Sethi, Tahir, Zia Aftab, Abdul Halim, Mohammed Haseeb, and Razaq Moghal. The rest of the information is not available.

All the activities and programs of this association follow. One could look at the period of the board and date of institution of the program or the activities to note under which period those were instituted. The work is done by all members of the community. Also, the community continues and so do its programs. Some overlap from one period to the other such as buying a building. However, a person is recognized where he or she was primarily a founder or contributor.

Muslim Association of Swift Current

Founding

An attempt was made by Dr. Haque in 1971 to either initiate an organization in Swift Current, or join the Regina chapter. They were not interested in Swift Current. They were happy to continue with the Arab Association. Another attempt was made by the Habib group in 1979. Naiyer Habib, while the president of the IAOS, Regina, and accompanied by Abdul Qayyum, Mohammad Sadeque, and Zubair Akhtar, traveled to Swift Current. On the way, they offered Zuhr prayer by the side of the highway, led by Zubair Akhtar.

A meeting was held at Abdullah Gader's house. Lunch was served. Gader invited Dr. Bhaba, a dentist and a Christian by faith, and actively involved with the Arab and Lebanese community.

Others like Zaineadin Sr., and Hindas joined. Naiyer Habib started reciting the Qur'an and speaking of some aspects of Islam. Zaineadin Sr. interrupted him. He said, "We know this and read the Qur'an. We need to know what we should do for our children who are going away from Islam." He was emotional while saying this. It was understandable. Abdul Qayyum said that he wanted to hear what they should do for the children. We had a discussion.

Subsequently, Dr. Habib invited Dr. David Russell, the late Dr. Zahir Alvi of Saskatoon, and Br. Salim Ganem. Dr. Russell was a professor at the University of Saskatchewan and the vice-president of the Council of Muslim Communities of Canada. Salim Ganem, after residing in Regina, was in Swift Current for a period before moving to Edmonton. He came from Edmonton. Some of our family had also accompanied us. There was a community meeting in the community hall of Swift Current. It ended with ideas and suggestions to initiate an organization of Muslims. They were assured that they would be helped by the Regina and Saskatoon communities.

Meanwhile, Br. Mohammed Afsar had moved from Hamilton, Ontario, to Swift Current as engineer for the city of Swift Current.

He assumed the charge to form the Muslim Association of Swift Current. He also had experience of community service in Hamilton.

It was prayer time. The community members wanted to watch the prayer along with their Muslim friends who had not seen a Muslim prayer. It became a moment for all to think and reflect. Prayer was offered.

This led to the initiation of the Muslim Association of Swift Current. Mohammad Afsar became the president and chairman of the Muslim Association of Swift Current, formed in 1980, and looked after the affairs of this association. His story is below under *Swift Current Mosque.*

Later a centre was established. A church was purchased and renovated, and an opening ceremony was held. The communities of Regina and Saskatoon also participated. Dr. Ahmed Sakr, a well known Islamic scholar, was chief guest. Hamid Sheikh attended as a representative of the Council of Muslim Communities of Canada. A subsequent story is noted below in the words of Mohammed Afsar.

Swift Current Mosque
Mohammed Afsar

Looking back at my life's journey, I had no idea that God had a special purpose for me when (in 1980) I moved from Ontario to accept the City Engineer/Planner's job in Swift Current, Saskatchewan.

To our pleasant surprise, we discovered that a sizeable community of Muslims lived in and around Swift Current. They were second and third generation immigrants from Lebanon, who homesteaded in the area in the early 1900s.

While they held pride in being Muslims, religion was not part of their practice in daily life. However, they showed a genuine desire to revive their faith and wished to establish a Mosque. Edmonton, Alberta too had a large Muslim community, mostly of Lebanese origin. Many in Edmonton were personally known to families in Swift Current.

Acknowledging the desire and enthusiasm for a Mosque, I called a meeting in mid-1980, which was also attended by guests from Edmonton and Regina Muslim communities. Bylaws were passed to provide a structure for the "Muslim Association of Swift Current". Sam Hattum was elected as first president of the association, and I took upon the role of chairing the Mosque Committee with a challenge to raise funds to establish a Mosque.

Islamic Education for Children & Adults

Parallel to the fundraising campaign, my wife Zia Afsar began organizing an Islamic education program. The local United Church graciously made space available in their church for classes once a week. Friday congregation prayers started being held in the local library.

Mosque Opening in 1983

In addition to the local community, funds started pouring in from individual donations by Muslims in Saskatchewan, Edmonton, Lac la Biche, and from some Islamic organizations, notably Rabitatul Islami. Because of the influence of Al-Rashid Mosque in Edmonton, a sizeable donation was received from the Islamic Dawa Society based in Libya.

Shaikh Sharkawi's (Imam in Edmonton) fundraising efforts deserve a special mention here. On his visit to Mecca, he made an appeal in one of the local Mosques, namely Masjid Al-Khair, and then went door-to-door raising $10,000 for the Swift Current Mosque. For this reason, the Mosque was given the name of Masjid Al-Khair.

One hundred thousand dollars was collected, enough to purchase an unused church building in 1983. Thus, in May 1983, the Swift Current Mosque's opening ceremony was held with great pomp. Ahmed Sakr, a well-known Muslim scholar, was the guest speaker. Representatives from Muslim communities in Hamilton, Regina, Saskatoon, Edmonton, Lac la Biche, and Vancouver also attended. Included in the local dignitaries were Pat Smith, Deputy Premier of Saskatchewan and John McIntosh, Acting Mayor of the City of Swift Current. Shaikh Sharkawi conducted the religious ceremonies. Swift Current Mosque now became the focus of all Islamic activities including daily and Jumuah prayers, Islamic

Education, hosting of sister Muslim communities from Regina and Saskatoon, guest speakers and interfaith dialogue.

Later, Rabitatul Islami loaned an Imam from Lebanon, but he did not suit the community due to his culturally conservative approach.

In 1991, I moved to Regina. What a great privilege to be able to play an important role in establishing the first Mosque in southwest Saskatchewan. It continues to be a strong focal point for Muslims. The Mosque also plays an important economic role, as it provides an added attraction for new Muslim immigrants to locate in the area. (September 28, 2013).

Hameed Sheikh (CMCC) and Ahmed Sakr, guest speaker

Shaikh Sharkawi in white cap

First Islamic Centre and Mosque at 240 College Avenue, Regina

This building was previously a business building. It was bought in January 1982. The plan was initiated in 1979, when Dr. Habib was the president. We were fewer in number, and there were financial constraints.

We did not want to get money from foreign sources to avoid any influence of the foreign countries on our affairs. The cost of the building was $135,000, which we could not afford. The need was essential. Hisham Badran, an Islamic scholar and frequent invited visitor to Regina, particularly for children and youth, helped secure a grant from the Rabita office in New York. The cost was still high. Dr. Habib spoke to the board members and the community. He told them, asking forgiveness from Allah, to get the building by taking out a mortgage on a temporary basis. He emphasized the dire need for a building of their own. There would be greater benefit for the Muslim community to observe their Islamic duty—Friday Prayer, and to provide a school for children and youth. He asked to ask Allah to forgive them if there was any sin for this reason.

After heated discussion, it was approved to get the loan. The building purchase was completed while Dr. Haque was the president. He registered the building with the Corporation Branch in January of 1982. The opening was celebrated while Abdul Qayyum was the president in 1984, with Hisham Badran as the chief guest. He was told about the mortgage and reason for it. He criticized but was not harsh. He participated in the opening ceremony. A year later, the loan was paid. A person who is knowledgeable about Muslim law said recently that this was an acceptable act under the circumstances. (Source not available).

First Islamic Centre and Mosque at 240 College Avenue: Opening Ceremony in 1982

Effort Started in 1977 by the Community

Opening with Qur'an recitation

Welcome by Abdul Qayyum, President

Greetings by Mohammed Afsar, Chair of Muslim Association, Swift Current

Hisham Badran (Toronto), guest speaker

Left: (3) Sadeque with daughter, Aijaz Hussain, Khatri, Riffat Hussain, Ahmad Qureshi; *Middle:* Khalid A., Adnan H., Riaz A., Majid K., Adnan Q. in check shirt, Nasir B. (only face)

Riffat Hussain (against wood wall), my mother (in sweater and white saree), Yasmin Habib (behind mother), Mariam Khatri (folded hands on knees), Ali Sethi (only face in front)

3273 Montague Street Islamic Centre and Mosque

Nasir Butt, then a member of the board, found a church building for sale. The asking price was $242,000, which was negotiated to be $204,000, plus an add-on renovation estimated to be $10,000. He worked hard to raise the funds from the community. The board approached the Canadian Islamic Trust (CIT).

Sajjad Malik was the president. Other members of the board included Dr. M. Anwarul Haque, Hazem Raafat, Naushaba Habib and Nasir Butt.

There were rigid and unacceptable conditions laid down by the CIT. There was considerable discussion by the board and members of the association. A final Agreement of Trust was reached and signed on behalf of the association. A sum of $95,000 without interest and payable to CIT was agreed. Islamic Society of North America (ISNA) issued an advertising letter for donation to the "Mosque Project of Regina" across Canada. The rest of the money was raised from the community. A donation came from Winnipeg. Two members of the community donated $20,000 each.

Finalization of the agreement was signed between the Canadian Islamic Trust Foundation and the Islamic Association of Saskatchewan, Regina, during the presidency of Naiyer Habib, and was signed by him as well as by Nasir Butt on behalf of the association, and Mohammad Ashraf of Canadian Islamic Trust. This contract included 22 points of agreement between the two organizations. This was notorized.

The Agreement of Trust and Promissory Note were placed in the file of the association. Dr. Habib handed over the original to the new president elected in 1998 with all documents, obtaining a signature from him, and Dr. Habib signed as well on all pages of the list. Refer to *Charge of Documents 1998* in the Table of Contents.

By the grace of God we now had our own Islamic Centre and Mosque. The signed and notarized document page is shown on the next page. It was signed by Naiyer Habib and Nasir Butt on behalf of IAOS and Mohammed Ashraf on behalf of CIT.

IN WITNESS WHEREOF, Trustee and Beneficiary have executed this Trust on this 1st day of November, 1989, and if this Trust is executed in counterparts, each shall be deemed an original.

THE CANADIAN ISLAMIC TRUST FOUNDATION

Per: _____

Per: _____

THE ISLAMIC ASSOCIATION OF SASKATCHEWAN, REGINA, INC.

Per: _____

Per: _____

PROVINCE OF:

COUNTY OF:

Before me a Notary Public in and for said County and Province, personally appeared __

_____

_____

who acknowledged the execution of the foregoing TRUST.

Witness my hand and Notarial Seal this 1st day of November, 1989.

My commission expires: Signature: _Roberta M. Robertson_

Oct. 31/92   Printed: _ROBERTA M. ROBERTSON_

40

ICM 3273 Montague Street, Regina
November 1989

Renovation Activities:

Nasir Butt and Sajjad Malik

Youth: unidentified, Faisal Sethi, Arsalan Habib,
unidentified, Kamran Qureshi, unidentified

Riaz Ahmed and Samina Ahmed sitting and Munirul Haque leaning

Arranging for school

Nilofer Haque and Naushaba Habib

Zarina Sardar and Aisha Catikkas

November 10, 1989—Rabiussani 11ᵗʰ 1410 Program

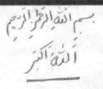

ISLAMIC ASSOCIATION OF SASKATCHEWAN
REGINA INC.

ISLAMIC CENTRE AND MOSQUE
3273 MONTAGUE ST.
REGINA, SK.   S4S 1Z8
RABI-2ND 11, 1410
NOVEMBER 10, 1989

SALATUL JUMA

12:20   ADAAN: BR. MUSTAFA BARRE
12:30   KHUTBA: BR. SAJJAD MALIK
12:45   PRAYER: IMAM: BR. SAJJAD MALIK

NOTICE

THERE WILL BE ISLAMIC BOOKS ON SALE ON:
RABI-2ND 13, 1410
NOVEMBER 12, 1989

Mustafa Elbare saying Call to Prayer, Sajjad Malik to lead the prayer

Mustafa Elbare calling Adhan, Sajjad Malik to lead prayer
Left to right: M. Jamil, Abdul Qayyum, Hazem Raafat, Jihad Rasheed,
Anwarul Haque on a chair, Riaz Ahmed praying and standing in the back

Get-together after prayer

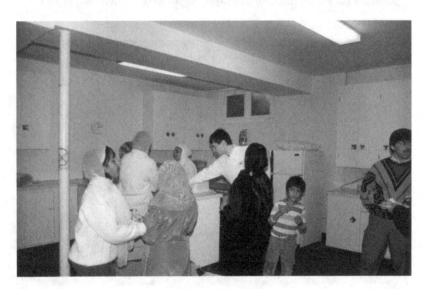

Naushaba Habib serving

Policy of Utilization of the Islamic Centre and Mosque

The established policy of utilization of the Mosque was lost along with other documents. See also Charge of Documents 1998 to the President Elect. These documents are lost as per my discussion with Dr. M. Anwarul Haque. This was officially communicated to the existing board in 2013, for the needful.

As we recollect from our memory, they were:

- all prayers
- Islamic, social, and cultural functions in keeping with Islamic tradition
- Islamic education
- marriage solemnization
- funerals

It was fully understood that women would be equal participants and interfaith groups were to be welcomed.

Opening Ceremony of the Centre at Montague Street

We clebrated the opening ceremony of the newly established centre on November 12, 1989.

A Reception Committee was formed. Guests were invited from ISNA Canada, ICNA, Council of Muslim Communities of Canada, Muslim Associations of Winnipeg, Swift Current and Islamic Association of Saskatchewan, Saskatoon.

Br. Imtiaz, Vice-President of ISNA Canada, represented ISNA, Dr. Mir Iqbal Ali, President of CMCC, sent a congratulatory letter. The president of the Muslim Association of Winnipeg also sent a donation. Br. Mohammed Afsar represented the Muslim Association of Swift Current and presented Toghra in a large frame which was hung on the wall of the Prayer Hall.

Gift of Fareda and Arif Sethi

An individual gift of Kaaba and Prophet's Mosque on a large carpet was presented by founding members of this association, Sr. Fareda Sethi and Arif Sethi. It was hung on the wall of the Prayer Hall.

Documents showing the reception committee, program, and presidential address appear below. Speeches of all are available on video recording till our survival.

Reception Committee

In the name of Allah, Most Kind, Most Merciful

Opening Ceremony of Islamic Centre and Mosque

Assigned personnel for the program

Coordinators: Naushaba Habib, Nasir Butt, and Hazem Raafat

Reception: Abdul Qayyum and Riazuddin Ahmed

Food in-charge: (Ladies) Naushaba Habib, Mustafa Bar, Saqid Ahmed, and S. Malik

Children supervision: (parents) O. Waseem, Rasekh Rifaat, and Jihad Rashid

Families from out of town wishing to stay or needing assistance are requested to contact the Reception Committee for any assistance.

In the name of Allah, Most Gracious, Most Merciful

ISLAMIC ASSOCIATION OF SASKATCHEWAN, REGINA, INC.

OPENING CEREMONY OF THE NEW ISLAMIC CENTRE/MOSQUE
3273 Montague St., Regina, Sk.

Rabie the Second 13, 1410 A.H.   November 12, 1989 A.D.

PROGRAM

12:00 Noon	Arrival
12:45 P.M.	Zuhr - Adaan: Br. Wa-el Sawan
1:00	- Iqama: Br. Wa-el Sawan
	- Imam : Br. Hazem Raafat
1:15	Pot-Luck Dinner - Community Hall
2:15	Function (Part I) - Community Hall

Chairperson: Br. Naiyer Habib
- Recitation of Qur'an : Brs. Khalid Tuwaty & Munir-Ul-Haque
- Announcement of Program: Secretary (Br. Nasir Butt)
- President's Welcome Address: Br. Naiyer Habib
- Short Address: Representatives of Visiting Communities and National Organizations
- Recognition of Founding Members of The Islamic Association of Saskatchewan, Regina Inc.
- Recognition of Past Presidents
- Recognition of Founding Members of Islamic School
- Recognition of Past Principals of Islamic school
- Recognition of Founding Members of Muslim Youth Group
- Address by Guest Speakers:
    - Role of Islamic National Organizations in North America: Br. S. Imtiaz Ahmed
    - Role of the Mosque in the Community: Br. Mostafa Abd-El-Barr

3:30 P.M.	Asr - Adaan: Br. Mohammad El-Zawie
3:40	- Iqama: Br. Mohammad El-Zawie
	- Imam : Br. Rasheek Rifaat
3:50	Function (Part II) - Community Hall

Presentation of Muslim Youth
Chairperson: Br. Ziad Malik
- Announcement of Program: Secretary (Br. Faisal Sethi)
- President's Address: Br. Ziad Malik
- Role of Muslim Youth: Br. Arsalan Habib

4:05	Presentation of Islamic School

Chairperson: Sr. Nasim Ahmed

4:50	Word of Thanks: Secretary (Br. Nasir Butt)

Dua'a and Official Ending of the Program
Snack - Community Hall

5:25	Maghrib - Adaan: Br. Jihad Rashid
	- Iqama : Br. Jihad Rashid
	- Imam : Br. Mostafa Abd-El-Barr

43

Opening Ceremony of New Islamic Centre and Mosque Program

Recitation of Qur'an: Khalid and Munirul
Chairman: Naiyer Habib
Program Coordinator: Nasir Butt
President: Naiyer Habib, Takbeer, Darood and speech

Welcome to the communities and their representatives:

1. Winnipeg
2. Swift Current
3. Saskatoon
4. Malaysia

Invitees of national organizations:

1. ISNA and Canadian Islamic Trust brother Imtiaz Ahmed, Islamic Circle of North America, Brother Aqib Muhammad. Saqib Amir of ICNA sends regrets with Salam and greeting
2. Council of Muslim Communities of Canada, letter from President, Dr. Mir Iqbal Ali

This vibrant organization has disbanded.

Council of Muslim Communities of Canada

CONSEIL DES COMMUNAUTÉS MUSULMANES DU CANADA

1521 Trinity Dr. Unit 16, Mississauga, L5T 1P6

(416) 672-1544

Dr. Nayyar Habib,
President Islamic Association of Saskatchewan, Regina.

Dear Dr. Habib,

As Salamu Alaikum wa Rahmatullah;
I was delighted to hear from you about the Islamic Association
of Saskatchewan having acquired a new place for the mosque and
Islamic Centre and the opening ceremony on Sunday the 12th of November 1989

Please accept our hearty congratulations and best wishes on this
very happy occasion from the Executive of the Council of the Muslim
Communities of Canada.

It is indeed an indication that the Muslim community in your city
is active in establishing and promoting the deen of Allah and the
Islamic culture and our great heritage from which all mankind will
benefit.

Let us pray for the unity and success of all the Muslim Ummah of our
great prophet Mohammed Rasul-Allah Sallallahu Alaihe Wasallam.

With love and regards,

Your brother,

Mir Iqbal Ali.
President.
Nov. 7, '89.

Introduction of IAOS Founding Members, Past and Present Presidents:

1. Anwarul Haque, Founding President 1971–1977
2. Founding members in attendance: A. Sethi for Fareda Sethi, F.M. Al-Katib. Absent: Basil Ramadan, Zackary Haymore, Sultana J.T. Rafay(deceased)
3. The past presidents:

   1977–1981 Dr. Naiyer Habib
   1981–1982 Dr. M. Anwarul Haque
   1982–1984 Abdul Qayyum
   1984–1986 Dr. Naiyer Habib
   1986–1989 Sajjad Malik
   1989–Now Dr. Naiyer Habib

Recognition

1. Founder of Islamic School, Mrs. Mahlaqa Naushaba Habib
2. Chairpersons of Islamic School:

   1976-1984 Mrs. M. Naushaba Habib
   1984-1986 Brother M. Jamil
   1986-Now Sister Naseem Ahmed

3. Recognition of founding youth:

   Adnan Habib
   Andaleeb Qayyum
   Samiul Haque
   Adnan Qayyum

Out of these four youths, Adnan Habib and Andaleeb Qayyum represented the Islamic Association of Saskatchewan, Regina, at the first Youth Conference arranged by the Council of Muslim Communities of Canada in Toronto.

4. Guest speakers: Imtiaz Ahmed introduced by Anwarul Haque; E. Mustafa introduced by Hazem Raafat
5. Salat-Ul-Asr
6. Presentation by youth and Islamic School

All have been videotaped and will be available for viewing. Unfortunately, the beginning of the recitation of the Qur'an that was done for the opening was missing from the video recording.

Presidential Address by Dr. Naiyer Habib

Presidential address on the occasion of the opening ceremony of the new Islamic Centre and Mosque at 3273 Montague Street, Regina, Saskatchewan, Rabi 2nd, 13, 1410 AH, November 12, 1989 AD.

Dr. Naiyer Habib

President (past and present: 1977–1981, 1984–1986, 1989–1992, 1996–1998)

In the name of Allah, Most Kind, Most Merciful.

My dear brothers and sisters in Islam and our guests, Assalam-O-Alaikum: It is my pleasure to welcome you on behalf of the Islamic Association of Saskatchewan, Regina, as a third-time (not continuously) president of the Islamic Association on this historic moment for which we are grateful to Allah (SW).

We pray for all who put their efforts in establishing Islam in this part of the province, going back to the first Muslim who came to this part of the world, whoever he or she may be, to those who are present today, that Allah accept their efforts and reward them for their deeds.

The various organizations and individuals who were supportive in one way or another for our community may be named. They are Rabita-Al-Alam, CMCC, Saudi Arabia via Rabita al Islamia (NY), Brother Hisham Badran, David Russell (Hisham Ahmed), Asad Dawud in the past. Canadaian Islamic Trust this time with the effort of brother Ashraf of Canadian Islamic Trust associated with ISNA. I offer thanks to all our past presidents with their boards, and all members of the community of the past and present for their help, and pray for them that Allah accept their efforts and award them for their good deeds.

I would like to bring the following facts that I feel important to express on this occasion:

Our leadership is important and has to evolve continuously to lead us in this part of the world. Old or ex-leaders who served us are very valuable. It is important we utilize their experience – not that as newcomers come and may put the old ones away.

Newer and younger generations must be incorporated in leadership under guidance of the most experienced ones. Remember "the present generation" who came from old countries who have strived to maintain and flourish Islamic values with their families—are our treasures having the Islamic values of old countries and how to follow Deen in this Western world—please associate with them with your family.

We have another treasure: new Muslims. They know the negativity of the society they left because of what they experienced. They came to Islam because they were convinced of its values—please love them, respect them and adore them more than our own blood relatives. They have sacrificed a lot. To the new Muslims, I have to say that your belief in Islam, your achievement of Taqwa is enough for you to be helped by Allah (SW).

Our neighbors, contacts, non-Muslim wives are our responsibility to demonstrate Islam to them by our practice—not theory—invite them to Islam with wisdom.

Our action or deed (Fail) must be in accordance with our words (Qaul), which must be representation of our Deen—Islam.

Remember two things:

1. Allah watches all the time and everywhere—with helping hands extended to us.
2. Our children, no matter how small they may be, watch us, don't they?

Parents who are casual in the practice of Islam are dual harmers:

1. Harm to their own family.
2. Harm to the society by adding children whose Islamic values will be diluted to future degenerations, leading to the extinction of Islam from them and the society they will form—(I hope and pray to Allah that this does not happen). Do we not see this happening?

By giving Islamic values to our children—from infanthood when they are like a green stick for molding, not when they are mature and become a hard stick which will break if you bend it, there will be society for all enriched with Islamic values.

It is hard or easy to practice Islam the way we want to look at it. If it is hard one can begin now with the least he or she can do—start with saying Allah, La Ilaha Illallah at bedtime with all sincerity. Ask Allah (SW) for forgiveness. Ask him to make it easier—the result has been and will be obvious. He will help to achieve Taqwa in due course.

Why can it not be possible to offer Fajr Prayer and start our daily activity from then on? Question yourselves how can you get up at 4 a.m. to catch a plane at 6 a.m. Why not Fajr Prayer? Why not get up to offer prayer and go back to sleep? Question yourself—as parents - about the bellyache in our children at midnight and rush to hospital or call a doctor or for problems at home with plumbing, getting help of the plumber at odd hours of night. As routine for prayer or others is adopted all becomes easier while asking Allah SW to make it easier for us!

Let us change our lifestyle without interfering with the working need of the Western society—make consultation among us.

Inhibition is a dangerous ailment of our society. Inhibition, I mean some of us are too shy even to say we are Muslims, not to speak of offering prayers in public. The answer to inhibition is communication with persons and society about our values and their significance.

Laziness is another ailment—be it in ablutions, offering prayers, recitation of Qur'an—leave the copies of Qur'an in your home wherever you sit—their dollar value to acquire the invaluable Qur'an is very little. It will not be a costly deed.

My dear brothers, sisters, and children, we live in the Western world—make our presence known as individuals becoming politicians, lawyers, journalists, doctors, farmers, laborers, volunteers, and all—make your presence known as Islamic society. Make your voice known on day-to-day issues, be it abortion, alcoholism, child abuse, and what not. We have answers. Discharge your duty to the country, province, city and the society you live in. After you have established that, ask your right, as a Muslim society without jeopardizing others, to follow Islam. Islam is so flexible that it will not jeopardize individuals, neighbors or others. Ask for things, keeping comfort and need of others around you, for example, a demand to call for prayer on loud speakers disturbing the neighborhood when you can use many modern ways and means to wake up and let others come to Masjid without disturbing others.

We as individuals make a contribution to the development of this society as a whole, but little is known to this society. Our contribution as an Islamic society via news media is not known. Look at today, that no news media has come to publicize our opening ceremony, despite me contacting them well in advance.

An immigration officer has been heard saying, "They are leaches to this country"—is that true? There are biases and they are because of misunderstanding or otherwise. *Satanic Verses*—problems arising out of it, are as alive to me today as on day one when this issue surfaced.

Many lessons to learn from, many steps to build on such lessons. Many things have been done and are being done—they must be done with wisdom. Can you imagine the writer's association reading the book in public! Ask if the writer's association has been able to prevent the agony of the author of this blasphemy that he is going through because of the sin he has committed. Remember the word of our own prime minister, Mr. Mulroney, in March in London, which I have recorded, saying when the border authorities did not allow the book to enter Canada, "Who are they to decide what we can read and what we cannot read?" Remember our foreign minister with swift action to call the ambassadors of Muslim countries to condemn Iran (*Fatwa of Ayatollah on Rushdie*), but not a word—not a word for Muslims to console them or any word against the author.

These will change and are changing as we make our presence known with wisdom. Our population must increase by birth and by sponsorship. And the issue of economy is to be solved by mutual effort. Individuals migrating should have quality and not quantity. However, the quantity which does not have quality led by quality will not become quality.

It is not practical to have a single Muslim organization—which would have been ideal, but as long as the goal is to act in accordance with Qur'an-i-Karim and Sunnah of our Prophet Muhammad (SAW)—there is no problem. These organizations may complement and supplement one another in jobs that are done, but not compete for power or politics or ridicule one another. Therefore, my brothers and sisters—children come together, come to the Masjid, resolve each and every day's issue, be it religious, social, family or politics, as good citizens of the West as dictated by Qur'an and Sunnah.

Hold the rope of Allah (SW), which He has extended to us, together. Help yourself and help one another whoever you are to whichever sect you belong and whatever views you hold. Carriage of Islam goes on—will go on. That is the promise of Allah (SW). Please join it.

And those of you who are not of Islamic faith, you are our brothers and sisters in the human race—we extend our values to you; please use them and be benefited by them, whether you accept Islam—the choice is yours. Islam does not impose conversion on you, it does invite you. Jazakallah Khair, Allah bless you all!

Thank you.

N Halil

Dr. Naiyer Habib, FACP, FRCPC, FACC
NH: aql

Past-Presidents' Speeches

They all welcomed the guests and wished success of the centre. The contents of their speeches, where available, are noted below:

Dr. M. Anwarul Haque

Founding President and Past-President: 1971–1977, 1981–1982

Dr. M. Anwarul Haque was an ear, nose and throat specialist. A native of Bangladesh, he completed his MB and BS from Dhaka Medical College in Bangladesh in1958. He left Bangladesh in 1959 and received training in Wales, UK; Minneapolis, USA; and Montreal, Quebec. He finished his training in otolaryngology in Buffalo, New York, and finally settled in Regina in 1969 and practiced the specialities of otolaryngology and allergy.

Address: *"History of Early Muslims in Regina"* (see in *Early Muslims of Regina*)

Abdul Qayyum

Past-President: 1982–1984

Abdul Qayyum was born in the Province of Bihar, India. He studied civil engineering and migrated to Canada in 1972. He first came to Thompson, Manitoba. He earned a master's in civil engineering (ME) in Winnipeg, Manitoba, and worked for the government of Manitoba as a civil engineer. He moved to Regina in 1978, and worked at the Provincial Highway Department in Saskatchewan.

Address:

Assalam-O-Alaikum,

It gives me immense pleasure today to be in this building and to see our guests from out of Regina and our people from other communities from within Regina and other members of the community as guests. We moved in 1978 to Regina from Thompson, Manitoba, which was a place which I felt was not enough civilized for different provider of civilizations. I always longed to move my children and family south and here I came, or we came in 1978. My involvement in the beginning was to study as to how we can go for that. Good enough we took up the responsibility. In fact, the beginning of what you see today was already made in late 60s or early 70s by the previous Muslim people and the community building is a continuous process. We are still in the building stage.

So however, whatever small involvement we have, we love to participate actively and we thank God for the achievement that we have today in front of us and we congratulate ourselves. More so, we congratulate those people, who were actively involved, they would spend time there for whatsoever. I have got a couple of words to add before I make my speech too long because time is short.

The unity of the community we must keep in our mind as number one objective and number one goal. On an individual basis, whatever affiliation we have, I know each organization in North America whether it is ICNA, ISNA, MSA, CMCC, and whatever. Each one of them has got very good intention, and I have got nothing to speak against them or about them. Members of our community are involved in those organizations; that is well and good, no problem, but as we go along with the community, let us move together without bringing the name of affiliation because when I recall the Islamic history and the fact in period the other sides in Baghdad, the Muslims were quarrelling, arguing on trivia as to whether the meat of the owl is legal, or whether it is proper to say prayer behind Imam Abu Hanifa or Hanifa's disciple or Imam Abu Shafi or Shafi's group, and these trivia disunited the Muslims and what happened when Halaku came to Baghdad. The other side was just run over, so let us remember that as we go along with the community that has peace or unity as number one because this unity is the basis of Islam. The God is one and this amalgamation in the unity of God made different religions. God is one, Muslim should be one, whatever schools we belong to, they are all good; I have got nothing to speak against or about, but as a community, we should move to get one.

Another point I would like to bring to the focus of our local members is that in this new building when we come, we have extra responsibility to pay a little more attention and teach our children as to how to behave in public, how to take care of the facilities of the building, the walls, and so on, so that those kids, right from day one, know how to behave and what is responsibility. The responsibility remains in the parents and with all of us. With these words gentlemen, I congratulate you, and we thank God together. God bless you.

Sajjad Malik

Past-President: 1986–1989

Sajjad Malik is Pakistani Canadian. He studied civil technology in Germany. He migrated to Canada, settling in Regina, and worked in a concrete plant as a Lab-in-charge. He served as president of the Islamic Association of Saskatchewan. He was a very sincere and devoted worker in the association.

Address:

Assalamualaikum Warahmatullahi Wabarakatuh: In the Name of Allah Most Gracious and Most Merciful. He is Who is having Authority and Power over all, Who created the Death and Life so that He may try us.

Mr. Chairman, honorable guests, brothers and sisters, and dear children in Islam: once again Assalamualaikum Warahmatullahi Wabarakatuh.

The blessing of God Almighty can reach you all; it gives me this honor as well as a distinct pleasure to be here among you all at this auspicious occasion to celebrate this historic event taking place in the history of the followers of Islam in this part of the world. I would like to take this opportunity to remind you all as the followers of Islam, we know that Islam is a complete code of law. It teaches us to lead a purposeful life to be rewarded in the life hereafter. Islam means voluntarily surrendering to the will of Allah Jallay Shana Ho and obedience to His commands. The Islamic way of life is based on sole obedience to Allah Subhana Wa Ta'ala. This is the way to obtain peace here and in the life hereafter. It is here that I would like to remind you, the favors of Allah Subhana Wa Ta'ala bestowed upon us as Muslims are great. In Surah Al Imran verse 110, "Ye are the best of peoples, evolved for mankind, enjoining what is right, forbidding what is wrong, and believing in Allah. If only the People of the Book had faith, it was best for them: among them are some who have faith, but most of them are perverted transgressors."

It is high time for us to think seriously about striving back for Allah Subhana Wa Ta'ala, in our mind and heart.

Islam teaches us decency, humanity, and good manners. Greeting Muslims is a must. Greet the follower of Islam with kindness and enthusiasm. We need to keep our promise, be truthful and just, faithfully. We ought to help the poor and the needy and respect the parents, teachers, elders, and leaders of the community. We should love the children and have good relations with our neighbors. These characterize the virtuous Muslims. These are the straight paths to Allah Subhana Wa Ta'ala and Islam. Last but not least, you are one of the millat-e-Ibrahim Sallalah-o-Alayehe Wasalam. So keep up the good work.

Dr. F. M. Al-Katib

Founding Member

Added information about first Muslims in Regina: Ta Haynee. See *Early Muslims of Regina.* Dr. Al-Katib came from Turkey and practised Family Medicine in Davidson. He was involved in the community at large in Davidson, as well as the Muslim communities of Regina and Saskatoon. His wife was the mayor of Davidson.

Guest Speakers

Imtiaz Ahmed, ISNA, Canada

Address: *Role of Islamic National Organization in North America*

Mostafa Abd El Barr, University of Saskatchewan, Saskatoon

Address: *Role of the Mosque in the Community*

Ziad Malik: President of Muslim Youth

Address: *Muslim Youth Presidential Address*

On behalf of Muslim Youth of Regina, I would like to welcome you all to this glorious and memorable occasion. It is indeed a historic day in the history of Islam in this area of the world. It is by the grace of Allah SWT, Who enabled us to establish a purely Islamic institution on this very land we call home. Every community has to strive very hard to establish itself. Allah reminds us that only the good hardworking people are the ones who are to rule and establish themselves on this earth. The establishment of an Islamic institution is a symbol of the presence of Islam and also a symbol of a prominent Muslim community in society. We have a moral responsibility to represent Islam, to contribute to the success of this country, and to establish the institutions so that the Muslims and non-Muslims may benefit from the results of our efforts. We are here as Muslims to solve many of the problems that exist here. We have dreams, we have hopes, and we have visions. We have a dream that by the year 2000, Muslims will be considered as pioneers in problem solving. Our dream for 2000 is that every single citizen is to have a house of his own, means of transportation, a business of his own and job without an employment, education without trouble of paying tuition, and many more, Insha Allah, like in my case. Our dreams are not those of hopes and wishes, but our dreams are those of reality of our Prophet SAW and his companions 1400 years ago. What is needed for Muslims as Muslims in North America is to take the initiative and assume the responsibility of establishing a society of morality. We have to make Dawa to inform people about the true message of Islam. We should participate, and take the initiative to establish Islamic institutions. The future of Muslims in North America is bright. The number of Muslims has increased by 200% in the last decade. The increase is also due to a high rate of individuals who are accepting Islam. The quality of activities has improved. In the early 1960s, Muslims were busy in search for identity by having conferences and building Masjids and centres. They were trying to establish professional societies and business enterprises. In the 1980s, they had established educational schools and colleges and also in this decade they were hoping to establish Islamic hospitals, clinics, and Islamic banks. So far, we have been talking about it. Insha Allah it will happen in the future.

Let me talk a little bit about the past. Muslims were exploited and enslaved. Crusaders invaded them, and they are up till now being exploited by the powers of the world. Muslims in their homeland are killed, persecuted, tortured, and jailed by their self-imposed leaders or by others. It seems that many of us talk about the past and present but very few of us are talking about the future. What have we done for the future so that our children would be proud of us? It is not enough to talk about the past and it is not only appropriate to talk about our present life. We are not to live in the past, but we are to benefit from the past and save the future. There is an old proverb, "They planted and we eat and we are planting so that they in the future will eat." There is also a Hadith by Prophet SAW: "Work for your worldly affairs as if you are here to live forever and work for hereafter, as if you have to die tomorrow." and I leave you with this.

Next, I would like to call Arsalan Habib.

Arsalan Habib, Youth Representative

Address: *Role of Muslim Youth in North America*

Assalamo Alaikum Wa Rah Matullahe wa Bakatahu,

The Muslim Youth has been an organized group in Regina for many years. Unfortunately, during the past three or four years, the youth group has degenerated to almost nonexistence. Although youth enjoys one another's company, the actual organization and board meetings had been placed on the back burner.

This year, the youth has re-organized and re-established. Our major aim at present is to keep the Muslim Youth in Regina an active branch of the Islamic Association. By doing this, the foundation of future youth will be set, and the organization will remain active for many years to come, but for this goal to be substantial, all of the youth must be involved. We must strive for unity and extend invitations to all the youth in Regina who are 13 years of age or over, but unity should not remain within the youth of this city but extend to the cities of Saskatoon, Swift Current, Winnipeg, Calgary, and Edmonton. Once this network is built, it will be possible to become involved in the rest of Canada and Insha Allah all of North America.

Youth who will be united now will, when they are community leaders in the future, also be united as a strong Muslim ummah. Another aim of the Muslim youth is that of learning; learning about our religion, learning how Islam complements the world around us, and learning of the good and the bad of the society in which we live are very important. It is true that learning takes place throughout our lives, but the most intense and most significant learning takes place during childhood and youth as it builds character, morals, and our Islamic identity. Through these major goals of learning and unity, many other goals might be achieved. We become leaders in the community, role models for the young, and builders of the future. Insha Allah the future for Islam is bright just by looking at your faces today. Keep the spirit that is in your heart now alive when you leave and not only will the goals of youth be achieved, but those of Muslim ummah as well.

All praise is due to Allah, the Most Kind, the Beneficient, and Merciful.

A Glimpse of the Opening Ceremony

Chairman, ICM Opening Ceremony

M. Sardar   Dr. Jaffery Talking to Alam Qureshi

Mahlaqa Naushaba Habib
Founder and first past principal
1976–1984 Islamic School

Mohammad Ejaz, President, IAOS,
Saskatoon

Mohammad Afsar, President,
Muslim Association of Swift Current

Dr. M. Anwarul Haque giving a
helping hand

A gift from Swift Current

Letters of Thanks

February 5, 1990

The President
Muslim Association of Swift Current
P.O. Box 1076
Swift Current, Sask.
S9H 3X1

Dear Brother in Islam: السلام عليكم

This is just a letter of thanks and appreciation for your donation in acquiring ou
new Islamic Center and Mosque. We also appreciated your excellent gift which w
have installed in our prayer hall. Please accept our thanks for that.

We will hope that Muslims of Swift Current will visit us on a more regular basis an
in larger number. Please take some time off for visiting us.

This is to inform you in advance that the get together of the three communities thi
time will be held in the 4th weekend of May. We have arranged a special program
Yoy may come on Friday night and attend the activities throughout Saturday an
may return on Saturday night or stay over and return home on Sunday. .
workshop on How to Create Islamic Environment at Home is being arranged b
Muslim authorities expert in this field. Quiz competition for the students of th
three communities will be arranged on the same day. The more formal program wil
be circulated in due course. Please announce to each and every member in th
community to reserve that weekend for such a gathering. It is very important.

Wishing you the best.

Your Brother in Islam.

Dr. Naiyer Habib
President
Islamic Association of Sask., Regina Inc.

NH:hm

Naiyer Habib & Mahlaqa Naushaba Habib

February 5, 1990

The President
Manitoba Islamic Association
Manitoba Islamic Centre
247 Hazelwood Road
Winnipeg, Manitoba
R2M 4E5

Dear Brother in Islam:

Assalamalaikum!

This is just a letter to express our appreciation and thanks for the generous donation and encouragement that you as Muslim brothers and sisters have shown which helped us acquire our Islamic Centre and Mosque. We missed your presence because of the bad weather on the day of the opening ceremony but we will hope that you will visit us on a regular basis. Our association has developed a very close link with yours.

Wishing you the best of all in your service and work for Islam. Allah raward you all.

Your Brother in Islam.

Dr. Naiyer Habib
President
Islamic Association of Sask., Regina Inc.

NH:hm

66

Aisha Catikkas

Sultana Qureshi, Samina Ahmed

Nilofer Haque

Naushaba Habib

Norlela (Adnan)

Saba Qayyum, Naeema Bhabhi

Sadeque

Najaf Bhimji, Samiul
Haque, Abdul Jalil

Abdul Jalil

Naiyer Habib, Anwarul Haque

Anwarul Haque

Islamic School Presentation

Naseem Ahmed, Principal

Nasir Butt was instrumental in acquiring the Islamic Centre and Mosque at Montague Street. He was a professional accountant, and a realtor in Regina, and served on the board of the association. He offered a vote of thanks at the conclusion of the opening ceremony, and initiated the welcome of the ceremony as well.

Vote of Thanks

Nasir Butt

Assalam-O-Alaikum Wa Rahmatullahi Wa Barakatahu, Brother Habib just mentioned and already thanked everybody on behalf of the board.

I really appreciate the people who came from outside of Regina. I like to say thank you to those who stayed here till 1:30 AM and many nights to put things together. I like to say thank you to those who have not been counted for hours and hours of discussion with each other to put the things together for the Islamic Centre. I thank you those who contributed. I thank you those who even guided. I thank you those who thought about their own children to establish this centre, which is the Islamic Centre for their youth for tomorrow. It is a great occasion. It is a great pleasure to stand here and say thank you to the people who have started this many, many years ago, but this process started somewhere in April, and it ended beautifully. I like to again thank the ladies, who spent hours and hours of their time. Remember that we already had lunch. We had our sweets, and we are going to have our supper, and we have been invited for another supper for tomorrow. Do you know how many hours that takes to just discuss even? I know how many hours it takes even to decide what to do and so I can understand how people will decide what to cook, where to cook, and who is going to cook. We will appreciate their efforts in putting things together and many of those sisters who were here hours and hours in this Mosque to clean the Mosque, to prepare for today along with the youths whose names have not been mentioned. I have a long list; I am not going to start thank you Mom that I was born, but I do say thank you to those who really help the association, help the community. It is your community. This we accomplished together. This was not a task of one person. This was not a contribution of one person. This is a contribution of all of you and you should be very proud and I see that you are proud and be proud and continue the good work and again I say to the sisters, thank you so much for all that you have done to make my life or the life of the board of directors easier. I appreciate and thank you so much.

Assalam-O-Allaikam Wa Rahmatullahi Wa Barakatuh.

Hazem Raafat: Concluding supplication

Guest book showing the list of guests courtesy of Jihad Rashid

Jihad Rashid

❧ GUESTS ❧

Date	Name	Address
Nov 12, 1989	NORAINI AHMAD	320 CUMBERLAND AVE. N, SASKATOON
Nov. 12. 89	NORLELA AZIZ	403.3, 103 Cumberland Ave. S, Saskatoon
	Suzanna Kassim	403.2, 103 Cumberland Ave. S, Saskatoon.
Nov 12 89	MOHAMED SADJANI	#104 - 335 Kilburn Blvd Sask.
Nov 12, 1989	QURAINI OSMAN.	401-5 Cumberland Ave. S, Saskatoon.
	NORMALA MOHAMAD.	403-4 " " ".
	NORELY ABD · RAHMAN	726, 13th STREET EAST, SASKATOON
	ADIBAH ABD RAHMAN	401·6 · 103 CUMBERLAND SASKATOON
	Zaheer Awi	12 Kirk Cr. Saskatoon
	Ijaz Ahmed	1-4219 Degeer St. Saskatoon
	Mohammad Khalid Hajj	101-355 Kingsmere S.toon.
	ABDULBASET ETTUKKI	204-365 KINGSMERE Saskatoon

⋇❀❀GUESTS❀❀⋇

Date	Name	Address
Nov 12	ADIL HASSAN	7-1514 Main St E. (Saskatoon)
''	INTISAR Nurdayem	101-105 Cumberland Ave N.
''	SAID ELFAKHANI	1222 McKercher Dr. Sarkahon
''	HANA NACHAWATI	'' '' '' ''
''	MOHAMD Elamin Khalid	7-1910 Main St ('')
''	Muhammad Abd·El·Barr	355 Charleton Dr.
Nov. 12	Imtiaz Ahmad	9875 Esplanade Dr·, Windsor, ON N9R 1W7
	M. Anwarul Haque	Regina.
N N	Mostafa Abd-El-Brr	355 Carleton Dr. S7 H3P2, Saskaton
'' ''	Amer M. Kassem	#31-20 Summers Place.
'' ''	MUSTAFA Barre	#31-42 MUNRo Place.
''	Mohammed Sharif	2124·C Robinson St

❧❧ GUESTS ❧❧

Date	Name	Address
	Jihad RASHID	Box 241 Regina
Nov. 12.	K. A. Qureshi	12- McDougal Rd Regina.
Nov 12/89	Samuil Hague	129 Westfield Dr. Regina
Nov. 12, 1989	W. Dawan	P.O. Box 241 Regina. Sask.
Nov. 12/89	K. Qureshi	56 Arlington st. Regina
Nov. 12/89		435 Elgin Rd Regina
Nov. 12/89	Khatoon Ahmed	127 Plains View Dr. Regina
Nov. 12/89	Dalia Noureldin	2234 Wascana Greens
"	A. Qayyum	4227 Castle Road, Regina
"	TAG TAGELDIN	3606 Wetmore Cres, Regina
	ALEX E Fatma Karauto Adua	Radville Sask
Nov 12/89	M. Naeem Khalid	1109. Ave T.S Saskatoon.

❦ GUESTS ❦

Date	Name	Address
NOV 12, 1989	MOHAMMED ARIF SETHI	21 CULLITON CRES REGINA
NOV. 12, 1989	FAISAL SETHI	21 CULLITON CRES. REGINA
NOV. 12, 1989	RAZA HASANE	1450 PARKER AVENUE. REGINA
NOV 12, 1989	Mohamed Elhadi (zawe)	Box 3782 Regina S4P 3N...
NOV 12 1989	SAJJAD MALIK & FAMILY	4505 ELGIN ROAD
	Qasim Ahmed.	127 Plainsview DR.
	Maryla Rahman.	4235 Montague...
No 12 1989	Sana Kashid.	R. 013 241 Regina
Nov 12 1989	Mohammad Ali Sethi	21 Culliton Cres
"	M. K. Rehman	4235 montogm St.
Nov 12 '89	SYED SHAFQAT HUSSAIN	809 SHANNON R...
Nov. 12 89	Akbar Moulavi & Farhad	3033 Grant Road

❧❦ GUESTS ❦❧

Date	Name	Address
S	Nary Habib	Regina.
Nov. 12. 1989	Farhad Moulavi	303 Grant Road
" " "	Mohamed Saleh	#414-193 Lockwood Rd.
" " "	Nadia Qureshi	56 Arlington St.
" " "	Shabnam Ahmed	4168 Rae st.
" " "	Sarah Khan	3414 Foster Bay
" " "	Zahra Aweigei	15 Vaughn Street Regina
" "	SABA Qayyum	4227 Castle Rd, Regina
"	QUDSIA "	"
4	Aboubakr Luseline	148-1128 McBeacher Dr
"	Saffad M. Malik	4505 Elgin Rd.
S	Talat S. Malik	"

❧❦ GUESTS ❦❧

Date	Name	Address
12 November 1989	كُرّم احمد	1330 Jubilee Dr. Swift Curren
Nor. 12. 89	شميم شاة	101- 193 Lockwood Rd. Reg
Nov 12 /89	نجم سِدّقی	1626 cumberland ave Sas
" " "	NURULAIN -JAFFERY	56, ARLINGTON .Str.
" " "	Sana-Axa Ahmed	99 Michner DR
" " "	Mohammad SARDAR	Rejina
" " "	M. Zea Hosan	SASkatoon,
"	ashraf Nourldin	2254 Vearana Greens
"	FIRDAUS PANCHASI	2935 RAE ST. REG
"	Mohmd. Kalam Panchasi	" " " "
	N Hasan .	SASKATOON
	Sara Siddiqui	"

❧❦GUESTS❦❧

Date	Name	Address
Nov 12, 1989	Kitty C Lahmidi	2724 Quinn Dr, Regina
"	Khalil Lahmidi	"
", "	Shahid Khan	1637 Admiral, Moose Jaw
" "	Hisham Ahmed (David Russell)	Apt A2, 320-5th Ave N. Saskatoon
" "	Sadeque Ahmed	4164 Rae St. Regina
	Karen Cappeller	403 Edward St. Regina
" "	Fathi Hamad	1107 Flexman Cr. Regina
	Muhammad Abdullah Hassan	3552 Allev Ave
" "	Mr & Mrs. Ghousia Riffat Hussain	809 Shannon Rd. Regina
" "	Mr & Mrs. Saba & Hussain	" " "
" "	Shafqat Hussain	" " "
	Raza Bhimji & Nargis	2667 Crocus Dr. E.

GUESTS

Date	Name	Address
Nov. 12	Mr. & Mrs. Ayaz Husan	2811 Peppa St. Regt.
	Mr. & Mrs. Md Rais uddin	123 Killan away
" "	MOHAMED SWENIA	58 MUNROE #434 Regina sk.
	Mohamed & Shamin Jail	567 Sangster Blvd
	Nadeem & Sharon Isfia Kelly	#8-8900 Sangster st
	R.I. AHMED.	Regina.
	Ayesha Ahmed	Regina .
	I. Ahmed	Regina
	M. Fatih al Katib	DAVIDSON
	Fayhan AlKatib	
Nov. 12, 1989 Rabie the 2nd 13, 1410	Hazem Raafat	13 walden cr. Regina
NOV. 12, '89	GHAZANFAR NAQVI and family	1331 FLEET St, REGINA.

❧❦ GUESTS ❦❧

Date	Name	Address
Nov. 12/89	NASAF BHIMJI	2667 Croods REGINA
"	Aisha Catilekas	2449 Winnipeg St, Regina
"	Laila B. Rifaat	214 Doiron Rd. N.
"	Abdulhakim HUMMAD	3920 ROBINSON REGINA
"	LUKMAN HUMMAD	" " "
"	FOWZI ABDULLAHI	
"	MOHAMMAD SALIM KHAN (5)	3414 - FOSTER BAY REGINA
"	Junaid Husain	2811 Pepper Dr.
"	RASEKH RIFAAT	214 DOIRON RD.
	JACKIE L JAVED JOSEPH	92 - BOBOLINK Bay
	Bahra Rao.	91 - CARDINAL Crook
	Laila Rahm	
	Mumtaz Rana.	

GUESTS

Date	Name	Address
12, 11, 89	HAROON KHATRI	35 MARKWELL DR. REGINA
12/11/89	Khalid Tuwaty	12 McDougall Rd. Regina.

Ejaz Ahmed was president after the opening ceremony of the ICM at Montague. He is pictured here with his introduction:

Dr. Ejaz Ahmed was president of the Islamic Association of Saskatchewan from 1994–1996. His main contribution was raising a large amount of funds for Bosnia.

He was a professor and head of the Department of Mathematics and Statistics at the University of Regina. He progressed to be the dean of the Faculty of Mathematics and Statistics at Brock University. He was a gold medalist. He has multiple publications on his subjects in national and international journals, and serves on editorial boards of various national and international journals. He has authored and co-authored several books—*Introduction to Probability and Statistics,* co-authored by him is adopted by several Canadian universities as a text book.

Islamic School

1976-1998

First Islamic School at 308 Habkirk Drive established in 1976 Residence
of Mrs. Mahlaqa Naushaba Habib and Dr. Naiyer Habib as founders

According to Dr. Haque, three years after the formation of
the association in Regina, a decision was taken to start an Islamic
School in Regina. There were only two or three students at that time.
The decision did not materialize and remained in abeyance. Our
family moved to Regina in August of 1976. During the function
of Eid prayer in the basement of the Red Cross building, while Dr.
Haque was presiding, I asked, "Why is there no arrangement for
teaching the children here?" In answer, Dr. Haque told me that he
had tried, but people did not show interest. So this was not pursued.
I said that I would offer my house for school, my wife as teacher,
and my children as students. All others could send their children to
be taught. So the first school was formed in 1976 at our home, 308
Habkirk Drive, with my wife as the principal of the school.

The school used to be every Tuesday evening, and continued for
eight years with Mrs. Habib as the principal. Fareda Sethi, Qudsia
Qayyum, Masood Hasan, Aftab Ghani, Nilofer Haque, and I also
taught for a period from time to time.

Students included as noted in the picture: Ali and Faisal Sethi, Adnan and Arsalan Habib, Adnan and Andaleeb Qayyum, Samiul, Munirul and Sabreena Haque, Ziad, Natasha and Samad Malik, Rizwan Masood, Farzana and her younger sibling Rahman, Sheela, Arsalan Aftab, two sons of Aftab Ghani, Usra Siddiqui, Nasreen Khatri, Sajid and Jameel Khatri. The Khatri family joined earlier, but later left.

The school held an annual function with certificates and awards to the students while my wife was the chair and principal. They were presented with a Qur'an and a Certificate of Completion of Islamic School as well as completion of their high school. A farewell function was held for them. The students also participated in the Islamic Association's functions.

Evaluation of Teaching

We had an established process to evaluate teaching in the school, getting feedback from students.

Mahlaqa Naushaba Habib
Founder and Past Principal
1976–1984 Islamic School

First Islamic School
Islamic Association of Saskatchewan, Regina
308 Habkirk drive (Habib residence)

- 1976-1984
- Founders:
- Principal 1976–1984: Mrs. Naushaba Habib, MA
- Chairman 1976–1984: Dr. Naiyer Habib

Islamic School Function at 308 Habkirk Drive

Left to right: (*above the front*) Natasha, unidentified, Farzana, Faisal, Raza, Rizwan, and Arsalan

Natasha Hussain, unidentified, Sabreena Haque, Nasreen Khatri

The school moved to 240 College Avenue East in June of 1984. Mrs. Habib stepped down as the principal in 1984, when the school moved after her eight years of service as the principal.

M. Jamil, Principal 1984 to 1986

Islamic School at 240 College Avenue

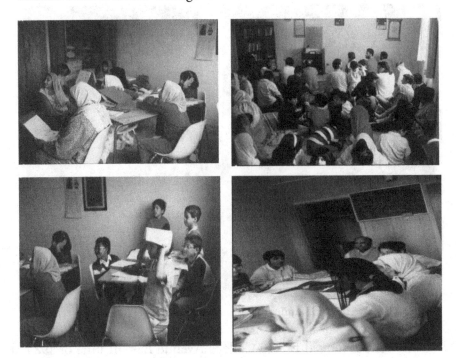

Annual Award Function at Islamic School

M. Jamil
Principal
1984 – 1986
President Naiyer Habib
An Annual Function of Islamic School
at Community Hall July 1984

Andaleeb Qayyum presenting on his graduation

Andaleeb is awarded Certificate of Graduation from President Naiyer Habib. Three ladies in-between (*left to right*), Naushaba Habib, Yasmin Habib, Uroose Hassanie. Nasreen Ajaz to the right of Andaleeb.

Adnan Habib receives award and Certificate of Graduation
from Principal M. Jamil and President Naiyer Habib

Munirul Haque receives annual certificate and award

Arsalan too. Mom in the back with a smile

Pictures of all others missing in the above were collected from family album.

Abbas Hassanie

Nasim Ahmed, Principal 1986 - 1998

Sr. Nasim Ahmed was appointed in 1986. She remained as the principal when we moved from College Avenue to Montague Street Centre in 1989. She stepped down in 1992. During her time as principal, students took part in a function at the Muticultural Event at the University of Regina, participating with Canadian Council of Muslim Women.

Left to right (back): Ziad Malik, Junaid and Azam Hussain, Munirul Haque,
Natasha Hussain
Front left to right: Farzana Rahman, Natasha Malik, Raza Hassani, Faisal Sethi,
Arsalan Habib
Naushaba Habib standing off to the right

From the fall of 1992, Br. Hazem Raafat took over until he left Regina (date unkown). Among others, Br. Abdul Qayyum taught from 1984 - 1991, K. Rahman, Sajjad Malik, Riazuddin Ahmed, Samina Ahmed, and Br. Rasekh Rifat, Naushaba Habib and others. Abdul Jalil was chair in 1998.

Abdul Jalil
Principal, 1998

Naiyer Habib
President 1996–1998

During the period of Dr. Abdul Jalil, there was an annual school function with distribution of certificates by teachers to the students, and an address by Principal, Abdul Jalil and President Naiyer Habib in the centre at Montague Street.

Opening: Abdul Jalil

Address by Principal Abdul Jalil

President N. Habib

Riaz Ahmed, teacher with the principal

Nargis Bhimji distributing certificates

Mrs. M. Naushaba Habib distributing certificates

Sajjad Malik helping

Various teachers at the Islamic School included the following, with dates known and unkown:

Abdul Qayyum, 1984–1991
Riazuddin Ahmed, 1981–1998
Samina Ahmed, 1988–1998
Sajjad Malik
Nargis Bhimji
Mahlaqa Naushaba Habib
Naiyer Habib

Projects

Friday Prayer
Luther College Annual Seminar
Muslims in Focus: Formerly Cable Regina
Sunday Monthly Islamic Symposium
Monthly Family Islamic Discussion

Friday Prayer 1978

Before using the College Avenue building as a Mosque, we used to offer Friday Prayer in an assigned room at the old university campus at the corner of Broad Street and College Avenue.

Friday Prayer was initiated a little later in 1978 at the recommendation of Dr. Masood-ul Alam who was the first Imam for Friday Prayer. He was from Bangladesh, and had moved to Regina from Saudi Arabia. A place for Friday Prayer was arranged by Dr. Naiyer Habib, President of the association at that time. He had a university appointment at the College of Medicine and therefore was able to arrange a room at the college campus free of charge. It was an inconvenience for prayer there, as the room would be found locked from time to time, needing a search for the security man to open the room.

It should be noted that we wanted those youth to perform Friday Prayer who could get a break from school between 12:30 to 1:30 p.m. So the time for Friday Prayer was fixed for all year around at 12:30 p.m., which was supported by the Hadith from Imam Hanbal. Thus, this exception was used for this exceptional need in this part of the world.

This continued till 1998, when it changed to 1:30 p.m. The youths then disappeared from Friday Prayer with the exception of one or two students. The others attended only when school was closed.

Supporting Evidence to Fix Time of Friday Prayers Including before Zawal (Midday) (see www.namcc.org/prayertimes.php)
North Austin Muslim Communities, 11900 North Lamar Blvd. Austin, TX 78753. Ph: [512] 491-7148

First Jumuah (Friday Prayer)	12:15 Khutba:: 12:45 Prayer
Second Jumuah (Friday Prayer)	1:30 Khutba:: 2:00 Prayer
Third Jumuah (Friday Prayer)	2:30 Khutba:: 3:00 Prayer

NOTE:

- We currently hold 3 Friday Congregations due to the limitation of the Parking Lot compared to the number of attendees. Our Parking lot holds 275 cars per congregation. We ask that you try to car pool to the prayer as much as you can.
- The times of the Friday Prayer are constant throughout the year, regardless of summer time.
- Please note that in some days during the year, the First Friday Prayer will be held before the Zawal* time. Our Imam agrees that this is permissible. This is also the opinion of the great scholar Imam Ahmad Ibn Hanbal. However, the second prayer will always be after the Zawal time. So if you prefer to pray after the Zawal, please attend the second prayer.
- At the end of the prayer, please leave immediately and remove your car especially if you are blocking anyone. Violators will be towed at owner's expense.
- When you leave the Friday Prayer, NO LEFT TURN is allowed on Lamar Blvd. ALL TRAFFIC MUST TURN RIGHT. You can make a left only when you drive on Lamar Blvd. until North Bend Drive.
- For your safety and our kids' safety, please be observing the speed limit inside the Masjid which is 5 miles per hour.

*Zawal time: is the time when the sun is in the middle of the sky. In general, Zuhr prayer time starts after Zawal time.

North Austin
Muslim Community Center

The Earliest Time for Jumuah Prayer

Is there any proof from the Qur'an or Sunnah that it is permissible to perform Salatul Jumuah (khutbah and salaah) before the time of Salatul Zuhr? For example, the time of Zuhr begins at 1 p.m., the khutbah of Jumuah begins at 12 p.m. and salaah is finished before 1 p.m. Are there any conditions or circumstances that would make this permissible?

Praise be to Allah.

The scholars differed as to the earliest time for Jumuah prayer. There are two views:

1. When the sun passes the meridian, like the time for Zuhr prayer, and it is not permissible to pray Jumuah before that. This is the view of the majority of Hanafi, Maaliki and Shaafa'i scholars, and al-Nawawi attributed it to the majority of the Sahaabah, Taabi'een and those who came after them. Imam al-Shaafa'i (May Allah have mercy on him) said: "There is no difference of opinion among all those whom I met that Jumuah cannot be offered until the sun has passed the meridian." Al-Umm (1/223)

2. It is permissible to pray before the sun passes the meridian, i.e., the time for it starts before the time for Zuhr.

This is the view of Ahmad ibn Hanbal and Ishaaq ibn Raahawayh. See al-Insaaf, 2/375-376, *Differences of the Hanbalis* concerning the beginning of the time of Jumuah, when the sun has risen to the height of a spear or in the fifth hour or sixth hour.

Those who hold this view quoted a number of Hadiths as evidence:

Shaykh Ibn Baaz (may Allah have mercy on him) said: The best time (for Jumuah) is after the sun has passed the meridian, so as to avoid an area of scholarly dispute, because most of the scholars say that it is essential for Jumuah prayer to be after the sun passes the meridian. This is the view of the majority.

Some scholars are of the view that it is permissible to pray Jumuah before the sun passes the meridian in the sixth hour, and there are Hadiths and reports indicating that, which are saheeh.

So if a person prays Jumuah shortly before the sun passes the meridian, his prayer is valid.

But it should only be done after the sun passes the meridian, following all of the Hadiths and so as to avoid an area of scholarly dispute, and so as to make it easy for all people to attend together, so that the prayer will be at the same time. This is what is better and more on the safe side.

End quote. (Majmoo' Fataawa Ibn Baaz, 12/391-392 and Allah knows best).

The need for a building for our objectives was felt essential. We started our effort.

The Imams Leading Prayers for Us

Members of our community, in rotation, led our prayers during our period of leadership. We could not afford full-time Imams. Local Imams were not available either. Imams were offered from Muslim countries. We had noticed that their preaching was not acceptable to us. We also learned that they were exerting influence of their countries of origin by having the force of finances from such countries.

Individuals who led the Friday and Eid Prayers on rotation included:

Ayman Aboguddah
Naiyer Habib
Anwarul Haque
Sajjad Malik
Hazem Raafat and a member of the Youth Group

Luther College Annual Seminar, University of Regina

With the rising interest and participation of our association, under our leadership, in Outreach Program we were invitees for participation in educational activities of organizations of repute.

On invitation of Dr. Ronald E. Miller* of Luther College, University of Regina, we were regularly participating in Islamic Seminars at the college on topics of his choice. He wanted his students and others to have discussion on Islamic topics with Muslims. Occasionally the session was held in our Islamic Centre and Mosque.

Our co-ordinator was Naushaba Habib. The participants for discussions included: Mohammad Anwarul Haque, Mahlaqa Naushaba Habib, Masood Hassan, Naiyer Habib and Norlela Aziz. Some of community members also attended.

{*Luther is able to do occasional teaching of courses in religion, under the university's rubric of a "Humanities" program. Luther's faculty, under the leadership of Dr. Roland E. Miller, plays a significant role in establishing the university's Religious Studies Department. (https://www.luthercollege.edu/public/files/100th%20 Anniversary%20issue.pdf 1977)}

Following is a letter of appreciation from Dr. Miller. He presented his authored Book, *"Mapilla Muslims of Kerala"*.

LUTHER COLLEGE
University of Regina, Regina, Saskatchewan, Canada S4S 0A2 Phone (306) 584-0255

(Memorandum)

TO   DATE   June 3, 1977

    Mrs. Naushaba Habib

FROM

    Roland Miller

RE: ....

I am sorry that I have delayed in sending you this note of thanks
for your kind participation in the Islamics Colloquium. I have been
waiting for the enclosed volume to reach me. Please accept it as a
token of the appreciation of our College and of my own gratitude.

Yours sincerely,

Roland E. Miller.

Muslims in Focus: Formerly Cable Regina
(Courtesy of Access Communications Cooperative of Regina)

We established the *Muslims in Focus* program on Cable Regina. Nurulain Jafferey was the introducer. Riazuddin Ahmed was the anchor person. The objective was to introduce the Muslim community of Regina to the population at large.

There were interviews about topics such as Riazuddin interviewing Dr. Haque and Dr. Habib about the history of Muslims and associations, Riazuddin interviewing Adnan Habib and Samiul Haque about their pilgrimage to Mecca, Sabreena interviewing Zia Afsar and Mariam on women's issues. Riazuddin Ahmed interviewing Mohammed Afsar, Abdul Qayyum, and Sajjad Malik as well.

Subsequently, *Islam in Focus*—a series by Dr. Jamal Badawi of Halifax, replaced *Muslims in Focus*. It was broadcast for a while. Cable Regina then did not want to continue the program, as it was not produced locally. Pictures that were available are included here, representing the program.

Note: My regrets for not being able to include others due to unavailability.

ICM, Regina

Nurulain Jafferey
Anchor Person

Riazuddin Ahmed
Interviewer

Riazuddin Ahmed, Dr. M. Anwarul Haque, Dr. Naiyer Habib

Sabreena Haque, Zia Afsar
Mariam Farooq

Samiul Haque, Adnan Habib
Riazuddin Ahmed

Sunday Monthly Islamic Symposium

Old University of Regina campus on College Avenue, Regina, SK

A monthly Islamic symposium was arranged, and held at the old university campus on College Avenue. Various subjects were chosen for presentation. They were delivered and discussed in this symposium on a monthly basis. The participation of the speakers was from the community on rotation. It included the adults and youth members of the community. It was well-received. However, over the course of time, this was discontinued because of the poor number of people participating in the symposium.

We also offered Friday Prayer in this building before acquiring our Islamic Centre at 240 College Avenue.

Monthly Family Islamic Discussion

For the ongoing learning of Islam and for their participation in the community and national affairs, a few families joined together at their homes in the evening, once a month. Children, youth, men and women presented various topics. Discussion followed under a co-ordinator elected for each session irrespective of age and gender. Socialization followed.

Participant families included: Asif and Najma Mann, Dr. Abdul and Nusrat Jalil, Dr. Abdur and Rizwana Rahman, Dr. Naiyer and Naushaba Habib, Riazuddin and Samina Ahmed.

Muslim Youth of Regina

The founding members of Muslim Youth were Adnan Habib, Adnan Qayyum, Andaleeb Qayyum, and Samiul Haque.

Other members were Saba Qayyum, Sabreena Haque, Usra Siddiqui, Arsalan Habib, Munirul Haque, Ali Sethi, Raza Hasni, and Faisal Sethi. These youths developed their own program and were participating in the efforts of the Islamic Association for programs and various celebrations.

Founding members of Muslim Youth:

- Andaleeb Qayyum
- Adnan Habib

They attended the first Muslim Youth Conference, organized by the Council of Muslim Communities of Canada in Toronto.

Top to bottom:

Samiul Haque

Adnan Qayyum

Munirul (head–part of face)

Andaleeb Qayyum

Adnan Habib

The Youth of Regina was established by the four founders mentioned above. Two of these, Adnan Habib and Andaleeb Qayyum, attended the first Youth Conference arranged by the Council of Muslim Communities of Canada in Toronto in the early 1980s.

Activities:

Pot Luck—monthly potluck and get-together at parents' houses, on rotation.

Volunteering—voluntary active participation in the functions and programs of the Islamic Association as well as Islamic School. Educational—the boys used to visit the Masjid at 240 College Avenue after its establishment. They recited the Qur'an and its translation. They listened to Islamic tapes and had mutual discussion. Subsequently, they would go to restaurants such as McDonald's, Dairy Queen, etc., to have coffee and fun. Girls participated at their homes.

Youth Camp—Camp Monihan

Al-Adhan Magazine Publication—monthly issues, first magazine attached.

Camp Monihan August 1985—this was the most important historic event arranged by the Muslim Youth of Regina. They made preparations by arranging the camp. This was a Christian camp, but they were happy to allow the facility to be used by our youth for a small donation. It is of note that the youth as seen in the next pictures, prepared a fence to put between the boys and the girls for the swimming purpose. Primarily, the girls were involved in making food, which they could take to the camp.

Fun!

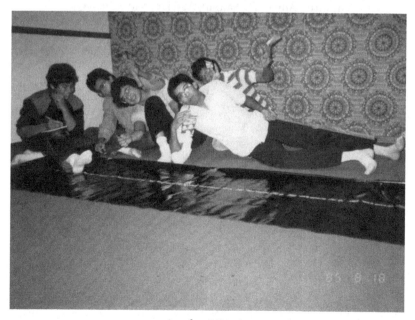

Arsalan joins in

Get to work
Munirul, Adnan H., Samiul, Arsalan, and Adnan Q.

Adnan and Arsalan Habib

Shahla Qayyum

Saba Qayyum, Usra Siddiqui, and Sabreena Haque

Sabreena

Camp Monihan 1985

All this was managed by the youth group. Parents assisted. Some parents stayed with them at the camp. They started the camp with a prayer. Subsequently, there were games, swimming, lunch, dinner, and snack. The participants were from Winnipeg, Swift Current,

Saskatoon, and of course, the host being the Regina Youth. On the last day of camp, they invited their parents for lunch and presented a program in the open with speeches and skits.

It was a very successful camp. All the communities were very happy to see the interest of the youth (boys and girls), big and small.

Unfortunately, this was the first and last camp for the youth. With new management, the youth camp changed to a kid's camp and then it vanished. This was also the first and the last. It was sad.

The day begins with a prayer

Saba Sabreena Shahla

Adnan Habib and Andaleeb Qayyum at camp

Left: Samad Malik, *Middle*: Arsalan Habib

Shahid Jamil, Adnan Habib, Riaz Alvi, Andaleeb Qayyum, Adnan Qayyum

The big brothers

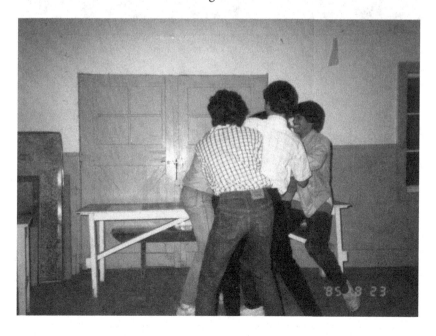

The team of mothers too

A lonely mom, "Where are you going, Naiushi?" says Naiyer

Wandering!

The boys' team and a father too

The boys

Limitless fun and relaxation

Skit

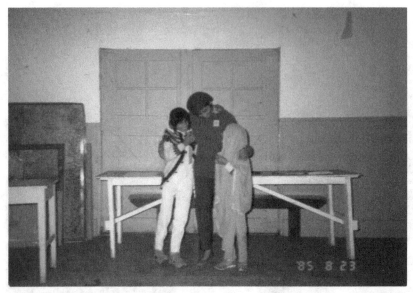

Sisterly cuddle...

...and brotherly game

The chat

Campfire

Parent's Day at the Camp

Welcome parents

A youth presentation

Buses dropped them to our home, so pleased we were. Thanks to Allah (SWT) at 440 Habkirk Drive, Albert Park, Regina, Saskatchewan.

Exhaustion and then sweet dreams!

After their departure, and with change in leadership of the association, the Youth Camp was changed to Kids' Camp and vanished all together.

Allah, Bless Our Prairie Youth

The Youth participated in the opening ceremony of the Centre at Montague Street. President Ziad Malik addressed the community and Arsalan Habib presented the goal of the youth in North America.

The Youth Group also initiated a monthly magazine. Its initial issue is presented below. These youth grew up and went to universities, and hence the Youth Group of Regina ended. But after a time, the second age group revived the group. However, this activity also ceased after a short period, with the change in the demographics of Regina.

These Youth Group of Regina members chose their careers as follows:

- ★ Adnan Habib: a lawyer in Abbotsford, BC
- ★ Arsalan Habib: MD, a nephrologist in Utah
- ★ Andaleeb Qayyum: BA (with honors) and post grad diploma in Economics. Now working as an economist with the federal government
- ★ Adnan Qayyum: PhD in Education and professor at Pen State University, USA
- ★ Shahla Qayyum: BS (with honors) and post graduate in Clinical Research. Now a pharmaceutical researcher at the University of Alberta
- ★ Saba Qayyum: MD, FRCPC, a psychiatrist in Saskatoon
- ★ Sabreena Haque: B. Ed. and BA in History, and educator in
- ★ Saskatoon
- ★ Samiul Haque: MD, FRCPC, a pediatric psychiatrist in Regina
- ★ Munirul Haque: architect in Regina
- ★ Usra Siddiqui: a lawyer in Toronto

First Issue of Al-Adhan
by Youth Team

Contents

Editorial

BY ADNAN HABIB

Among the five pillars of Islam, Prayer is the second. It is performed five times a day – at dawn, in the early afternoon, in the late afternoon, just after sunset, and at night. The essence of Islam is the consciousness of and submission to Allah, and the most direct means of developing these qualities is through prayer. It is clear that prayer once a week or once a day is not enough, as we become so absorbed in our activities that we tend to forget the Creator. That is why prayers are prescribed five times each day.

Apart from the five daily prayers, the Jum'a (Friday) congregational prayer is obligatory upon muslim men and boys. Women, due to their household responsibilities are excused from praying Jum'a prayer in congregation and can pray Zuhr prayer at home. Jum'a prayer consists of two rakkats, substituting for the four rakkat of Zuhr, preceeded by a khutba(Sermon) and is observed at Zuhr time on Friday, always in congregation.

"O! you who believe! when the call is proclaimed to prayer on Friday (The day of Assembly) hasten earnestly to the Remembrance of Allah, and leave off business; That is the best for if you knew!"
(69:9)

Friday is the Day of Assembly, that the weekly congretional meeting of Muslims of a locality, when they demonstrate in public their unity through common worship. The Khutba is delivered by the Imam where he might throw light on the spiritual life of the community and also call Muslims to follow pure living. The occasion also offers an opportunity for the largest social contact for muslims, because Friday congregations take place in the principal mosque of a township where as the five daily prayers are offered in the local mosques within various habitations of a town.

The objective of the weekly Day of Assembly (Friday) in Islam is different from the Jewish Sabbath (Saturday) or the Christian Sunday. In the Jewish belief, Sabbath is a commeration of God's day of rest after completion after the creation in the preceding six days. This resting day was supposed to be a Saturday. The ... To Pg. 5

In the name of Allah, the Beneficent, the
Merciful

124. If anyone does good works, be they male
or female and has faith, they will enter Paradise,
and not the least injustice will be done to
them.

125. Who is better in religion than one who
submits his whole self to Allah, does good, and
follows the way of Ibrahim, the true in faith?
For Allah (Himself) chose Ibrahim a friend.

126. To Allah belongs whatsoever is in the
heavens and on earth. And He encompasses all
things.

127. They consult you concerning women. Say:
Allah gives you decree concerning them, and the
Scripture which has been recited unto you,
concerning female orphans who give not that
which is ordained for them though you desire
to marry them, and concerning the weak among
children, and that you should deal justly
with orphans. Whatever good you do, Lo! Allah
is ever aware of it.

128. If a woman fears ill-treatment from her
husband, or desertion, it is no sin for them if
they make terms of peace between themselves.
Peace is better, even though men's souls are
swayed by greed. But if you do good and keep
from evil, Lo! Allah is well-acquainted with all
that you do.

SURAH AN-NISA:124-128

136

SISTER'S PAGE

Part I:The Status of Women Before Islam

BY 'MONA AL-HAQUE
(SAGGAM)

Historically,a woman has been looked down apon and degraded just because she was born as a female.She did not hold the status that she deserved and her natural role in society was degraded.

During the days of Jahiliyah,before the coming of Prophet Muhammad(p.b.u.h),women in Arabia were not considered human.She was thought to be something between a human being and a beast.Because she was was not thought of as human,the birth of a female child was a disgrace to the family.The custom at that time was to bury alive a female child.The Holy Qur'an describes how a man felt when he recieved the news that he had a daughter:

"When news is brought to one of them of(the birth of)a female(child),his face darkens and he is filled with inward grief!With shame does he hide himself from his people,beacuse of the bad news he has had!Shall he retain it an(sufference and)contempt,or bury it in the dust?Ah!What an evil(choice)they decide on!"(16:58-9)

This was only part of the degration women suffered during this period.Open prostitution was prevaledin this society.The prominent men in the society owned brathels,filled with young slave girls in order to earn money and to entertain their guests.

The condition of women in other nations was no better.The ancient Greek civilizations is thought of as a glorious one,but in

3

marriage.He could do as he wished with it.Slowly this changed and men
had to ask the wife's permission to sell her property.He was still
the manager of all the property and he got the money it produced.

With the advent of Prophet Muhammad(p.b.u.h) and the message of
Islam that he brought,women's status was raised and her rights were
what she deserved.Women were granted by Allah,spiritual equality,and
social,economic and political rights.

FROM P.6

Christians have fixed Sunday
as the day of rest. It is
presumed by them to be the day
of creation of the universe by
God. Sabbath and Sunday are
observed by the Jews and
Christians, respectively, as a
holiday. The conception of
Friday in Islam is completely
different. It does not
stipulate rest or rejoicing.
Friday coincides with the
creation of Adam and hence it
is considered blessed by the
muslims. The importance of
Friday is explained in the
Quran which refers to Friday
prayer in continuation of the
earlier cited verse:

"And when the prayer is
finished, then may you
dispense through the land, and
seek of the bounty Allah, and
celebrate the praises Allah
often (and without hint)that
you may prosper."
(62:10)

In the next verse Allah
tells Mohammad of the people

who will be distracted by the
craze for amusement or gain.

"But when they see some
bargain or some amusement,
they disperse head long to it,
and leave thee standing. Say:
"The (blessing)from the
presence of God is better than
any amusement or bargain! and
God is the best to provide for
all needs."
(62:11)

In effect if you lead a
righteous and sober life,
Allah will provide for you in
all senses, better than any
provision you can possibly
think of.

5

VIEWPOINT
Establishment of Islamic Communities
By Dr. Hammudah Abd Al-Ati. (AN-NUR)

The Muslims of North America face difficult problems. Some of these are common to all modern industrial societies, others are peculiar to special groups.

The general problems of North Americans are also our problems. We are members of this society and are affected by it in various ways. But in addition, the Muslims in North America face some unusual problems and are beset by special difficulties. There are many reasons for this perplexing situation.

To begin with, the Muslims in North America are a minority of minorities. They represent different national origins, racial features, ethnic backgrounds, socio-cultural styles, linguistic groups, and a multitude of diversities. They have not yet felt the kind of crisis that usually consolidates the endangered minorities. Nor have they recaptured the classical Islamic spirit that overrides all other identities and is the rallying point of all Muslims of whatever national origin, station in life, language, or ethnicity.

As a minority, the Muslims are subjected to the disadvantages of American minorities. They do not even enjoy the simple benefits and compensations available to these minorities. They have no viable national organization to represent them, no pressure groups to speak on their behalf or protect their rights, no real representation in the power structure. They profess a religion which, for centuries, has been associated in many a Western mind with numerous misconceptions. They come primarily from under-developed or developing areas where corruption, chaos and divisiveness reign supreme, or where conflict with the North American governments is sharp and acute. They are branded with undesired socio-cultural traits of African and Asian origin. The national and religious identity of the Muslims is a constant ridicule-theme in the North American media.

To compound these problems, the identity of the Muslims is diffused. It gravitates in many uncertain directions. Some Muslims do not even realize that they are a minority. Some realize it but do not wish to admit it because of shame, apprehension, or lack of character. Some want to "pass" as Anglo-Saxons and, to achieve that goal they over-indulge. Some live in North America, but they are not of it. They cling to traditional and distorted values, and mistake them for Islam. They alienate themselves and persist in their misconceptions, frustrations, and bitterness. In addition, many Muslims in North America are not critical enough to distinguish true Islam from what is alien to it, or to free Islam from the intrusions that have tarnished its brilliance. They are unable to utilize the good constructive forces in American society. This is a double jeopardy, to say the least.

The fact that Islam is all-inclusive, cosmopolitan, and international seems to work against the Muslims in North America rather than for them. Since America is a secular society with a pluralistic social structure, many Muslims seem to think it impossible to make Islam an effective social force in this highly complex, pragmatic secularized environment. On the other hand, Muslims are tempted for various reasons to emphasize the similarities between Islam and the other prevailing religions. This tendency exhausts a good deal of Muslim energy and endeavor, and may overshadow the uniqueness of Islam. As a result, many Muslims may think that, since all divine religions are essentially the same, nothing much will be achieved by propagating Islam in a strange, pluralistic land. When one adds to this the dire need for concerted efforts, personal sacrifice, persistent and exemplary work, despair becomes a foregone conclusion or self-fulfilling prophecy. With regard to the non-Muslims, who are pre-occupied with many instant problems, who think little of religion anyway, and who are used to a special style of life, they may find it burdensome to change their religious orientation or expand their spiritual frontiers. The multiple effect of this situation is that Islam, the all-inclusive, cosmopolitan religion, will be contained in the remote corners of the Muslim minds, committed to memory or admired in the abstract. And when Islam does not find its way to the troubled world as a dynamic force of reform and hope, surely this causes every committed Muslim distress, tension, and pain.

Some Suggestions

But what then? Shall we despair and resign to fate, come what may? If we know Islam well enough or care for it, the answer will be an emphatic no! We must realize that ideologies are not self-promoting. They need committed believers and practitioners. We, as committed Muslims, must act to reduce the tension, surmount the problems, and live as a community of Muslims. You must have heard this many times and raised the question; yes, but what can we do, and how?

Without appearing presumptuous and without over-simplifying what is a very complex problem, I would like to submit that we attack the problem on three fronts: on the individual level, the family level, and the community level.

A. To begin with, every individual Muslim must try to restore his true identity. He must constantly ask himself the serious questions: Who am I? What are my real life goals? My priorities? My potentials? Liabilities? Limitations? To whom am I responsible? For whom and for what am I accountable? In addition, the individual Muslim must cultivate a strong sense of discretion to sustain his regained identity. He must try to be highly selective and judicious with respect to his associates, his actions and his whole style of life. In mate selection, one must seek the pious mate and trust Allah.

In his adaptation to the American way of life, one must discriminate between the proper and the improper, the sound and the unsound to adopt the former and avoid the latter.

B. On the family level, the members of the family unit must try to follow the teachings of Islam in their treatment of each other. Many centuries ago, the Qur'an pointed out that

To page 9

6

139

COMMUNITY SERVICES

PORK CONTENT IN NATIONAL FOOD BRANDS RESEARCHED

MANUFACTURER	PRODUCT	INGREDIENTS	USE
Procter & Gamble Co.	Kirk's Coco Hardwater Castile	Coconut Oil	Good
	Ivory	Beef & Pork Tallow	Bad
	Camay	Beef & Pork Tallow	Bad
	Safe Guard	Beef & Pork Tallow	Bad
	Zest	Beef & Pork Tallow	Bad
	Coast	Beef & Pork Tallow	Bad
	Lava	Vegetable Fat	Good
Lever Brothers Co.	Lux	Beef Tallow	Good
	Lifebuoy	Beef Tallow	Good
	Phase III	Beef Tallow	Good
	Dove	Beef Tallow	Good
	Caress	Beef Tallow	Good
Colgate Palmolive Co.	Palmolive	Beef & Pork Tallow	Bad
	Cashmere	Beef & Pork Tallow	Bad
Andrew Jergen Co.	Jergens	Beef Tallow	Good
	Woodbury	Beef Tallow	

DEFINITION. Dentifrice: Any powder, paste, or other preparation for cleaning teeth.
EXPLANATION. Of the many dentifrices sold on the open market, the following two categories listed below show only those products we know to be good or no good for use.

Lever Brothers Co.	Pepsodent	Vegetable Fat	Good
	Close Up	Vegetable Fat	Good
	Aim	Vegetable Fat	Good
Colgate Palmolive Co.	Ultra Brite	Lard	Bad
	Colgate Paste	Lard	Bad
Procter & Gamble Co.	Crest	Lard	Bad
	Gleem	Lard	Bad
Vicks Chemical Co.	Fix-a-dent	Vegetable Fat	Good

CHEWING GUM

Dynamint Co.	Dynamint	Candelilla Wax	Good
Wrigley's Co.	Chewing Gum	100 per cent Mineral or Veg. Base	Good
Warner Lambery Co.	Chewing Gum	100 per cent Mineral or Veg. Base	Good
	Chiclets	100 per cent Mineral or Veg. Base	Good
	Dentyne	100 per cent Mineral or Veg. Base	Good
	Trident	100 per cent Mineral or Veg. Base	Good
	Freshen Up	100 per cent Mineral or Veg. Base	Good
Beech-Nut	Chewing Gum	Glyceol Monostearate or Ester of gum	
		from any animal fat	Bad

VENDOR	PRODUCT	INGREDIENTS	USE
Dixie Bakeries Div. of Borden Foods Inc.	Honey Bun	Lard	Bad
Entenmanns	All Products	Vegetable Shortening	Good
Giant Foods	Bread	Vegetable Shortening	Good
Huber Baking Co. Bakers of Sunshine Bread	Roman Meal Bread	Soybean Salad Oil	Good
	All Products	Veg. Shortening, Oleo and Lard	Bad
Koehler	All Products	Lard	Bad
Nabisco	Rolls, Bread, Cakes	Veg. shortening or Butter	Good
Pepperidge Farm	Layer Cakes	Note: Even though this cake is made with good shortening the gelatin used is made from pigskin.	Bad
Pillsbury Co.	1869 Brand Buttermilk Biscuits	Vegetable Shortening	Good
Stroehmann Brothers Co.	Hillbilly Bread, White Bread	Lard	Bad
Sunshine Biscuit Co.	All Products	Vegetable Shortening	Good

FROZEN PIZZA PIES

BRAND	CHEESE	COAGULANT	USE
Jeno's	Mozzarella	Vegetable	Good
Beloni	Mozzarella	Vegetable	Good
	Mozzarella	Vegetable	Good
Little Chef	Mozzarella	Vegetable	Good
Ellio's	Cheddar	Swine Pepsin	Bad

CHILDREN'S PAGE

PRAYER

NAME: _____

Can you help Tariq and Hoda unscramble the words
and then find their way to the mosque for prayer.

HUZR   _ _ _ _   HUSNNA   _ _ _ _ _ _

RAS   _ _ _   DARF   _ _ _ _

RAFJ   _ _ _ _   LAFN   _ _ _ _

GAIBMHR   _ _ _ _ _ _ _

HISA   _ _ _ _

CHILDREN'S PAGE

By Rukhsana Khan

WORD SEARCH: ADAM AND HUWA

R	A	F	E	L	B	U	O	R	T
D	N	A	T	I	A	H	S	N	F
C	W	A	B	T	R	E	E	P	S
K	L	L	M	T	W	M	R	F	T
B	I	A	S	E	E	O	V	O	N
S	G	H	V	G	S	E	A	R	E
N	I	A	O	T	T	J	N	Q	R
F	L	U	R	N	J	E	T	A	A
I	J	A	N	D	M	W	S	V	P
R	T	I	U	B	E	T	T	E	R
E	J	W	F	J	K	N	S	L	B

1. Adam was _____ Man.
2. He was made of _____
3. Huwa was his _____
4. Angels are Allah's _____
5. The Angel's leader was _____
6. Angels thought man would cause _____
7. Allah taught Adam the _____ of things.
8. Allah ordered the Angels to _____
9. The Angels' leader refused because he thought that he was _____ than Adam.
10. The Angels' leader was a _____
11. And he was made of smokeless _____
12. But Allah expelled the Angels' leader but granted his request for _____ until the day of _____
13. Allah warned Adam and Huwa to stay away from the _____
14. _____ tempted Adam and Huwa and they disobeyed Allah.
15. _____ Adam and Huwa were expelled from the _____
16. Allah _____ Adam and Huwa for their sin.
17. Adam and Huwa became the _____ of all mankind.

ESTABLISHING ISLAMIC COMMUNITIES from p.4

parents, children, spouses, and kin may become one's enemies. They may stand in the way of Allah and force the individual to go against his conscience. To put things in proper perspective, Islam makes a clear distinction between the rights of Allah and the rights of kin. It shows the way to harmonize these rights and to resolve any conflict that may arise along the way. To the parents, it says in effect: love your children with discipline; be decisive but compassionate; attend to their well-being in every respect. To the children, it says in effect: be considerate, thoughtful, and far-sighted; attend to the needs of parents, but cultivate your own sense of personality and guard your own conscience. To every one it says: render unto God what is God's and unto man what is man's.

C. On the community level, we must search for one another, relate to one another, think and act together. We must organize ourselves, coordinate our activities, mobilize our resources, and revitalize our energies. We have to arrange our priorities, start our recruitment with the most committed Muslims, and adapt our means to the desired ends. We have to search our own souls before we condemn others. We have to conserve our energy for future construction instead of wasting it on fighting windmills or offending and attacking innocent people. In short, we have to follow the example of the Prophet, in his call to Allah, by words of wisdom, advice of compassion, argument of substance, and spirit of noncompromise on principles. We, the workers for Islam in North America, must educate ourselves in every field, be persistent, charitable, compassionate, and kind. We must set our own house in order. Wherever two or more Muslims live in the same community, this should become a great asset and

blessing. It should be utilized to strengthen the community spirit and foster the brotherhood of Islam. For it is no conceit or exaggeration to say that the true brotherhood of Islam is the greatest hope for a lasting, genuine brotherhood of man.

The modern age presents us with a challenging opportunity to test our integrity, try our resources, and call upon our moral strength. The contemporary scene of North America holds for us the threat of extinction as well as the promise of glory. It is crying aloud for those who have the courage to stand out, to be constructively different and unique, to defy the stereotypes, and lend a helping hand to the troubled society. We can do it. In fact, we must try, because if we do, we will preserve our identity and help our troubled fellow men. Above all, we will please Allah, enjoy His infinite blessings and aid, and stand as true sons of Islam, conscientious servants of Allah, and a living hope for humanity. □

LOCAL NEWS AND EVENTS

by Munir Haque;

Brothers and Sisters Assalam Alaikum

This year's Islamic Camp,overall was a success dispite the low number of campers.There was a turnout of 27 campers,6 junior boys,9 junior girls,11 senior boys and 1 senior girl.Inshallah next year there will be more participants.

The camp began on Thu.Aug.20th and ended on Sun.the 23rd;at Camp Monahan in the Qu'appelle Valley.The camp was sponsored by the Islamic Association of Saskatchewan,Regina Inc. and was organized by Br.Anwarwul Haque & Br.Hazem Rafaat with additional help from Br.Yousef Siddique of Winnepeg.Sessions were held by Br.Yousef Sidique,Br.Waheed Moustapha(of Winnepeg),and Br.Hazam Rafaat and the main speaker was Abdul Idris Ali,principal of the fulltime Islamic School in Toronto.Br.Idris was an excellent speaker who was good with both the children and the youth.He helped prepare a skit which was presented on the last day.

Special Note
Special thanks to the organizers,speakers,out of towners,kitchen helpers,counsellors,and the sisters who baked all the deserts.We would like to thank those who supported the Islamic Camp and Inshallah next year with your continued support we will have an even better camp.

by,Arslan Habib

& Munir Haque

10

THE DO'AA WHEN ENTERING THE TOILET

اللَّهُمَّ إِنِّي أَعُوذُ بِكَ مِنَ الْخُبُثِ وَالْخَبَائِثِ

(O Allah, I seek protection from the evil of the male and female devils.)

THE DO'AA WHEN LEAVING THE TOILET

When a Muslim leaves the toilet, he will always step out with his right foot first.

Whenever A Muslim leaves the toilet, he will praise Allah for removing all the waste and filth from his body, he will say :

غُفْرَانَكَ

I ask You forgiveness

Then recite this Do'aa:

الْحَمْدُ لِلَّهِ الَّذِي أَذْهَبَ عَنِّي الْأَذَى وَعَافَانِي

(All praise be to Allah, who has removed from me the filth, and gave me sound health.)

ISLAM:
MYTH & REALITY

Prof. Jamal Badawi
St. Mary's Univ., Halifax

Date: Friday Nov.27, 1987
Time: 7:30 p.m.
Place: Recital Hall, College
       Bldg., Univ. of Regina
       (old campus)

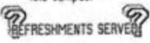
REFRESHMENTS SERVED

Public Policies (Stand Taken)

Bosnian Crisis

Condoms in School

Islamophobic Anti-Islam Conference

Gay and Lesbian Week Proclamation

First Gulf War

Lord's Prayer in Public School

Satanic Verses

Bosnian Crisis

The Bosnian crisis was an ethnic conflict after the collapse of Yugoslavia. In the words of Hartmann (*Crimes of War*), "The conflict in Bosnia-Herzegovina, which began in April 1992 and ended in November 1995, has come to be seen as the model for wars of ethnic cleansing throughout the world. This was the most violent event Europe experienced since World War II."

Slobodan Milosevic in Serbia and Franjo Tudjman in Croatia planned the creation of Serbia and Croatia of their own states with their ethnicity. Milosevic put all his resources together. He intended to include Bosnia-Herzegovina and Croatia.

The war began on April 6, 1992, with the siege of the capital, Sarajevo, of Bosnia-Herzegovina.

In 1993, Croats initiated war against the Muslims. Muslims facing two enemies entered the war as well. According to Hartmann, they never entered into ethnic cleansing.

Serbian forces killed men and boys and eliminated their intellectuals. They raped Muslim women and deported women and elderly with children to neighboring countries.

In an exhaustive report to the United Nations, a special Commission of Experts, chaired by Cherif Bassiouni of DePaul University in Chicago, concluded that globally, 90 percent of the crimes committed in Bosnia-Herzegovina were the responsibility of Serb extremists, 6 percent by Croat extremists, and 4 percent by Muslim extremists. These conform roughly to an assessment drafted by the American CIA (see www.icty.org/x/file/.../un_commission _of_experts_report1994_en.pdf).

According to *Wikipedia,* the number of casualties varied according to the sources. The number quoted varies according to the source of collection as follows:

> If a narrow definition of genocide is used, as favored by the international courts, then during the Srebrenica massacre, 8000 Bosnian Muslim men and boys were murdered and the remainder of the population (between 25,000 and 30,000 Bosniak women, children and elderly people) was forced to leave the area. If a wider definition is used, then the number is

much larger. According to the ICTY demographic unit, 25,000 Bosniak civilians and 8000 Bosnian Serb civilians were killed in the war, with 102,138 casualties for all sides involved, both military and civilian, between the Bosnian Croats, Bosnian Serbs, and Bosniaks.[62]

In a statement on 23 September 2008 to the United Nations, Dr. Haris Silajdžić, as head of the Bosnia and Herzegovina delegation to the United Nations 63rd Session of the General Assembly, said that, "According to ICRC data, 200,000 people were killed, 12,000 of them children, up to 50,000 women were raped, and 2.2 million were forced to flee their homes. This was a veritable genocide and sociocide."[63]

However, such estimations have been criticized as highly inaccurate and analysts such as George Kenney have accused the Bosnian government and the international community of sensationalism and of deliberately inflating the number of fatalities to attract international support for the Muslims.[64]

In October 2009, the Research and Documentation Center in Sarajevo published its findings and found that 97,214 persons of all ethnic groups were killed in the war, of whom 57,529 were soldiers.[65]

It was not until July 1995, when NATO intervention in Bosnia-Herzegovina was at hand, that the tribunal indicted political leader Radovan Karadzic and military commander Ratko Mladic for genocide. Debate was going on whether the massacre in Bosnia was genocide, failing to establish that NATO was not willing to intervene. Bosnia-Herzegovina was free finally at such human cost besides economic cost.

1991 - OIC calls on UN Security Council to take all necessary steps against Serbia and Montenegro, including military intervention, in order to protect Bosnian Muslims.

1993 - OIC calls on UN Security Council to remove arms embargo against Bosnian Muslims in order to allow them to defend themselves against Bosnian Serbs; OIC members pledge 80 million dollars in emergency assistance for Muslims affected by the war in Bosnia; seven OIC states commit themselves to providing up to 17,000 troops to the UN peacekeeping force in Bosnia (UNPROFOR). http://www.crimesofwar.org/a-z-guide/bosnia/ and *Wikipedia*.

Remark so true: Abdul Jalil, noted to be in a very thoughtful mood, said, "I am wondering if this may happen to us here!" Dr. Habib smilingly replied, "No, this will not happen here. People in the West are broad minded and educated. They apologized to the Japanese for their treatment in World War II."

Now look how Jalil's prediction came true after 9/11; the effect of it has not dwindled at all on Muslims. In fact, it is on the rise.

The following comment in *A Toxin in the Blood* on *YellowTimes. org* by John Chuckman, (a Canadian columnist) on Monday, November 11, 2002 at 11:21:02 EST haunts me. "The Attorney General of the United States tells Arab Americans they are fortunate not to be treated the way Japanese Americans during World War II were - that is, fortunate not to be thrown into concentration camps and have most of their property seized, never to be returned." **(Author's Note: John Ashcroft, 79th Attorney General, served under President George Bush from 2 Feb 2001 - 3 Feb 2005).**

In 1995, a young man started a fundraising tour for Bosnia on bicycle across Canada and arrived in Regina. This was during the presidency of Ejaz Ahmed. IAOS and Canadian Council of Muslim Women, Regina joined hands to raise approximately $12,000 for Bosnia. The bicycle tour was sponsored by Human Concern International. Canadian Council of Muslim Women, Regina took a leading political role against the rape in Bosnia (see CCMW chapter in this book).

Bicycle Tour for Bosnia

Welcome address by Ejaz
Ahmed, President

Address by the cyclist volunteer

Cycle tour by the community led by RCMP

Condoms in School

The Regina School Board was to recommend placement of condoms in public schools. It was an attempt by the school board to prevent teen pregnancy. This step was in the right direction, seeing the prevailing problems of teen pregnancy.

However, from the Islamic point of view, it is the basic preaching of Islam that such practice should not come into play of the society. Lack of this aspect of education and its practice was the root cause of teen or unwanted pregnancy.

The placement of condoms in schools was perceived as an encouragement and acceptance of the acts leading to it by an institution responsible for teaching the children.

In view of this, the Islamic Association expressed its concern to the board of education with a response. The outcome of this is not available to me and is not recalled.

The correspondence is shown here:

In the name of ALLAH, Most Gracious, Most Merciful

ISLAMIC ASSOCIATION OF SASKATCHEWAN
Regina Inc.

March 10, 1992

Mrs. Margaret Fern
Chairperson
Public School Board
1600 4th Avenue
Regina, Sask.
S4R 8C8

Dear Mrs. Fern:

I am writing to you on behalf of the Muslim Community regarding the issue of placement of condoms in the school. Public school system represents a broad public interest in the matters of education and is not to follow the mores of particular group.

It is realized that teenagers are sexually active. Some parents want the school take their responsibility to dispense condoms in schools or even teach sexuality school from kindergarten. These are the parents who spend time in acquiring material success and have no time to spend with the family to raise the children with high moral and character. The family value is lost. It should be the responsibility of these parents to provide condom to their children themselves by organizing a volunteer place or home or as they consider fit outside the premises of the public school.

The public school funded by tax payers belonging to various cultures and religion must take into consideration views of all and must not act to support the views a segment of the society only. If it has to involve itself it must give due consideration to the views of broader groups of the society based on cultur religion and morality respecting the principle of virginity.

We Muslims are a segment of the society. Our children attend the public school I enclose here the following brief information which are self explanatory:
1. A brochure on moral system of Islam.
2. An editorial from Muslim Parent Magazine.
3. A recent statement of 'Magic' on virginity.

The subject in itself is vast. If the Department of Education wishes to have input of Islamic expert in developing any guideline we will be more than happy to provide you with list of resource personnel and will be happy to participate in any discussion that you may have.

151

I will hope that the Board will give due consideration to all above matters and help us raise better children and citizens.

With personal regards.

Yours truly,

Dr. Naiyer Habib
MBBS,MD,FACP,FRCP(C),FACC
President
(306) 584-6707

NH:bm

Encl.

Copies to: Trustees, Public School Board
              His Worship Mayor Doug Archer
              Hon. Mr. Roy Romanow
              Hon. Mr. Grant Devine
              Hon. Mrs. Linda Haverstock

THE BOARD OF EDUCATION OF THE

REGINA SCHOOL DIVISION
NO. 4 OF SASKATCHEWAN

J.A. Burnett Education Centre
1800 4th Ave., Regina, Sask., S4R 8C8   (306) 791-8200

March 20, 1992.

Dr. Naiyer Habib,
President,
Islamic Association of Saskatchewan,
Regina Inc.,
3273 Montague Street,
Regina, Saskatchewan.
S4S 1Z8

Dear Dr. Habib:

Thank you for your letter of March 10, 1992, and the information provided about the Islamic faith which I personally found most interesting.

For your information, the Board is in the process of establishing a review committee to examine our family life education program.

The opinions of the Islamic Association and your kind offer to provide input will be conveyed to the committee. I agree with you that our public system must be sensitive to the many cultures represented in our students, and I am sure that any future decisions by our Board will reflect this.

Your interest is much appreciated.

Yours sincerely,

Margaret Fern,
Chairperson.

MF:am
c.c.   His Worship Mayor Doug Archer.
             Hon. Mr. Roy Romanow.
             Hon. Mr. Grant Devine.
             Hon. Mrs. Linda Haverstock.

Naiyer Habib & Mahlaqa Naushaba Habib

Office of the
Leader of the
Opposition

Saskatchewan Legislative Assembly

265 Legislative Building
Regina, Canada
S4S 0B3
(306) 787-9434

March 18, 1992

Dr. Naiyer Habib
President
Islamic Association of Saskatchewan
3273 Montague Street
Regina, Saskatchewan
S4S 1Z8

Dear Dr. Habib:

On behalf of Mr. Grant Devine, Leader of the Opposition,
I would like to thank you for providing our office with
a copy of your letter to Ms Fern.

I know the Islamic Association takes this issue very
seriously and we appreciate being made aware of your
views.

Yours sincerely,

John Weir
Principal Secretary

PREMIER OF SASKATCHEWAN

LEGISLATIVE BUILDING
REGINA, CANADA   S4S 0B3   (306) 787-9433

May 25, 1992   Our file: 6568/92

Dr. Naiyer Habib
President
Islamic Association of Saskatchewan
3273 Montague Street
Regina, Saskatchewan
S4S 1Z8

Dear Dr. Habib:

I write to acknowledge receipt of a copy of your letter dated March 10, 1992
to Mrs. Margaret Fern, Chairperson, Public School Board.

Thank you for keeping me informed in this way.

Yours sincerely,

Roy Romanow
Premier

Naiyer Habib & Mahlaqa Naushaba Habib

Legislative Office
140 Legislative Building
Regina, Saskatchewan
S4S 0B3
Tel: (306) 787-0860
Fax: (306) 787-0250

Constituency Office
#330-2900 8th Street East
Saskatoon, Saskatchewan
S7H 5W5
Tel: (306) 374-0029
Fax: (306) 374-0065

Lynda Haverstock – MLA   Saskatoon-Greystone

April 07, 1992

Dr. Naiyer Habib
MBBS, MD, FACP,
     FRCP(C), FACC
President
Islamic Association
     of Saskatchewan
3273 Montague Street
Regina, Saskatchewan
S4S 1Z8

Dear Dr. Habib:

Thank you for your letter of March 10, 1992 and the accompanying
material you enclosed on the Islamic Association.

Your letter presented some interesting perspectives on the issue of
condoms in schools which may affect not only school children but
all the residents of Saskatchewan. Your observations on the
complexities of this issue are worth noting.

Once again, I thank you for writing and I am grateful that you
chose to take the time to inform me of your association's concerns
and aims.

Yours sincerely,

Lynda Haverstock

Lynda Haverstock
Leader
Saskatchewan Liberal Party
MLA – Saskatoon-Greystone

LH:se

Islamophobic Anti-Islam Conference by Counter Terror Group

Such activities against Islam and Muslims are on the rise, and this conference was held. Dr. Sadiq, the president of Islamic Circle of North America in Edmonton, raised concern with the group and informed us so that we may do our part.

The following is the correspondence from Dr. Sadiq and documents forwarded to us. The outcome of the effort of Dr. Sadiq was also nil, but I am not aware of the responses to his letters.

Naiyer Habib & Mahlaqa Naushaba Habib

March 28, 90

FROM: DR. SADIQ

To: MOHAMMED ATEEQUE

Assalamo Alaykum,

Here is a copy of the Winnipeg Conference
I talked to you about along with a copy
of my letter to the Counter - Terror Study Centr.
Copies of this letter are being sent to:

1. Rt. Hon. Brian Mulrony
2. Fed. Minister of Culture
3. Premiere of Manitoba
4. Culture + Educa. Ministers of Manitoba
5. President of Univ. of Manitoba

Pl. convey this info. to Muslim Alert if you
think it is necessary.   Wao-Salam

H. Sadiq

[ORGANISED BY " COUNTER TERROR STUDY CENTRE "
                     200 DROMORE AVE
                 WINNIPEG MANNITOBA   R3M-0J3]

ISLAMIC TERRORISM IN THE 1990S AND THE THREAT TO

NORTH AMERICA

April 20-22, 1990

****

Friday April 20 -	7:30	Registration and Reception at St John's College (Coffee and Desert)
Saturday April 21 -	9:00 - 10:30	"Islamic Fundamentalism and Hezbollah." Professor Ron Miller
	11:00 - 12:30	"The Relation between Internal Iranian Politics and External Revolution." Sean Andy Anderson.

LUNCH

	1:30 - 3:00	"Islamic Terrorism: the Threat in the 1990s." Professor Jerrold Green
	3:15 - 4:30	"Panel Discussion on Islamic Terrorism" Chairman - Professor Jim Ferguson.
	7:00 - 10:00	Dinner at Holiday Inn South. Keynote address: Professor Jerrold Green
Sunday April 22 -	9:00 - 10:30	"The Threat to Canada." Federal, Academic and Specialist speakers
	11:00 - 12:30	"The Threat to the USA." Federal, Academic and Specialist speakers

LUNCH

	1:30 - 3:15	Panel discussion: "Islamic Terrorism and the Threat to North America." Chairman - Professor Peter St John

CONFERENCE ENDS

Naiyer Habib & Mahlaqa Naushaba Habib

Phone: (403)-455-4313

ISLAMIC CIRCLE OF NORTH AMERICA
(ICNA) Edmonton Unit

13103 - 113 Street, Edmonton, Alberta, Canada, T5E-5A9

March 26, 1990

Counter Terror Study Centre
200 Dromore Avenue
Winnipeg, Manitoba
R3M 0J3

Dear Sirs:

I came across your announcement regarding the conference on "Islamic Terrorism in the 1990s and the threat to North America" which is scheduled to take place on April 20, 1990.

I must say that I was deeply disturbed with your conference theme. While I appreciate your organization's concerns regarding terrorism, I cannot understand the reason why, apparently highly educated and well informed people like yourselves would choose to tie terrorism with Islam alone. Have you ever considered to hold a conference on Jewish Terrorism in Middle East, especially in Lebanon?

As educators and knowledgable people, you must know that the terrorism rampant in the world today is not limited to Muslims, and that in all such acts, there are political motives more prominent than religious. What name would you give to the terrorist activities in South American countries backed by United States, and those in India and Phillipines?

How many terrorist acts are you familiar with in Canada in the last decade and in how many of them did you find Canadian Muslims involved? The facts speak for themselves. I fail to see what threat does your organization feel from Islam or Canadian Muslims and based on what? If you are concerned about what you call "Islamic Fundamentalism", are you equally worried about "Christian and Jewish Fundamentalism" as well?

I was utterly shocked to hear that people like Professors Jerrold Green, Ron Miller and Peter St. John would participate in lop-sided and clearly prejudicial activities like this. I am further concerned that these people are in very influential teaching positions and the opportunity it provides to them to spread their biases and prejudices against Islam as a religion and it's followers. As it is, there is an unbelievable amount of ignorance about Islam and Muslims in North America. Your conference will simply fuel this further.

1

160

4R 28 '90 12:55   FROM YYC 422-2811   PAGE:004

While Federal and Provincial governments are spending millions of
dollars to promote understanding and brotherhood among the people of
this country who all come from various religious and cultural
backgrounds, organizations like yours may potentially undo these
efforts if you do not exercise extreme caution in the way you go about
dealing with terrorism.

Terrorism has no place in Islam. All of us are as concerned about it
as you claim to be, but to associate it with one religion and it's
followers does not reflect either a true understanding of the problem
or a genuine concern.

Therefore, on behalf of all the followers of Islam in North America, I
urge you to reconsider the consequences of your conference theme. It
is not befitting for highly educated people like yourselves to set
things up so as to create a strong negative reaction among Muslims
against your conference giving you an opportunity to prove your point,
unless, of course, if that was the whole idea.

I ernestly hope that you will change the title of your conference and
your programs which single out Islam and it's followers. Your efforts
will well serve the cause if you instead include some talks about the
root causes of such activities around the world.

Sincerely yours,

Mohammed Sadiq, Ph.D.
President, ICNA
Edmonton Unit.

Phone: 403-455-4313

ISLAMIC CIRCLE OF NORTH AMERICA
Edmonton Unit

13103 113 Street, Edmonton, Alberta, Canada T5E 5A9

March 28, 1990

Right Honorable Brian Mulroney
Priminister of Canada
Room 309, South Centre Block
House of Commons
Ottawa, Ontario
K1A 0A6

Dear Mr. Mulroney:

I am writing to you on behalf of the Muslim Community of
Edmonton to bring to your attention a matter of grave concern
to our community.

An organization called "Counter-Terror Study Centre",
situated in Winnipeg, Manitoba, is in the process of organizing a conference on April 20, 1990. The title of this conference is "Islamic Terrorism in 1990s and the threat to
North America". I have enclosed a copy of their announcement
for your ready reference.

The Muslim communities around North America, as well as all
reasonable people of this country, find the title of the proposed conference by the above group quite offensive and not
in the best interest of the cause they claim to serve.

We are all equally concerned about terrorism rampant around
the world. Terrorist activities have been going on in many
parts of the world, such as, South America, Philippines, India, Pakistan, South Africa, etc. We all know that underly-
ing all such activities are political motives rather than religious. It seems highly unfair, therefore, to attach this
phenomenon to a specific religion and it's followers.

I was utterly shocked to hear that people like Professors
Jerrold Green, Ron Miller and Peter St. John would participate in lopsided and clearly prejudicial activities like
this. I am further concerned that these people are in very
influential teaching positions and the opportunity it provides to them to spread their biases and prejudices against
Islam as a religion and it's followers. As it is, there is
an unbelievable amount of ignorance about Islam and Muslims
in North America. These types of conferences further feed
into this ignorance.

162

While Federal and Provincial governments are spending millions of dollars to promote understanding and brotherhood among the people of this country who all come from various religious and cultural backgrounds, organization like Counter-Terror Study Centre may potentially undo these efforts if they do not exercise extreme caution in the way they deal with their subject.

Terrorism has no place in Islam. Islam promotes universal brotherhood and peace for all. Associating terrorism with a religion and it's followers does not reflect either a true understanding of the problem or a genuine concern.

I, therefore, urge you to take whatever action in your power to direct/convince this organization to reconsider the title of their workshop and some of their presentations. If they go ahead with the conference as is, it is likely to create a strong negative reaction from the Muslim Communities, the scenario for which is nicely set up by this organization in their proposed conference.

Hope to hear from you favorably at an early date, I remain,

Sincerely yours,

Mohammed Sadiq, Ph. D.
President, ICNA
Edmonton Unit

My correspondence with the organizer of the conference and with the premier of Manitoba is shown below:

The outcome was nil. The conference was held and no recommended Islamic scholar was invited by the group.

In the name of God, Most Gracious, Most Merciful.
ISLAMIC ASSOCIATION OF SASKATCHEWAN, Regina Inc.
3273 Montague Street, Regina, Sk. S4S 1Z8
CANADA
Tele: (306) 585-0090

April 12, 1990

Counter Terror Study Centre
200 Dromore Avenue
Winnipeg, Manitoba
R3M OJ3

Dear Sirs/Madams:

Re: Islamic Terrorism in the 1990's and
___Threat to North America___

We came to know about the above conference lately. Although it is late for me to write to you about it because the conference is already scheduled to be held from April 20th to 22nd 1990. However, I could not shun this away and it is my responsibility to pass my comment to you on behalf of the Muslims of Saskatchewan. I am sure each and every Muslim of North America has the same feeling.

The theme of the conference is directed against Islam and Malign the Muslims in North America. We, those North Americans, loyal citizens of this part of the world have duty, to find such organization and group and do needful to save our countries from their evil plans not only against the Muslims but directed against anyone in this part of the world.

There is no terrorism in Islam. Islam teaches to live in peaceful co-existance according to the law of God and the guidance of the prophet, Muhammed (Peace be upon him). Islam protects the right of minority. We have materials and scholars in Islam. If you need to educate anyone or group about Islam we will be more than happy to assist you. This will remove various misunderstandings that exist in the western world because of the media and because of the west relying on information obtained from western non-Muslim sources. One must judge a Muslim on the criteria of Islam and one must not form opinion about Islam by looking at a Muslim who is Muslim by name and not in virtues. This also holds true for followers of other religions.

The definition of terrorism depends on which side of the fence one stands. Is Israeli terrorist for Palestinian making them homeless or are Palestinian terrorists against Israel to liberate their own land or even to find a home for themselves? There is no threat to North America from Islam (or Muslims). Islam is a society of people free from gayism, lesbianism, abortion, alcoholism, child abuse, drug addiction or trade. We Muslims are maintaining this kind of society in our homes and in our communities.

Page 2

We wondered how educated people like the speakers and those who are taking part in panel discussions could take part in such a conference with such a theme to represent a unilateral biased opinion without inviting a single Muslim scholar from North America. This reflects a bias and giving one sided view of a group.

At this time if it is not possible for you to cancel this conference as it is too late, which is my demand you should kindly consider changing the name of the conference and its theme and invite a Muslim scholar from Muslim organization such as Islamic Society of North America or Islamic Circle of North America or Muslim Association of Manitoba who could analyze the discussion and will be able to give the views of the North American Muslims the way they will look at the content of the Conference.

The other alternative will be to arrange a conference in consultation with Muslim organizations under the heading of "Islamic Terrorism in the 1990's and the threat to North America – Counterview of North American Muslims, sponsored by Counter Terrorist Study Centre and Muslim Organizations of North America".

Please come together as human race and make the world a better place to live for all but not only for a group of people at the expense of another group of people.

I will hope we can count on your work towards just cause and with broad mindedness in future.

Yours truly,

Dr. Naiyer Habib
MBBS,MD,FRCP(C),FACP,FCCP,FACC
President
Islamic Circle of North America, Regina Unit

(306) 584-6707
NH:bm

ADDENDUM: I enclose a glimpse of the views of two non-Muslims of the West: H.G. Wells and George Bernard Shaw.

cc: Hon. Prime Minister Bryan Mulroney
Hon. Marcel Mass, Minister of Culture. Federal Government
Hon. G. Filmon, Premier of Manitoba
Minister of Culture, Government of Manitoba
President, Islamic Society of North America
President, Islamic Circle of North America
President. Muslim Association of Manitoba

Dr. Naiyer Habib
MBBS; MD; FRCP(C); FCCP; FACP; FACC

CARDIOLOGY

PLAINS HEALTH CENTRE
4500 WASCANA PARKWAY
REGINA, SASK., CANADA
S4S 5W9
TEL: (306) 584-8707

September 30, 1990

Honorable Premier Mr. Gary Filmon
204 Legislative Building
Winnipeg, Manitoba
R3C 0V8

Dear Mr. Filmon:

Re: Islamic Terrorism in 1990's and the Threat to North America

I congratulate you on being re-elected as Premier of Manitoba and I am sure you will be an asset to your province and to Canada as a whole.

I highly appreciated your response to my letter regarding the issue. Meanwhile, we had taken necessary step to change the situation and that the topic was changed to Terrorism in the Middle East. This is a very unfortunate happening and we expect that these things may prop up from time to time.

Although I agree with you and accept your regret that because of the arrival of my correspondence too late to persue this matter from your side.

However, it would have been nice if a letter should have gone to the Group from your side with appropriate comment expressing your views on the issue.

I personally feel that we Canadians respect one another as individuals whether they are black or white, Muslims or non-Muslims, Indians or non-Indians for their values and share common good ground to develop our society.

From our side we are getting increasingly watchful for such incidences and will take necessary step as time will go by. Certainly support of the politicians will be needed.

With kind regards.

Yours truly,

Dr. Naiyer Habib
FACP, FRCP(C), FACC
President
Islamic Association of Sask., Regina Inc.
Islamic Circle of North America, Regina Unit

NH:bm

THE PREMIER OF MANITOBA

Legislative Building
Winnipeg, Manitoba, CANADA
R3C 0V8

October 10, 1990

Dr. Naiyer Habib
FACP, FRCP(C), FACC
President
Islamic Association of Saskatchewan, Regina Inc.
Islamic Circle of North America, Regina Unit
Plains Health Centre
4500 Wascana Parkway
Regina, Saskatchewan
S4S 5W9

Dear Dr. Habib:

On behalf of The Honourable Gary Filmon, Premier of Manitoba, I would like to acknowledge your letter dated September 30, 1990.

Please be assured that your correspondence will be brought to the Premier's attention.

Yours sincerely,

Aline Zöllner
Correspondence Secretary
to the Premier

Naiyer Habib & Mahlaqa Naushaba Habib

THE PREMIER OF MANITOBA

Legislative Building
Winnipeg, Manitoba, CANADA
R3C 0V8

May 14, 1990

Naiyer Habib
MBBS, MD, FRCP(C), FACP, FCCP, FACC
President
Islamic Association of Saskatchewan, Regina Inc.
3273 Montague Street
Regina, Saskatchewan
S4S 1Z8

Dear Dr. Habib:

Thank you for your letter which arrived in my office on April 23, 1990 regarding the recent conference held at the University of Manitoba, titled "Islamic Terrorism in the 1990s and the Threat to North America"

I appreciate knowing your concerns about this conference and regret that the correspondence on this topic came too late for me to pursue this matter.

Please be assured that I share your desire to promote greater understanding between people of different races and religions and that I hold the highest regard for the members of the Islamic community who have contributed so much to our society.

Again, thank you for taking the time to write.

Yours sincerely,

Gary Filmon

168

Gay and Lesbian Week Proclamation by the City of Regina

Gay and Lesbian Pride Week was proclaimed in the *Leader-Post* on June 23, 1989, as approved by the city, and the news was published.

The *Leader-Post* on June 24, 1989, published an article, *Gay Proclamation Survives*.

The association sent its views to the mayor as did others.

First Gulf War

The First Gulf War, under President Bush Sr., came into being after Saddam Hussein invaded Kuwait on August 2, 1990. Saddam Hussein proclaimed Kuwait as a province of Iraq.

This raised international issues. Iraq declared this step as a signal to the USA on meeting with a USA official prior to the invasion. This was denied by the USA.

Operation Desert Shield began and was led by the USA. On August 7, 1990, the first US Forces arrived in Saudi Arabia. On November 29, 1990, the UN authorized whatever force necessary to remove Iraqi forces from Kuwait. Iraqis were given until January 15, 1991 to leave Kuwait. Congress granted President George H. W. Bush the authority to use military force on January 21, 1991. Iraqis did not agree to walk out of Iraq. Other incidents followed according to the following timeline:

> 16 January 1991—Air campaign began against military leadership targeted in Kuwait and Iraq (concentrating on Baghdad).

> 24 February 1991—Desert Storm began as coalition ground forces drove on Iraqi forces in Kuwait.

> 28 February 1991—After 100 hours, Iraq agreed to a ceasefire. Iraqi forces retreated from Kuwait. The United States (under the leadership of President George H.W. Bush, Defence Secretary Dick Cheney and Chairman of the Joint Chiefs Colin Powell) was satisfied with UN objectives and did not push on to Baghdad.

> 3 March, 1991 – Iraq accepted conditions for a permanent ceasefire. Summarized from *Google* search and *Wikipedia-* First Gulf war and timeline Desert Storm.

Iraq stated that an attack on Iraq would be a holy war. This had an adverse effect on Muslims in the West. The Islamic Association of Saskatchewan, under my presidentship, felt its duty to raise a voice against the war as a Canadian and Muslim organization representing Muslims. Prayers were held regularly in the Masjid for peace.

A peace coalition was formed of the Interfaith group in November to December 1990 initiated by the association and led by Riazuddin Ahmed. Most faith groups joined the effort.

There were media interviews and a petition to the government against the war for a negotiated settlement of the problem. There was a large peace rally at City Hall against this war on January 12, 1991. I was the president of the Islamic Association, and I, as well as others, addressed the rally as a speaker.

As the cloud settled, it came to surface by a *CBC Fifth Estate* documentary that the USA, joined by Kuwait, dramatized the killing of babies in their incubators, as well as others in the hospital of Kuwait, to get USA public support for the war. This was enacted by the daughter of then ambassador of Kuwait who gave an interview, testifying the false story to the media with tears. *The Fifth Estate* showed that a media expert was hired for the enactment.

Seeing what went on and what may happen to Muslims, I felt it mandatory to have a North American organization, including the USA, of a confederation of Muslims. I wrote letters to all the organizations including the Islamic Societies of North America, USA and Canada, Islamic Circle of North America, Council of Muslim Communities of Canada and others, but received no response, let alone an acknowledgment. I also addressed the Muslim communities of British Columbia in a Richmond Masjid, as arranged by Azhar Syed and was welcomed by President Ali Mihiring of the British Columbia Muslim Association. There was no outcome of that initiative.

Activities of the Islamic Association

MEDIA – ISLAMIC ASSOCIATION – MIDDLE EAST CRISIS

-Jan 9, 1991 6:00 p.m.

Live interview: CBC TV with president of the Islamic Association of Saskatchewan, Regina (Naiyer Habib)

-Jan 10, 1991 10:00 a.m.

News conference at Islamic Centre/Mosque

Interfaith-Intergroup Peace Committee: STV, CBC, CKCK TV, radio, newspapers

-Jan 10, 1991 6:30 and 10:30 p.m.

STV interview with president of the Islamic Association (Naiyer Habib)

"Why Interfaith-Intergroup Committee Formed"

-Jan 12, 1991

Peace Rally City Hall – president of Islamic Association as speaker (Naiyer Habib)

"Muslims Caught in Gulf Crisis – a Response"

"Holy War?"

-Jan 14, 1991

Prayer for peace in Mosque and churches (see Leader-Post)

-Jan 16, 1991

CBC Radio – open line guest for the Islamic Association (Hazem Raafat)

-Jan 17, 1991

Interview: CKTV with president of the Islamic Association (Naiyer Habib)

-Jan 18, 1991

Live interview: STV with president of the Islamic Association (Naiyer Habib)

-Jan 22, 1991

Interview: CBC Radio with president of the Islamic Association (Naiyer Habib) (Broadcast Jan 23, 1991)

-Jan 26, 1991

Leader-Post interview: "Most Muslims Seeking Peace" (Hazem Raafat)

-Jan 27, 1991

CBC TV: Broadcast on "Prayer for Peace" – Islamic Centre and Mosque, and interview with members – Br. S. Haseebuddin, Br. A. Qayyum, Sr. V. Catikas (Excerpt is available and if needed may be sent to you on request)

<u>Media Interviews and Broacasts</u>

CBC, Regina on January 9, 1991
Dr. Naiyer Habib and Holly Preston

Holly Preston of CBC-Regina Interviews Dr. Habib

HOLLY PRESTON: Later in the program, I will talk to a Regina Muslim leader and get his thoughts on the Gulf crisis. Joining me now is Naiyer Habib, the president of the Islamic Association of Saskatchewan, Regina Chapter.

HOLLY PRESTON: Good evening, Dr. Habib. What is your reaction to the failure of these talks in Geneva today?

DR. HABIB: I hope that we should not say failure. I hope they go back to the table again and there should be some kind of negotiated settlement coming up, but if it does not then we are heading for problems as it appears from the news that we just heard and I hope that people do become wise; the Iraqi and the United States and Western allies and our own government should get involved into it to go for a peaceful settlement.

HOLLY PRESTON: Do you support Saddam Hussein or the United Nations?

DR. HABIB: I think it is a good question. We all along, all the Muslims and also all the peace loving people in the whole world are against the invasion of Kuwait by Iraq, there is no doubt on that. But what the problem we perceive is the United States; we expect United States to act as a big honest just brother, that perception we have not seen.

HOLLY PRESTON: What do you expect the US and the UN to do?

DR. HABIB: Well, I think first I have to say that we perceive United States to show double standard. Let's go to China; when Tibet was attacked by China and was taken over, what was done at that time? The same situation with the Palestinian issue and the Israeli conflict and now we have this problem.

HOLLY PRESTON: But the US is not acting alone; it is acting with the sanctions of a lot of other countries in the world.

DR. HABIB: Yes, I think the people are supporting, all countries are supporting to go after Saddam Hussein to get him out of Kuwait. But the way things are being done is not right. Things are being done quite hurriedly. The sanction has not been allowed to work. We have to allow the sanction to work excluding the food and medications. We have heard from the United States analyst that Saddam Hussein's army is not going to last too long, maybe 6-7 months and is going to go, so I think United States is hurrying the world to go for quick settlement, which he did not do for sanctioning the African problem in South Africa, that is hurrying up and we should not be doing that. Our government should get into it and show good leadership for a negotiated settlement. I think it can still be done.

HOLLY PRESTON: We have heard tonight about Joe Clark's effort to do that...what more can Canada do then? Will you support the action of the government taken in this part?

DR. HABIB: I think our government is now listening to us because we are forcing our government that we do not want war, majority of the Canadians do not want war. We have formed a group and you will be hearing that tomorrow there will be some ads in the news about the Interfaith-Intergroup, so I think the attitude of our government is changing, but we would have expected this attitude to start with, for the Canadian government to follow its own agenda right from the beginning. The perception we have is that it went along with the United States.

HOLLY PRESTON: Thank you very much for coming in.

DR. HABIB: You are most welcome.

CBC Interview with Peace Coalition—Interfaith Group about Gulf War (courtesy of CBC, Regina)

Steve McQuin, Riaziddun Ahmed,
Peter Neufeldt, and Naiyer Habib

HOLLY PRESTON: The Islamic Association of Saskatchewan says Canada should do more to promote peace in the gulf. The association and ten other groups condemn Iraq's invasion of Kuwait and they also condemn the rush to a military solution. Terry White reports:

HOLLY PRESTON: There are more than 1000 Muslims in Saskatchewan. Some of their families settled here more than 100 years ago. Some of them are asking the world not to rush to war.

This group represents 11 churches and social action groups.

PETER (Mennonite Church): What has frustrated me and I think many other groups here on the prairies, is what we should do to stop the bloodshed.

TERRY WHITE: What they can do is circulate a petition. It will be in tomorrow's paper. It starts with the condemnation of the aggression.

RIAZUDDIN: We condemn the immorality of the Iraq attack on Kuwait and consider it essential that Iraq use peaceful means to resolve its grievances with Kuwait.

TERRY WHITE: They also want the world to stick to peaceful means against Iraq. They say the economic embargo, which has cut Iraq's export by 97% and its import by 90%, should work.

RIAZUDDIN: The United Nation's sanctions do not include food and medicine, yet the American-led blockade is contrary to that resolution and that is illegal.

TERRY WHITE: For that reason, they want Canadian troops pulled out of the gulf.

PETER: We have not initiated potential peacekeeping solutions and we are urging our government to do that.

TERRY WHITE: The Islamic community wants Canadians to know they are members of a religion, not an ethnic group.

RIAZUDDIN: We are all Canadian and all we are seeking is Canadian government to play a more balanced and more constructive role.

TERRY WHITE: The petition will be in Saskatchewan papers on Friday and the national paper later if they can raise the money. Terry White, CBC News, Regina.

The multifaith group, inclusive of the Islamic Association, addressed the public in the City Hall.

Naiyer Habib's Interview with Steve Krueger, STV (Courtesy of Global TV [formerly STV])

STEVE KRUEGER: Joining us now is Dr. Naiyer Habib. He is the president of the Islamic Association of Saskatchewan Regina Chapter. Dr. Habib, thank you for joining us today. What is the feeling right now in the Islamic community in Regina about the events that are happening in the Persian Gulf?

DR. HABIB: Well, as any Canadian who loves peace we are really shocked. We are shocked and we are disappointed that all our efforts to resolve this issue peacefully have failed so we are in that shock. We feel very sorry for all our young people who are fighting there in the armed forces, what is happening to them, and the onslaught or the result of that what will happen to the families; they need a lot of support. We are quite concerned for people who are from the Middle East who have relatives there and they are much more shocked so we are going into a phase of shock as any Canadian peace loving people. As you know, with Islam being a worldwide religion, we have people from various parts of the world so that is the feeling we have. This war could have been avoided. Economic sanctions were going to work, maybe months as this war is out of our culture but things were hurried and we have run into such an escalation, I do not know the end to that.

STEVE KRUEGER: Saddam Hussein has called for Holy War involving the Muslims of the world and the people of Islamic faith; how are your people responding to that?

DR. HABIB: We do not consider this to be Holy War. There is no word like Holy War in Islam. It is a misinterpretation of the word Jihad which is an Arabic word, which merely means struggle. Struggle for the right cause; struggle for even within yourself if you have any ill feelings; struggle if a Muslim is prevented from performing his religious duty; struggle against that will be Jihad. Similarly, people of other faiths or other groups who were being oppressed by somebody and the Muslim people have the power to prevent that it will be also struggle.

STEVE KRUEGER: So Jihad is not a Holy War.

DR. HABIB: It is not. I think I have made a comment before that various leaders, whether it is of Christian sect or Islamic sect, in the past had played religion to draw the attention of the people, so this is not a Holy War, but there is so much great sentiment for the shrines which are in Baghdad and we are concerned - what is happening to those? Has United States spared those areas? So we have a lot of concern about that and similarly we have shrines in Saudi Arabia, so as world Muslims we are quite concerned and as Canadian Muslims we are quite concerned about that part.

STEVE KRUEGER: Is there anything that your community can do here in Saskatchewan to in any way express your concern or assist in what is happening here? I know that Iran this morning was saying that they are preparing to provide humanitarian assistance for the victims. They have opened their borders with Iraq and they are allowing refugees to come in. Being this far away, is there anything that your community can do to help or planning to do right now?

DR. HABIB: We have formed an interfaith group and through that we are working. Presently, we are providing moral support to the families who are from the Middle East and whose relatives are there. We are trying our best for a negotiated settlement by communicating with our government and if economic help we can offer, we are looking at those so we will try our best to do that and we hope that there is a ceasefire and renegotiation should occur and I hope that our government will take initiative as peacemaker rather than take part to escalate the war.

STEVE KRUEGER: How difficult is it right now for the Islamic community? Do they sense that there is any resentment directly toward your people because Canadian forces are in combat in this part of the world?

DR. HABIB: No, I have not perceived that in Regina, neither in Saskatoon, but I heard some rumor that somebody by the name of Hussein in Edmonton is receiving phone calls, etc. and my message to all Canadians is that whether it is Muslim or Christian or Jew or Iraqi or Arab they are all Canadian at this time and they should look at that, but if there is any person who is suspicious, we should be going after that or any group that is suspicious, we should be looking into that.

STEVE KRUEGER: I would imagine the same cases as we have with people who come here from every country of the world, hopefully, if problems at home are left at home.

DR. HABIB: We have to work as Canadians for the peaceful thing which is happening there. We should not be singling out an individual or any group for any matter.

STEVE KRUEGER: Any immediate plans right now in Regina area that you can have?

DR. HABIB: We do not have any plan, as I said that we are shocked; we are as confused as any peace loving people. We have joined the Interfaith group and we are working through them.

STEVE KRUEGER: Thank you very much for joining us and good luck and hopefully the tolerance that you are finding while staying in place here in Regina should pay.

Interview with STV, Gulf War:

Joanne D, *STV*

REPORTER: Canadian says that possibly this is the first time they have been involved in a war since the Korean conflict. That bothers a newly formed group here in Regina, as Grant reports. They hope to pressure Ottawa and to bring our troops home.

REPORTER: Most people may know Naiyer Habib, who has been here, as a heart specialist. Habib is dedicated to preserving life; that is why he has had to establish an interfaith group for peace in the Middle East. The group wants Canada to pull troops out of the Persian Gulf.

NAIYER: Our children, when I say our, it means every one whether it is Christians, Jews or Muslims, white or black, it does not matter, we are Canadian, so our families are being sent. I saw the picture of a man holding his baby, who is going to the war. So it is affecting us as a whole.

RIAZUDDIN: Our first meeting was on the 5th of December.

REPORTER: The group is starting a petition which calls on Ottawa to pull Canadian troops out of the gulf region. It is not the military acting in its traditional peacekeeping role, and backed up the statement by saying that the naval blockade that we are participating in and stopping things like food and medicine getting into Iraq.

MICHAEL QUINN: In one sense there is little difference between killing the Iraqi people with bombs and guns, and starving them to death.

REPORTER: Hazem Raafat (HR) is not a member of the group; he is also worried about the Gulf situation. His reasons though are personal.

HAZEM: Yes, I am originally from Egypt and am living in Canada. My in-laws are living in Qatar, which is in the Gulf area and I have a lot of family members and friends in Kuwait actually during the invasion.

REPORTER: The University of Regina professor says Canadian soldiers should never have been sent to the Gulf, and sanctions should have been given more time to try and force Saddam Hussein to give up on Kuwait.

HAZEM: We did not give them any time for the sanctions to work out. I think we are now sending our troops there and this was not a good decision.

REPORTER: With the deadline for Iraq to leave Kuwait just days away, they ask to pray for them. Joanne D, STV News.

The Leader-Post Regina Fri., Jan. 11, 1991

The Gulf WATCH

Peace group wants Canada to be referee

By KEVIN BLEVINS
of The Leader-Post

Canada is not doing all it can to avoid a war in the Middle East, says a new local group dedicated to peace in the area.

Riaz Ahmed, chairman of the Inter-faith, Inter-group for Peace in the Middle East, said the Canadian government has been a puppet of the U.S., blindly following it into a Persian Gulf conflict.

"All we want is for the Canadian government to seek a more balanced and constructive role," he said at a news conference Thursday.

The group, which includes various church and peace associations, thinks Canada could be a referee at the United Nations, ensuring the U.S. follows the proper rules when seeking support for war, Ahmed said.

"We think this is a role a middle power like Canada can carry out," he said.

The group, formed in December, also feels the Canadian government has ignored the wishes of most Canadians when pursuing its foreign policy in the Gulf, said Dr. Naiyer Habib, president of the Islamic Association of Saskatchewan, Regina chapter.

"Our government has been very

Riaz Ahmed

passive, following the U.S. agenda and not listening to the silent majority of Canadians," he said. "We feel Canadians do not want war."

To that end, the group has started to raise money to circulate a national petition, calling for Canada to re-

move its 1,700 troops from the Gulf in the hopes of creating a better atmosphere for a peaceful solution.

Copies of the petition appear in today's editions of The Leader-Post and Saskatoon Star-Phoenix. The group is also hoping to gather together enough cash to place a quarter-page ad in the Toronto Globe and Mail.

In addition to the petition, the group is conducting a public forum Saturday at city hall to hear the concerns of local residents.

Meanwhile, local immigrant families from the Middle East say they are not worried about their safety if war breaks out in the Gulf.

Ahmed said the six or seven families in the Regina area who hail from countries in the Middle East are more concerned about Canadian troops than they are about themselves.

"We are citizens of this part of the world. We are Canadians first, and like other Canadians, we are concerned for the safety of our troops there," he said.

Habib confirmed Ahmed's assessment of the situation, adding he has not heard of anyone suffering racial insults as a result of growing tensions in the Gulf.

Moreover, should war break out, the Middle East families do not fear hostile treatment from Canadians.

PEACE PROMOTING PETITION
PEACE IN THE MIDDLE EAST
DRAFTED BY INTER-FAITH/INTER-GROUP, REGINA & AREA

1. We are fundamentally committed to universal peace and therefore stand unequivocally against all and every aggression, including the forced annexation of lands.

2. We condemn the immorality of Iraq's attack on Kuwait and consider it essential that Iraq use peaceful means to resolve its grievances with Kuwait.

3. We deplore the present military build-up in the Middle East and the threats of war and consider it immoral for any country to wage war in the Middle East to protect energy dependant lifestyles.

4. We consider it essential to maintain Canada's internationally recognized role of a peace maker and peace keeper.

5. We consider it essential for the pursuit of a peaceful settlement of the Middle East Crisis that Canada not be involved in military actions in the Middle East.

6. Therefore, we urge the Government of Canada to withdraw all military forces from the Middle East and to use every possible diplomatic means to create the will and conditions required for a peaceful, negotiated settlement of the Middle East conflicts within the concept of a broad regional common security and justice arrangement.

Endorsed by:

Islamic Association of Saskatchewan
Wilma Wessel, United Church
Ken Powers, United Church
Jack Boan, Presbyterian
Muslim Association of Swift Current
Regina Committee for Peace for the
   Middle East
The Very Rev. Duncan Wallace,
   Anglican Church

The Rev. Patrick Tomalin,
   Anglican Church
The Rev. Wm. Portman,
   Anglican Church
Peace Mennonite Church of Regina
Members Pakistani Community
   in Regina
Social Justice Department, Roman
   Catholic Archdiocese of Regina
Grace Mennonite Church of Regina

NAME ADDRESS

_____

_____

_____

(NO POSTAGE IS NECESSARY)

PLEASE SIGN AND MAIL TO: and/or mail to your

PRIME MINISTER OF CANADA
Langevin Bldg., 2nd Floor
80 Wellington St.
OTTAWA. ONTARIO K1A 0A3

MEMBER OF PARLIAMENT
HOUSE OF COMMONS
West Block
OTTAWA. ONTARIO K1A 0A6

North American Muslim Confederation

A call for this much-needed organization received no response from any organization, but there was the formation of the American Muslims. Their role remained unknown as to such activities.

In the name of ALLAH, Most Gracious, Most Merciful

ISLAMIC ASSOCIATION OF SASKATCHEWAN

Regina Inc.

February 24, 1992

Dear Brother in Islam:

Assalamo Alaikum!

You may recall my communication at the time of Gulf War in which I had expressed my disappointments in our national organizations especially their inability to join hands together to provide national leadership of Muslims at a time like Gulf War. I had ~~also~~ spoken to some of you regarding the need and ~~perhaps~~ initiation to form Muslim Federation. I had also communicated to you what we did at the time of War with our small resources as to manpower and finance. We were pleased with the outcome.

Now it is noted that American Muslim Council has been formed. It is expected that this will be activated in Canada. Bearing this in mind I do not wish to pursue the idea of Muslim Federation separately. The aim and objective of American Muslim Council appears to be reasonable and good. It will be worthwhile that all Muslims should join hands to see its success and see that it functions with input from all according to Islamic democracy

From our local point of view we have continued to have our activity that we started at the time of War and we appear to have established ourself fairly well. Certainly I shall urge you that you must form your own local organization to deal with local matters and to cooperate and assist the American Muslim Council when that comes to being and extends hand to your area.* Local politically active group and national politically active groups are requirement of today for all of us.

Wishing you the best in your Islamic work.

Wassalam!

Yours truly,

[signature]

Dr. Naiyer Habib
FACP,FRCP(C),FACC
President

NH:bm

* Meanwhile we must not wait. ~~Sit.~~ I urge you to start linking yourself with your adjoining cities & provinces for political activity & mobilization/preparation. ~~I also request you to see~~ These could then become national organization in one name or two. We will be glad to join hands with you at any time. Still I see apathy towards us.

Note - new letter was retyped & sent out — that is missing

3273 Montague St., Regina, Sk., CANADA, S4S 1Z8 Tel:(306)585 0090

Lord's Prayer in Public Schools (Regina)

Regina Board of Education proposed to have the Lord's Prayer mandatory as an opening exercise in public school. Since the schools had students of multi-religious beliefs, it raised concern. The majority of the news released in the *Leader-Post* provided alternate suggestions.

Dr. Habib, as the president of the Islamic Association of Saskatchewan, raised our concern with suggested alternatives in a letter to the board of education. The letter was acknowledged by the board of education. Our concerns on behalf of the Muslims were published in the *Leader-Post* on Dr. Habib's call to them (dated January 31, 1981). The concern appeared in an interview with *Maclean's Magazine* on February 23, 1981 on page 31.

Jews felt that it was against their religion to recite prayers of any other religion. The Jewish group and others were not taken into account. A church group sympathizing with the faith of other groups suggested a dialogue with faith groups and others (*Leader-Post* week of March 14–29, 1981). Others made suggestions for a workable solution (*Leader-Post* week of February 02, 1981). Some okayed the concern of the minority groups suggesting accommodation, giving examples of the practices of other schools in other provinces.

It should be noted that the feeling of students who were left out of such an exercise was to have psychological effect as expressed by Dr. Habib.

A suggestion by a couple to conduct a poll by the parents in a questionnaire was rejected by the board. The board sent the results of a telephone survey by two radio stations with strong support for the Lord's Prayer and Bible reading. A trustee, Mary Hicks, did not put great faith in such a telephone survey saying, "If the poll was taken in Iran, what to do with the hostages, whether to kill or release them, they would probably all be dead." (*Board of Education Decides against Poll*—Matt Bellan—*LP*)

Finally, guidelines were set out for the opening exercise in public school. These in summary included:

- Members of minority groups may be excluded from participating in the opening exercise if they wish.
- Singing of "O Canada" should be included in opening exercise.
- Lord's Prayer may be included.
- Suggested Bible readings prescribed by the Department of Education may be used without comment or explanation.
- Principals of secondary schools should try to include singing of "O Canada" and "God Save the Queen" at some school functions held in the auditorium.

This was passed by the members of the board of education with a vote of four to three.

The outcome was that it was optional and not mandatory without considering the psychological impact on the left-out students from such gatherings. These are the costs of living in a major society. Dr. Habib says that, "a democracy by majority neglecting minority is akin to dictatorship."

Correspondence with the board of education, and publication in the *Leader-Post* courtesy of Marion Marshall on behalf of the *Leader-Post* of Regina are included here. Dr. Habib's opinion expressed in *Maclean's* magazine is also included, but not the pages of the *Maclean's* magazine.

The Lord's Prayer

Our Father
Who art in heaven,
Hallowed be thy name.
Thy kingdom come.
Thy will be done on earth,
As it is in heaven.

Give us this day our daily bread,
And forgive us our trespasses,
As we forgive those
Who trespass against us.
And lead us not into temptation,
But deliver us from evil;

For Thine is the Kingdom,
And the Power.
And the Glory, forever.
Amen

Naiyer Habib & Mahlaqa Naushaba Habib

بسم الله الرحمن الرحيم

THE ISLAMIC ASSOCIATION OF SASKATCHEWAN
REGINA

PHONE

P.O.B 3572
Regina, Saskatchewan
Canada

وَاعْتَصِمُوا بِحَبْلِ اللَّهِ جَمِيعًا وَلَا تَفَرَّقُوا

'And hold together firmly to God... rope and do not separate.'   The Quran 3:103

February 2, 1981

Chairman
Board of Education
Public Schools
1870 Lorne Avenue
REGINA, Saskatchewan.

Dear Sir:

I, on behalf of the Islamic Association of Saskatchewan (Regina), have been asked to express our concerns regarding the recent approval by the Board of Education of Public Schools, allowing the singing of Oh Canada, The Lord's Prayer and recitation of the bible as officially accepted practice in public schools from now on, as it appeared in the recent issue of The Leader Post. It is apparent that the Board did not consult any religious minority group while making this decision. It is also noted that this proposal was passed by the Trustees by a marginal vote of one only.

Approval of such practice is quite appropriate for any organization if all people come from the same background. However, Canada is enriched with people of various cultures and religions. All people, in whatever number they may be, are entitled to flourish equally and are not to be differentiated from one another on the basis of race, religion, culture, etc., Although the majority may not like to be dictated to by one or two (students/parents) people, majority also should not take steps to create circumstance to set aside the one or two persons from the mainstream of life. Those few persons could be of vital importance to the Nation.

Provision by the Board for the minority to be excused, yet asking the majority to proceed with its present recommendation as officially approved, creates considerable problem for the children of minority groups, particularly of a psychological nature. These children will be differentiated by other children in the schools. They may be suspected to be "unbelievers" when they may come from very religious communities. A vicious circle will be created. These schools which expected to bring up our children as good citizens, will become a source of differentiating one group of children from another and will become a centre of conflict for them. Children of minority groups thus singled out now and kept away from the main group of students with whom they have been united in performance of all activities, will be psychologically affected and tortured on a day to day basis if this proposal, which has been approved, is brought into practice.

I note the comments that many teachers conducted such exercises before and it is apparent that it was without approval of the Board. If it is so, the Principals of these schools, and the Board, should have tried to know the feelings of the minority groups in this context. If the Education Act allows the School Board to introduce both the Lord's Prayer and bible readings

190

in the schools as part of the opening exercises, we should look at this Act in the light of the views of the minority groups now.

After presentation of the above facts and comments, I put forward the suggestion of our organization to the Board for kind consideration and action for the public schools.

1. Singing of "Oh Canada" should be the opening exercise in all schools to stress Canadian nationalism, which we lack.

2. Although we realize that the Board is sincere to bring students to religion to make them better individuals, we feel that this approach should be left to individual families and religious communities, who should play active roles in our present Canadian set-up.

3. There should not be any recitation from any religious book, from any religion, either in the form of prayer or opening exercise.

4. The Lord's Prayer should not be included in the opening exercise. A prayer may be included on which all present or future minority group will agree. We would like to see the content of the Lord's Prayer for specific comment.

5. In view of the above discussion, all schools who are conducting religious exercises should be asked to discontinue such exercises.

6. The School Board should consult all religious groups whenever it considers any matter in relation to religion.

7. It is noted that Separate schools exist to bring up children of majority faith, whereas the minority lacks this facility and has to face much more hardship in teaching their children their religion and culture.

8. Our organization is apprehensive that if the Board does not take these points into consideration, and particularly if the Board continues to make decisions without consulting the minority religious groups, probably other religious difficulties may be encountered by the minority religious groups.

Having brought these points to your attention, some of which were amply focussed on by some members of the Board as well as some members of minority groups as it has appeared in the recent newspapers, it is our hope that the Board will withdraw its recommendation and will advise the various public schools accordingly.

We shall be waiting to hear regarding your action.

With sincere regards,

Yours truly,

Dr. Naiyer Habib
President.
4500 Wascana Parkway

THE BOARD OF EDUCATION OF THE

REGINA SCHOOL DIVISION
NO. 4 OF SASKATCHEWAN

1870 Lorne St., Regina, Sask., S4P 2L9 (306) 569-3610

February 12, 1981

Dr. Naiyer Habib, President,
Islamic Association of Saskatchewan,
4500 Wascana Parkway,
Regina, Saskatchewan.

Dear Dr. Habib:

Receipt of your letter of February 2, regarding
the Guidelines for Opening Exercises in public schools,
is hereby acknowledged. Your correspondence will be
brought to the attention of our Board at the first
opportunity.

As requested, we are enclosing a copy of The Lord's
Prayer for your information.

Yours truly,

W. B. Knoll,
Secretary-Treasurer.

WBK/so
Enclosure

THE BOARD OF EDUCATION OF THE
REGINA SCHOOL DIVISION
NO. 4 OF SASKATCHEWAN

1670 Lorne St., Regina, Sask., S4P 2L9 (306) 569-3810

February 17, 1981

Dr. Naiyer Habib, President,
The Islamic Association of Saskatchewan,
4500 Wascana Parkway,
Regina, Saskatchewan.

Dear Dr. Habib:

The Regina Board of Education approved the "Guidelines for Opening Exercises" at a meeting held on January 26, 1981. On that occasion, all members of the Board were in attendance to make the decision.

Your letter of February 2, 1981 has been circulated to the members for their information, along with the agenda for the meeting of February 16.

The Chairman advised that he would prefer to delay further consideration of the subject of opening exercises until all members are able to be present. Consequently, the topic will be deferred for several weeks since some members are out of the city for a short period of time.

This information is conveyed to you at this time so that you will know the Board has not had an opportunity to react to your suggestions.

Yours truly,

W. B. Knoll,
Secretary-Treasurer.

WBK/so

cc: J. A. Burnett

Naiyer Habib & Mahlaqa Naushaba Habib

THE BOARD OF EDUCATION OF THE
REGINA SCHOOL DIVISION
NO. 4 OF SASKATCHEWAN

1870 Lorne St., Regina, Sask., S4P 2L9 (306) 569-3610

February 17, 1981

Dr. Naiyer Habib, President,
The Islamic Association of Saskatchewan,
4500 Wascana Parkway,
Regina, Saskatchewan.

Dear Dr. Habib:

The Regina Board of Education approved the "Guidelines for Opening Exercises" at a meeting held on January 26, 1981. On that occasion, all members of the Board were in attendance to make the decision.

Your letter of February 2, 1981 has been circulated to the members for their information, along with the agenda for the meeting of February 16.

The Chairman advised that he would prefer to delay further consideration of the subject of opening exercises until all members are able to be present. Consequently, the topic will be deferred for several weeks since some members are out of the city for a short period of time.

This information is conveyed to you at this time so that you will know the Board has not had an opportunity to react to your suggestions.

Yours truly,

W. B. Knoll,
Secretary-Treasurer.

WBK/so

cc: J. A. Burnett

194

بسم الله الرحمن الرحيم

THE ISLAMIC ASSOCIATION OF SASKATCHEWAN
REGINA

PHONE

وَاعْتَصِمُوا بِحَبْلِ اللهِ جَمِيعًا وَلَا تَفَرَّقُوا

'And hold together firmly to God's rope and do not
separate.'   The Quran 3:103

P O B 3572
Regina, Saskatchewan
Canada

February 20, 1981

W.B. Knoll,
Secretary-Treasurer
The Board of Education of the
Regina School Division
1870 Lorne Street
REGINA, Saskatchewan
S4P 2L9

Dear Mr. Knoll:

I am in receipt of your letter dated February 17th, 1981. I am sure that the Board will look into the suggestion that we have forwarded and will take appropriate action.

We understand that these things do take some time. Please let me know if I can be of any assistance.

Yours truly,

DR. NAIYER HABIB
President.

NH:RD

Address:
4500 Wascana Parkway
Regina, Saskatchewan
S4S 5W9

584-6511

195

Naiyer Habib & Mahlaqa Naushaba Habib

The Leader-Post   Regina, Saskatchewan   Saturday, January 31, 1981

Moslems join protest against Lord's Prayer, Bible reading

By Matt Bellan
of The Leader-Post

Regina Moslems have joined the protest against guidelines allowing the Lord's Prayer and Bible reading in public school classrooms.

Dr. Naiyer Habib, president of the Regina chapter of the Islamic Association of Saskatchewan, called The Leader-Post Friday, saying his organization is upset about the guidelines, part of a package of procedures for opening exercises the board of education approved Monday.

"We favor the national anthem but do not favor any religious observance," Habib said. "Although we are Moslems and believe in God, we believe it should be kept separate."

Among other things, the guidelines give teachers the option of reciting the Lord's Prayer and reading passages from the Bible approved by the department of education.

Some trustees said many teachers already conduct opening exercises and board guidelines will standardize the practice.

The Education Act allows school boards to introduce both the Lord's Prayer and Bible reading in schools as part of opening exercises, they added.

Habib said although the guidelines allow teachers to excuse students from minority religious groups from participating, "I see a sort of psychological torture for those young children to be away from the majority."

He agreed with statements by Rabbi Sheldon Korn about the guidelines, he added. Korn, rabbi at Regina's Beth Jacob Synagogue, said in a Leader-Post interview this week that he objects to them partly because the Lord's Prayer is a Christian prayer.

"I suggest that the board of education, when it makes this kind of decision, should consult religious minorities." Habib said, adding that there are at least 100 students of Islamic faith in the city's public schools.

According to school board officials, total enrolment in the public school system is about 23,500.

Habib said his organization plans to write a letter to the board protesting the guidelines.

In a Leader-Post survey Friday of other religous minorities, Jack Hui, secretary of the city's Chinese Cultural Society, said he was also against allowing the Lord's Prayer and Bible reading in public schools.

"Even with excusing students I still say, in your heart you're isolated by the other people," said Hui, adding that he spoke for himself, not for the local Chinese community.

There are about 500 Chinese children in the city's public schools, he said. Some of their parents are Christian; the majority, including him, are of Buddhist background but not necessarily observant Buddhists.

His organization hasn't discussed the issue yet but may do so at a coming meeting. Hui added.

Dr. H. N. Gupta, a University of Regina professor and a Hindu, said parents should look at the Lord's Prayer before condemning its use in classroooms.

"Some prayers can be perfectly universal," he said, adding that he was speaking for himself, not for the local Hindu community. "One should not simply react angrily."

There are between 120 and 150 Hindu students in Regina public schools, Gupta said.

He said it's not just religious minorities who may object to religious practices in the classroom. Some parents of Christian background may also object.

"If anyone does not want to join in prayer, they should have a written request from parents," Gupta said. Teachers and principals should freely grant such students permission to be excused.

196

Board of education decides against poll

By Matt Bellan
of The Leader-Post

The board of education has turned down a suggestion that it poll parents on recital of the Lord's Prayer, Bible reading and other school activities involving religion.

Trustees at the board's weekly meeting Monday voted to receive and file a letter from a husband and wife who suggested the poll following the board's approval of guidelines last week for opening exercises in public school classrooms every morning.

The guidelines make singing O Canada mandatory, and let teachers decide whether to recite the Lord's Prayer and read passages from the Bible approved by the education department.

The letter-writing couple referred to some trustees' concerns last week that including the Lord's Prayer and Bible reading will be harmful to children from minority religious groups.

Worse effect

The couple said school preparations for Christmas and Easter have a much worse effect on non-Christian children than opening exercises that include religious activities.

They said too much time is spent on such preparation, quoting a principal saying his students don't do anything for "a month before Christmas" because of all the activity.

The couple added that children from minority religous groups some times feel left out because their parents don't want them involved in such preparations.

They said the board should send public school parents a questionnaire asking whether opening exercises including the Lord's Prayer, Bible reading and O Canada should be a regular part of the school program.

The couple also said the questionnaire should ask parents, among other things, how they feel about the amount of time schools spend on preparation for such events as Christmas and Easter concerts.

In rejecting the proposed questionnaire, trustees noted two local radio stations last week conducted telephone surveys on whether the Lord's Prayer and Bible readings should be part of public school opening exercises.

They voted to send the couple a letter with the results of the surveys, both of which showed strong support for including the Lord's Prayer and Bible reading.

Trustees also agreed to forward the couple's letter to an upcoming principals' meeting for discussion.

Referring to last week's radio surveys, trustee Mary Hicks said she didn't put a great deal of faith in "telephone surveys".

"If a telephone survey had been done in Iran on what to do with the hostages, whether to kill or release them, they'd probably all be dead," said Hicks, one of three trustees who opposed including the Lord's Prayer and Bible reading in opening exercises. "Just because groups favor something doesn't mean it's right."

She said she supports school Christmas concerts and preparation for them, but "perhaps not to the degree now being carried out."

Hicks added much of the celebration of Christmas in modern society is pagan rather than Christian. "Jesus Christ has in fact taken a back seat to Santa Claus."

197

Naiyer Habib & Mahlaqa Naushaba Habib

Board gives go-ahead to opening exercises in public schools

By Matt Bellan
of The Leader-Post

Amid sometimes heated debate, the board of education this week gave the final go-ahead to daily opening exercises in schools next September.

Trustees attending the board's meeting Tuesday approved a policy that encourages schools to hold the exercises but leaves it to principals and teachers to decide the format.

Among regulations approved:

• O Canada should be included in the exercises.

• The Lord's Prayer may be included. Bible readings prescribed by the administration department may be used without comment or explanation.

• The principal must inform parents at the beginning of each school year of the form of opening exercises to be used in the school. Parents may ask for their children to be excused from any part of the exercises.

• Teachers not wishing to conduct opening exercises may be excused.

Alex Robb, the board's superintendent of programming, said the policy and regulations approved are a more detailed version of guidelines for opening exercises that trustees approved in January. "There's a little more detail about informing parents."

Trustees decided last year to draw up a policy on opening exercises as part of an effort to promote citizenship among students but the issue has caused bitter debate since January.

Members of some minority groups and civil libertarians said that including Christian religious exercises in classrooms would be unfair to non-Christian children and that excusing children from the prayers would make them feel singled out.

Trustees voted on the issue Tuesday as they did on the guidelines in January. Dr. John Beks, Bill Rusztyk, Les Hammond and Eric Crosbie supported the regulations administration's proposal and Mary Hicks, Susan Currie and Marge Johnson opposed them.

Hammond said he knows some people are opposed to including the Lord's Prayer and a lot are in favor. "We are not making it compulsory for teachers or any minority group."

He quoted Rabbi Sheldon Karo of Regina's Beth Jacob Synagogue as saying there are only 66 Jewish students in the public school system. In contrast, the public school system has 22,000 students.

"Do we have to throw it (the Lord's Prayer) out because 66 don't want it when we have 22,000 who will accept it?"

Marge Johnson, an opponent of religious exercises, said: ". . . We talk about the majority and the minority. That majority is made up of minorities.

Hammond said Johnson has a "special interest" in opposing religious exercises referring to the fact that she had Jewish parents.

"My religious background has nothing to do with it," she replied, adding in an interview she is not a practising Jew.

Dr. John Beks said he favors religious exercises because the public school system is historically Protestant.

He also supports the exercises because the board last year vetoed a request for a religiously oriented Christian alternative program in the public school system, he added. "This is a small gesture in favor of those who wish to have some element of Christian faith involved in the schools."

Hammond quoted Dr. Morris Shumiatcher, a Jewish lawyer who supported including the Lord's Prayer in opening exercises in a story in The Leader-Post in January.

"Dr. Shumiatcher said schools without prayers are like towers without stairs," Hammond said.

"Dr. Shumiatcher doesn't know everything," Mary Hicks snapped.

The board noted and filed a letter from the board of directors of Beth Jacob Synagogue opposing religious exercises.

"The Lord's Prayer is not acceptable to members of the Jewish faith, who are in fact prohibited from the recitation of prayers of another religion," they say. "To separate and exclude non-Christian students for the purpose of religious activity in the public school system is divisive, whereas a public school should, in our humble opinion, foster unity and avoid division and exclusion on the basis of religion."

198

Guidelines set out for opening exercises

By Matt Bellan
of The Leader-Post

Singing O Canada, reciting the Lord's Prayer and Bible reading are officially accepted practices from now on in Regina public schools.

They were included in guidelines for opening exercises the board of education approved for classrooms at its weekly meeting Monday.

Among main features of the guidelines:

• Members of minority groups may be excluded from participating in opening exercises if they wish.

• Singing O Canada should be included in opening exercises.

• The Lord's Prayer may be included.

• Suggested Bible readings prescribed by the department of education may be used without comment or explanation.

• Principals at secondary schools should try to include the singing of O Canada and God Save the Queen at some school functions held in the auditorium.

Trustees Bill Hawrylak, Eric Crosbie, Dr. John Beke and Les Hammond voted in favor of the guidelines, while Mary Hicks, Marge Johnson and Susan Currie opposed them.

Ed Kucey, a board administrator, said in an interview the guidelines are the board's first official set of rules for opening exercises, although many teachers have long conducted exercises of some kind.

"It started out last spring as a survey to see how much of this was going on in the schools," he said.

Wording of the guidelines, drafted by a principals' committee, has led to debate among trustees during the past few months.

The board rejected an earlier set last November, saying they didn't provide for minorities who might not want to take part in such exercises as Bible readings.

New guidelines presented to the board Monday were an attempt to take minority views into account.

They called for including The Lord's Prayer and Bible readings provided that no student or parent objects to those practices — in effect, giving anyone objecting a veto.

Hicks said that could lead to students trying to find out who the objecting student or parent was. "I can see one child being picked out as different.

"I still don't understand why we feel it's necessary to say the Lord's Prayer . . .," she added. "I almost get the feeling it's done not because it's a matter of wanting to worship God, but so we can say, 'Look at me, I'm a good Christian'."

Johnson said she could accept some of the guidelines, but not the ones involving religious practices.

"I don't mean to sound unGodly," she said, adding she respected religion in a church and that's a wonderful place for it to be.

Beke said there is no easy way to satisfy all groups, including minorities, about recital of The Lord's Prayer and Bible readings.

"Probably the most equitable approach would be that prayers of minority groups be used at times too, and see how the majority react."

Hammond said reciting the Lord's Prayer and singing O Canada are a good way to start the day.

"We shouldn't let one or two (students or parents) veto our way of life in singing, prayers and that sort of thing," he added later.

Crosbie said students with "very strong beliefs" conflicting with the guidelines should be excused from opening exercises rather than given veto power. The board accepted his suggestion.

Kucey said the principals' committee that drafted the guidelines has prepared a package for each school, and it is available on request.

The package includes cassette tape with O Canada and the Lord's Prayer on it, guidelines for opening exercises, and an outline of Bible readings for schools approved by the minister of education.

Dr. Habib Speaks out to Maclean's Magazine on Call

The Regina School Board introduced guidelines to offer the Lord's Prayer as an opening exercise in the public schools. After input from various organizations, this was not made mandatory but optional for the students to participate or not to participate. Various media interviews and news are noted in this book under the heading of the Lord's Prayer in public school. The following is the comment of Dr. Habib published in *Maclean's* magazine under the heading of *Pray or Not to Pray* on February 23, 1981 on page 31:

"It could actually amount to a form of psychological torture" warns Naiyer Habib, president of Regina Chapter of the Islamic Association of Saskatchewan after officially complaining in a letter to the school board. He further remarks, "There are mixed religions now in public school and if some children do not join in, or walk out, they will feel they are not a part of the group, other students will see it and a feeling against the minority student might start seeding."

It was further remarked by the interviewer that like other minority spokesmen, Habib complains that a committee established by the board to study introduction of religious guidelines did not confer with parents or religious groups before reporting to the board.

This is the abstract from the magazine as one of the comments by Naiyer Habib against introduction of the Lord's Prayer in Public School.

Satanic Verses

Salman Rushdie, of Indian origin and living in UK, was a writer. He wrote a book, *Satanic Verses,* falsely accusing the marriage of the Prophet (his wives) and Islam in dramatic language. This led to protests by Muslims internationally. Some Western countries very humbly had some comments against the book. However, they were not opposed to its publication, claiming the right of the individual for self-expression in a democratic country. The British prime minister, Margaret Thatcher, had a humble comment but did not justify its publication. Canadian customs officers banned the book for entry into Canada. The former prime minister of Canada, Brian Mulroney, harshly criticized the customs officials while he was visiting Britain. He remarked, "Who are they to decide what we can read and what we cannot read?"

Imam Khomeini of Iran declared a million dollar reward for killing Salman Rushdie. Rushdie had to be securely confined by the British government and travel was considered to be dangerous.

Muslim organizations criticized but had no influence on the issue. Some British Muslims felt not to protest much with a view that it would further publicize the writing. Some non-Muslim countries banned the book.

The former board of the Islamic Association in 1989 did not take any initiative. (I assumed presidency again in September of 1989 but not during this crisis, which occurred in May–June of 1989). Having seen no action by the Islamic Association board, I (Dr. Naiyer Habib) being the chair of the Islamic Circle of North America, involved myself and was joined by a few members of the community to raise the issue. A large announcement was published on June 24, 1989, in the *Leader-Post*. This is included here. There were some media interviews, but that information is not available to be placed in this document. Islamic Circle of North America published flyers and brochures across the nation for distribution to the public.

Muslims in Canada perceived the remark of Mulroney to be very objectionable. He was the conservative prime minister.

There were books banned in Canada. See the following list. However, it was a lame excuse of freedom of speech not to ban the *Satanic Verses.* This was another double standard.

Naiyer Habib & Mahlaqa Naushaba Habib

The Leader-Post   Regina   Sat., June 24, 1989   Local   A 5

CANADIAN MUSLIMS
ON
"SATANIC VERSES"

In Canada we have a great respect for the freedom of expression. So when one group of people wants the book Satanic Verses withdrawn by its publisher (Penguin) we feel that this group wants to violate the freedom of expression, and we ought to stand for freedom of expression even though we may not agree with the material in the book. This is a natural reaction and is expected of all freedom loving people. However, every inquiring mind would ask that why in the world this group, also living in Canada, wants this book withdrawn. Recent media coverage does not provide a satisfactory answer to this question. Therefore, in this article a sincere attempt has been made to approach this issue in a systematic and logical fashion in a question answer format .

Q. Is Islam an intolerant religion which cannot stand any criticism?
A. Islam is neither an intolerant religion nor afraid of any criticism. Islam in fact is such a peace loving religion that one of the meanings of the word Islam is peace itself. Day in and day out anti-Islamic material is produced. Muslims do not take to the streets and say that this material or that material be withdrawn. So tolerant, reasonable and peaceful are the Islamic principles that, despite all the bad publicity, Islam is earning adherents right in the west.

Q. Then why Muslims cannot tolerate Satanic Verses?
A. This book is not based on any civilized criticism of Islam. This sacrilege is based on fabrication, slander, and extreme insult toward Prophet Mohammad, his family and other Islamic personalities, and pristine principles of Islam. And in turn it insults one billion Muslims of the world.

Q. Can any specific insults be cited?
A. Yes. We can have a brief review of the book in the following categories:
a) Blasphemous. Six out of nine chapters deal with Islamic theme, Islamic symbolism and with real Islamic characters. The whole of chapter two is about the life and mission of the last Prophet of Islam, Mohammad (peace be upon him). Prophet Mohammad is depicted as "Mahound" which means devil. Great Companions of Prophet Mohammad (peace be upon him) were described as "those goons" and "those F-- clowns" (page 101) and they also were called "bum" and "scum" (page 101). Wives of Prophet were called "whores" (page 381) and Islamic rituals and terminologies were ridiculed (page 104, 381 and others). The sanctity of Muslims' Holy Book, The Qur'an was damaged (page 363 and 364).
b) Racist. The book contains many racist remarks. For example, one of Prophet Mohammad's companions from Africa was painted as "an enormous black monster" (page 101). There were many negative remarks about Malcolm X, who was Muslim leader of the U.S. (page 413).
c) Anti-Semetic. Abraham, the great Prophet, common to Judaism, Christianity and Islam was called "the bastard" (page 413). May Allah forgive us even to quote these offensive excerpts.

Q. But this is a work of fiction, some names have been distorted or changed and the events occur in a sequence of a dream. What is the comment on that?
A. Everybody would agree that fiction and fantasy are no license for insult, slander and profanity. Anybody can dream or fantasize as he pleases but insulting others is the no go region.

Q. Did the publisher Penguin have any knowledge about the insulting nature of the book before its publication?
A. Yes, their own Indian editorial advisor Khushwant Singh (not a Muslim) advised them not to publish the book. He told them, "The Prophet had been made to be a small time impostor in the novel and that if the author could not see that the work would cause trouble he was out of touch with the Indian reality."

Q. But what about an author's right to freedom of expression?

A. All environmentally conscious people resist abuse of the environment. All energy conscious people oppose abuse of energy.
Similarly, all freedom loving people should stand against abuse of freedom of expression. Freedom of expression should not violate the right of one billion people to religious dignity. Even in Canada freedom of expression has not been absolute. Keegstra and Zundel cases have been recent example of that.

Q. Keegstra and Zundel cases involved promotion of hatred, but this book has been okayed by the Government of Canada!
A. Any reasonable person would understand the insult to one billion people is not going to promote love, peace and harmony in the world. Regarding the Government of Canada okaying the book, it must be said that to make a proper judgment on the book one must know about Islam. Probably a better approach in this regard would have been to form a board comprising of scholars from various faiths and Muslims should have been allowed to present their case before the judgment was passed.

Q. Does Islam believe in freedom of expression?
A. Yes. In fact, Islam has a complete system of basic human rights (for example, rights to: live, equality, personal liberty, religious freedom, economic protection, freedom from religious distress, justice, etc.). And the history of these human rights does not start with the Magna Carta or U.N.O.'s treaties and covenants. These rights were given fourteen centuries ago. According to Islam, freedom of expression is not only a right but exercising it for the good of mankind is part incumbent on all believers. Furthermore, Islam accords all religions and their followers freedom of religious dignity and the right of protection from religious distress. Qur'an commands, "Do not revile the deities which they invoke beside Allah" (6-108). That means to talk about various religions with reasons and criticizing them with respect or disagreeing with them is a part of freedom of expression. But ridiculing any religion for the purpose of insult is denial of the right to protection from religious distress and religious dignity.

Q. Has the author inflicted insult on somebody else before?
A. Yes. Regarding his novel Midnight Children both the author and his publisher had to give public apology to the late Prime Minister of India, Mrs. Indira Gandhi, in answer to her libel action. They also paid costs and gave an undertaking to remove from all future editions under their control the passages objected to by her. The author had suggested that Mrs. Gandhi was responsible for the death of her husband through neglect.

Q. Wouldn't withdrawal of the book make other authors and writers feel insecure?
A. No. All sensible authors and writers do not use insulting, abusive, and obscene language toward religions of the world and their revered figures. The issue is not the freedom of expression. The issue is the right to religious dignity. In fact authors and writers should be the first to denounce this book because it is a scar on their profession. Disciplinary action against abusers exists in all professions. And this does not weaken the profession but strengthens it.

Q. If the book is not withdrawn would it enhance the credibility of western freedom of expression around the world?
A. No. In fact it would be a set back for the credibility, at least in the eyes of the one billion Muslims. It will imply that under the pretext freedom of expression the right to religious dignity of any minority can be violated in the West any time.

Q. Is the demand that the publisher (Penguin) withdraw the book made only by a small number of Muslims?
A. No. All Muslims around the world want this book withdrawn. The Secretary General of the 46-nation Organization of the Islamic Conference (OIC), Syed Sharifuddin Pirzada supported this demand. Muslims need help from all Canadians in this peaceful campaign.

List of Books Banned in Canada

1) The Battle of Truth
2) Controversy of Zion
3) Hoax of the 20th Century
4) Know Your Enemies
5) The Real Holocaust
6) Rulers of Russia
7) Secret Societies and Suprasive Movements
8) The Talmud Unmasked
9) The Ultimate World Order
10) World Revolution
11) Zionist Factor

There were reasons to ban these books and we want to know:

—What about freedom of the press?
—What about freedom of speech?
—Where was the writers association at that time?

We invite the attention of all the people with no prejudice and ask them:

—why now there is such an uproar on our demand banning the book "Satanic Verses" which is another example of hate material, racism and distortion of real history and slander in the 1st degree?
—Why, all of a sudden, are we blamed to be against the freedom of speech and freedom of the press?
—Why now is the Canadian Government, especially the Prime Minister, saying that the board of a few people should not decide what Canadians should read and should not read (Statement of Prime Minister in London, England visit March, 1989)
—Why the elected leaders are not concerned for one specific group.

We want to see:
—Canadian Government take a lead in all matters of truth, fairness and justice.
—Canadian Government to be honest and sincere to its people within Canada in particular and everybody in the world in general.
—Canadian Government give priority to decent moral values over unnecessary and meaningless cooperation with indecency.

We are outraged, we are hurt and we are ignored, We feel that:
—You can help us in knowing the truth.
—You can help us in joining the truth.
—You can help in making this beautiful country even a better place to live.

We are determined to:
—Continue our effort until, our demands are met.
—Stand firm on our objectives.
—Solve our problems through democratic and peaceful process.
—Convey and propagate the message of truth.
—Maintain multiculturalism in our country by respecting one another.

All We Want Now:
—The book "Satanic Verses", the insult to common intellect, be banned in Canada, the book which is based on racism, profanity, slander and distortion of real history.
—An unqualified apology from the Writer, the Publisher and the Distributor.
—No publication in any other language.
—Task force from our Government to study problems arising out of Satanic Verses & Temptation of Christ, and perhaps more to prevent decay of our multiculturism.

Quotable Quotes About "The Satanic Verses"

The Satanic Verses goes much further (than The Last Temptation of Christ) in vilifying the Prophet Muhammad and defaming the Holy Qur'an.

Former President Jimmy Carter

The Western literary herd, of course, is thundering to Mr. Rushdie's defense, invoking the First Amendment, artistic freedom and all that, though, what the episode reveals is that the First Amendment has succeeded phony patriotism as the last refuge of the scoundrel. For Salman has written a defamatory novel, a blasphemous attack on the faith of hundreds of millions. Satanic Verses is an act of moral vandalism by an artistic delinquent.

Patrick Buchanan
Director of Communications in the Reagan Administration.

We understand that the book itself has been found deeply offensive by people of the Muslim faith. We can understand why it could be criticized.

British Foreign Secretary Geoffery Howe

We thank all book sellers, religious and other organizations as well as individuals who have shown their support. The blasphemous book cannot do anything to Islam in achieving its objective. It is not a matter of a protest making it a best seller, but it is a matter of principle to challenge such a blasphemous endeavour in a civilized society!

For more information write to
**Islamic /Circle of North America
Canadian Zone
404-815 4th Ave.
Calgary, Alta. T2P 3G8**

**Islamic Circle of North America
Regina Unit,
P.O. Box 6753, Regina,
Sask. S4S 7E6**

Column: Canada Customs Seizes Freedom of Expression at Border
Caroline Dobuzinskis

Canada Customs has decided to infringe upon our rights to freedom of expression to protect us from "obscene" literature. The censorship of books by customs continues to target gay and lesbian bookstores, despite a Supreme Court decision against this type of prejudice.

David Rimmer, owner of After Stonewall on Bank Street, was not able to import a lesbian-themed novel this month. *Cherry*, by Charlotte Cooper, was seized at the border because it was deemed "obscene" under Canada Customs guidelines.

The novel described lesbian sex scenes, including acts of "fisting." However, the troublesome novel was then released from customs due to its artistic merit. Its sufficient literary value was discovered after its British publication company launched a letter writing campaign to customs.

According to Rimmer, books allowed through customs can be extremely explicit as long as they do not delve into certain off-limit categories such as acts considered sado-masochism.

"It seems ridiculous to me that something that is legal to do in Canada is illegal to read about," says Rimmer. "Especially when some books, like books on S&M, can be educational."

Canada Customs' tailored guidelines on obscenity are subjective and arbitrary.

While they prohibit books describing illegal and non-consensual sexual acts, they emphasize unconventional sexual practices. These include bondage, submission, spanking and "extreme roughness of action."

According to these formal rules, Canada Customs wants to keep sex in literature good, clean, and simple—maybe they just forgot to nab all the Harlequin romances on their way to drugstore shelves.

Furthermore, customs has repeatedly made mistakes in seizing books, later rescinding with their tails between their legs. This happened in 1989, with the seizure and release of Salmon Rushdie's *Satanic Verses*. Then in 1998, the lesbian novel *Empire of the Senseless*, by Kathy Ecker, went through a similar process.

Customs' strategy on literature sounds like a running play that belongs on the football field—the seize and release.

This floppily ambiguous decision-making and targeted bullying does not belong at our borders—especially when it concerns freedom of expression and the literary arts.

Little Sister's Bookstore, which opened in Vancouver in 1993, made similar arguments against customs in the Supreme Court of Canada in 1994. Because of multiple incidents of book seizures at customs, Little Sister's felt that they were being unfairly targeted.

"While the laws for Canada Customs are not unconstitutional, they have systemic problems at customs such as a negative view of homosexual culture," says Mark Macdonald, a Little Sister's book buyer.

The Supreme Court found that the store had suffered prejudice and harassment at the hands of customs. The law determining obscenity in literature was reversed, putting the onus for proving the obscenity of a publication on customs instead of importers.

In March 2002, Little Sister's Bookstore filed yet another appeal with the British Columbia Supreme Court to have comics released from customs because they have not been proven to be obscene. The comics are from a series called *Meatmen*, that feature artwork by gay male artists.

The comics are considered to be male erotica but some are also humouristic takes on life in the gay community.

Little Sister's now has the largest selection of gay, lesbian, bisexual and transgender books in North America, most of which have to be imported from the United States.

According to Macdonald, Canada Customs continues to seize one in four of his shipments of up to 100 books at the border.

These actions harm small businesses, not only by holding stock and delaying transactions, but also by tarnishing reputations. Unfortunately, when these border seizures are made, the bookstores importing the books receive negative attention—not the bullies at Canada Customs.

The Muslim voices echoed across the world. Many died during the protest. It was not banned in the west but other books noted above remained banned.

http://centretownnewsonline.ca/archives/97to04/nov2202/arts4.htm

This Website is closed.

Media Representation

We attempted to respond to media publications related to Islam and Muslims.

These are in addition to *Public Policies (Stand Taken)*.

These letters are published courtesy of *Leader-Post*, Regina, Marion Marshall:

1. *Leader-Post* (courtesy of *Leader-Post*, Regina, Marion Marshall)
2. Response to *Time* magazine

The Leader-Post Regina Fri., Jan. 11, 1991

The Gulf WATCH

Peace group wants Canada to be referee

By KEVIN BLEVINS
of The Leader-Post

Canada is not doing all it can to avoid a war in the Middle East, says a new local group dedicated to peace in the area.

Riaz Ahmed, chairman of the Inter-faith, Inter-group for Peace in the Middle East, said the Canadian government has been a puppet of the U.S., blindly following it into a Persian Gulf conflict.

"All we want is for the Canadian government to seek a more balanced and constructive role," he said at a news conference Thursday.

The group, which includes various church and peace associations, thinks Canada could be a referee at the United Nations, ensuring the U.S. follows the proper rules when seeking support for war, Ahmed said.

"We think this is a role a middle power like Canada can carry out," he said.

The group, formed in December, also feels the Canadian government has ignored the wishes of most Canadians when pursuing its foreign policy in the Gulf, said Dr. Naiyer Habib, president of the Islamic Association of Saskatchewan, Regina chapter.

"Our government has been very

Riaz Ahmed

passive, following the U.S. agenda and not listening to the silent majority of Canadians," he said. "We feel Canadians do not want war."

To that end, the group has started to raise money to circulate a national petition, calling for Canada to re-

move its 1,700 troops from the Gulf in the hopes of creating a better atmosphere for a peaceful solution.

Copies of the petition appear in today's editions of The Leader-Post and Saskatoon Star-Phoenix. The group is also hoping to gather together enough cash to place a quarter-page ad in the Toronto Globe and Mail.

In addition to the petition, the group is conducting a public forum Saturday at city hall to hear the concerns of local residents.

Meanwhile, local immigrant families from the Middle East say they are not worried about their safety if war breaks out in the Gulf.

Ahmed said the six or seven families in the Regina area who hail from countries in the Middle East are more concerned about Canadian troops than they are about themselves.

"We are citizens of this part of the world. We are Canadians first, and like other Canadians, we are concerned for the safety of our troops there," he said.

Habib confirmed Ahmed's assessment of the situation, adding he has not heard of anyone suffering racial insults as a result of growing tensions in the Gulf.

Moreover, should war break out, the Middle East families do not fear hostile treatment from Canadians.

207

Naiyer Habib & Mahlaqa Naushaba Habib

The Leader-Post   Regina   Sat., Oct. 6, 1990

Readers' Viewpoints

Solutions must address Palestinian problem

Some facts were left out by the reporter on my comments under the headline "Dartboard draws critics" (Leader-Post, Sept. 29, Page A17).

I had added, "However, I wonder why Hussein and Khomeini were selected for dartboards and not the Zionists who are responsible for killing Palestinians on an ongoing basis and making them homeless. From the Canadian point of view, they stand on the same level."

The situation in the Middle East is a complex one. Because of the complexity of the problem, I add the following comments.

Many leaders do not represent the masses. The West, which also includes a large, ever-growing Muslim population, must realize this fact. There should not be double-standards by people who claim to be of high morals and character.

Canadians used to be respected in the world, and that respect is dwindling. There is no doubt that the aggression on Kuwait and its occupation are illegal. According to our present standard, so is the occupation of Palestine.

If Kuwait did belong to Iraq, Iraq had the option to solve the issue diplomatically through the United Nations. If the U.S. was inspired by the plea to protect Saudi Arabia and to liberate Kuwait, it should have shown its character by seeking a peaceful, honorable solution for the Palestinian people, rather than supporting wholeheartedly the state of Israel.

This comment is also for those western nations joining the United States in this endeavor. The solution must aim for a lasting peace with preservation of the home for Israel and creation of a homeland for the Palestinians.

It should be noted that the Muslim mass across the world is against the deployment of forces other than Arab ones in the Muslim holy land of Saudi Arabia. It is a serious matter.

We should all join together to seek a peaceful solution with honesty, justice and sincerity, so that we can all have a better world in which to live.

Let us not run in the race of competition of black or white, Muslim or non-Muslim, Indian or non-Indian. There is no end to that.

History shows us that the biggest powers do fall and the smallest rise. This rise and fall continues.

Dr. NAIYER HABIB
Habib is president of the Islamic Association of Saskatchewan, Regina Inc.

208

The Leader-Post Regina

Mon., Sept. 20, 1993

Wise, brave

The PLO leader, Yasser Arafat, and Israeli Prime Minister Yitzhak Rabin reached agreement. It is an unexpected, historic event. They are wise and brave. They have come to the realization of the facts of history. History never stops; the cycle keeps going.

It is now the responsibility of the pro-Israeli and pro-Palestinian allies, friends or foes, to lend them helping hands to walk ahead on a very critical and difficult path for a permanent settlement.

The principles of tolerance, reconciliation, and give and take are the essence of coexistence.

I know Jerusalem may become a critical point. I do not think it should be. If wisdom prevails, it can be solved.

I have proposed (as an individual) that Jerusalem, with all its sacred places for Jews, Christians and the Muslims — "the children of Abraham" — be declared as a neutral zone for all three religions.

This neutral zone should be administered by representatives of these religions. Its chairmen could be elected from the Jews, Christians and Muslims in rotation.

This area could be a model, like the United Nations Organization.

Let us hope and work for everlasting peace for the Middle East and elsewhere.

NAIYER HABIB

Regina

Dr. Habib suggests uniform support for sufferers and not only for one faction.

≥ ¬HDₑ-X PₑSₜ MAY21 93
Fₒily

'A new life'

The headline news on the front page of The Leader-Post, May 13, "Serbian refugee attacked", is inflammatory and is not in keeping with Canadian spirit. It is most important that when such a situation arises, we help people to reconcile their differences. They deserve our sympathy, from whatever background they come.

It is our responsibility to educate the people who come facing such circumstances in their old countries. The Canadian spirit, the spirit of beginning a new life in Canada, of respecting and tolerating one another for a new beginning, for the goodness of Canada and thereby for the goodness of the world as a whole.

People closely involved with such groups should sense the problems beforehand and take preventive measures. The media have a greater responsibility of what to publish and in what manner.

Dr. NAIYER HABIB

Habib is past president, Islamic Association of Saskatchewan, Regina. Inc.

12   The Leader-Post   Regina, Saskatchewan   Tuesday, January 23 1979

From left, Anna Watts, Charlie, Dr. Alexander Watts and David in Arabic dress   Leader-Post photo

Family enjoyed short stint in Emirates

By Andrew Kozma
of The Leader-Post

Dr. Alexander Reginald Watts, a Regina neurosurgeon, spent part of last year in the United Arab Emirates doing medical and missionary work for the Evangelical Alliance Mission (TEAM).

Watts, his wife, Anna, and two sons, Charlie, nine, and David, seven, lived at Al Ain, a conglomerate of 10 townships, each with a population of several thousand.

Watts said the Emirates consist of seven small sheikdoms, with a population of about 300,000 living on about 32,-000 square miles.

Thanks to its oil income, one of the sheikhdoms, Abu Dhabi, has the highest per capita income in the world — about $100,000.

Dubai, the other oil-rich sheikdom, has also been the world centre in gold smuggling.

Support others

"These two are supporting the remaining five sheikhdoms which have no oil but hope it will soon be found."

" Politically, the Emirates are in a position of a small country with a 'big brother'. About the shortest description of the situation would be to say that if the Saudis say jump — they jump," Watts said.

Watts said large portions of the Emirates are technologically highly developed, with technocrats and officials educated at foreign universities.

"Abu Dhabi, Dubai, Sharja and Al Ain are all modern cities with highways, highrises and all the comforts of modern life. "Still, the country as a whole is being run in what I called the Arab variation of IBM methods, where 'I' stands for Insh'Allah (it's God's will, or everything comes from God), 'B' stands for Bukhara (tomorrow, which may mean two weeks, next year, or never.) Finally, 'M' stands for Malesh (don't worry)."

He said, with these three phrases, people in the Emirates are able to solve or brush off any problem.

Watts said he had a sick little girl in the hospital, whose father wanted to take her out.

"I told him if he did the child would die. He shrugged his shoulders, said Insh'Allah and took her away. She was dead within a short time."

He said Arabs have a different set of values than people of the western world. Islamic is more than merely a religion. It is the leading force of the Arab world that regulates every facet of life, the law, administration of countries, the whole of social and family life."

Watts said the most common quality of the Arab character is hospitality.

"We visited a family that paid more than $100 just for the goat for the rice pilan. In Canada it would cost about $30."

Wives can be costly

Incomes are high but so are prices. A wife can cost about $25,000 and the groom can see her only after the wedding.

According to Watts, the 14- to 16-year-old brides are an improvement as, in old times, 10-year old brides were not unusual.

He said other prices are also high. A 12-ounce jar of honey is about $3.

"With a yearly income of $100,000, it's not difficult for a man to get married. Some have two or more wives," Watts said.

He said the Q'uran allows four, plus an unlimited number of concubines, if the husband is able to take care of them.

How do wives in such multiple marriages getting along?

"Just like they would here in Canada — like a bunch of cats in a sack".

He said the husband has to build a separate house for each and maintain a separate household.

"If you add to it that the poor guy has to put up with four mothers-in-law, the advantages of this polygamy become rather questionable," Watts said.

Most local Arabs are in government employment. Some higher officials are trained at foreign universities or at the U.S. University in Beirut, he said.

"There is a modern university of Islamic studies at Al Ain, attended by students from all over the Arab world."

He said laborers, truck drivers, mechanics, tradesmen come from Pakistan and India. They are Muslims and either Belujis or Pattanis.

3

All wages clear

"A truck driver in the Emirates makes $1,500 a month and there are no taxes."

"This may sound like a tale, but the colorful Orient of the Tales of the 1001 Nights, if it ever existed at all, belongs to the past," Watts said.

Al Ain, where they stayed, is a modern city with highways, highrises, a great many cars and modern stores.

There are still many goats on the streets but no mules. Camels are kept as pets.

Medical services?

There are many, physicians, mostly from India and Pakistan, practising in the Emirates and large, modern government hospitals in the cities of Burayami and in Jimi. A second, 500-bed hospital was under construction there during the Watts' stay.

Watts said Abu Dhabi has three large government hospitals and there is a big, modern hospital in Dubai.

"I worked at our mission hospital that has been in operation since the 1960s. It provides general medicine and basic surgery.

"I saw one or two cases of malaria and two or three suspected cases of malaria every day and a few advanced cases of trachoma.

"The general hygiene is getting better but there is plenty of TB. The Arabs are very clean people, though it's not easy because of the chronic shortage of water."

Watts said the Arabs have accepted the mission hospital with great confidence and trust.

Why?

"Because we always told them what's wrong with them and what they need. They said, in government hospitals, they were told nothing.

"I was doing mostly general medicine. Once, while I was assisting at the delivery of a baby in the presence of another woman — the hvastah — and the grandmother, granny started to hit me over the head. I asked why and was told she did it because I was a man. She did not take me as a doctor, obviously."

First disc operation

Watts said he did the first disc operation in the Emirates. Up to then people had to go to England for such operations.

Most of the population are Bedus, while in Oman there are visible African influences through the slave trade.

"When babies are born, the mothers pull their noses so they will not have short, stubby 'slave' noses," he said.

Among the oddities of the ancient medicine now being abolished is the practice of putting salt into the mother's vagina after childbirth.

"It was to prevent after-birth infection but the salt damaged the birth canal. The birthrate had therefore been low as most women could have only one baby."

He said one of the reasons the Arabs accepted modern hospitals willingly was that they stopped this 'salt treatment!'

"Many people are still wearing talismans, usually made of gold or leather."

He said there is plenty of 18-karat gold jewelry around.

"I saw a three-year-old naked girl with about $80 worth of gold around her neck. A woman who was visiting us regularly with her sick baby was always wearing at least $5,000 worth of jewelry and I never saw her wearing the same piece twice," Watts said.

He said the old souk, better known under the Iranian name of bazaar, is gone. The old style Oriental market does not exist but bargaining and haggling in the stores is still a part of the buying and selling ceremony.

He said the Maria Theresia silver dollars minted in Austria, the semi-official currency of the Arabs for almost 200 years, has disappeared.

Watts said each of the seven sheikhdoms has a local government and there is a federal government in Abu Dhabi headed by Shaikh Zayid.

"His Rolls Royce and guards wearing chrome-plated tommy guns are quite often seen driving through the country," he said.

"Men are still wearing the traditional khondura, a long white gown. Around the headcover they have the suffrah, a thick black rope. It was originally used to tie the camels' legs at night. During the day, the riders simply put it on the headcover.

"Women wear the long black cloak, the abbah over their dresses and their faces are covered with the burka, a black mask. Some Somali and Pakistani women are still wearing the thick, ancient veils," Watts said.

Prior to the discovery of oil the majority of the Bedu population just lived off the camel.

"Currently there are large imports of western technology and great efforts are made to modernize the ways of life though always strictly within the rules of Islam.

"It is still a land of contrasts. The custom of chopping off the hands of thieves seems to be still in use," he said.

How about the famous Arab coffee?

"They are adding lots of cardamon to it and it tastes just awful to us."

Watts said his wife was in charge of the children of the mission's staff. The two boys enjoyed every minute of their stay at Al Ain despite the 110 degree temperatures. On the hottest day it was 131 degrees.

"It was a valuable experience for the whole family and we are ready to go down there or to any other place where we can be of some help to people anytime," Watts said.

Naiyer Habib & Mahlaqa Naushaba Habib

Response to Dr. Watts from Dr. Habib

The Leader-Post Regina, Saskatchewan Monday, March 12, 1979

*Readers
Viewpoints*

Question of wives

In an interview published Jan. 23 Dr. Watts was quoted as saying Quran allows four wives plus an unlimited number of concubines, if the husband is able to take care of them.

We are sorry to note such a distorted remark.

Quran does not permit concubines — even one. A sex relation beyond marriage in Islam is punishable by death.

Quran permits marriage with one to four wives provided the husband can do equal justice to all wives and can maintain them.

Islam, as a religion, was the first to put a limitation on numbers of wives. It is a provision under conditions difficult to fulfill and not an encouragement. Looking at history it was a time when many women became widows after wars.

We agree many Muslims take advantage of the provision and do not fulfill the conditions. So they are in sin and punishable by Islamic law.

Our association has literature on these aspects.

NAIYER HABIB
President, Islamic Association
of Saskatchewan, Regina

214

Response to Time

Time magazine had a front-cover issue June 15, 1992.

Title: *Islam: Should the World Be Afraid*

It had a picture of half the top of a Mosque and that of a person apparently representing a Muslim from the Afghan area.

Response by Dr. Habib, as president of the Islamic Association of Saskatchewan, Regina was published by *Time* magazine in its issue on July 6, 1992 as follows:

LETTERS

ISLAM NEW MARCH

"By accepting Islamic model,
The world can be a better
place to live.
Naiyer Habib
Regina. Sask"

"ISLAM IS NOT A RELIGION OF RITUAL BUT a way of life. State and religion are not separate. Islam protects the rights of minorities and those who are oppressed as well. By accepting the Islamic model the world can be a better place to live"

Naiyer Habib, President
Islamic Association of Saskatchewan
Regina, Sask

Community Events

We celebrated events and invited others as an outreach to the society at large.

Canada's 125th Anniversary
Eid Milad un Nabi (Observing the Birth of the Prophet)
Four Seasons Hotel * Empringham Palace
Family Workshop
Mosaic Festival 1978
Ramadan or Eid
Eid al-Adha
Tri-Community Get-Together

Canada's 125th Anniversary
(1992)

This was celebrated at the Islamic Centre and Mosque at Montague Street. A flag was hoisted, and a sign was posted for its celebration. There was a community get-together. President Habib, Past-President Abdul Qayyum, and active member of the community Riazuddin Ahmed addressed the audience. This was initiated with recitation of the Qur'an by the children, and national anthem by all. Natasha Malik addressed the audience on behalf of the youth. The pictures are shown below.

ICM, Montague Street   Children

Naiyer Habib, President

Natasha Malik addressing the youth

Riazuddin Ahmed

Abdul Qayyum and Naiyer Habib

Socializing after Celebration

Ladies   Dr. Jafferey and Adnan Habib

Dr. Jafferey and Samiul Haque with others

Eid Milad un Nabi
(Observation of the Birth of the Prophet): Peace be upon Him

Eid Milad un Nabi (PBUH) on February 26, 1978 at Four Seasons Hotel

The tradition of Eid Milad un Nabi (PBUH) had been established by Dr. M. Anwarul Haque. He used to invite the majority of the members of the community to his home once a year to have dinner preceded by a program presented by the members of his family, that is himself and his children.

While he continued this tradition for a while, the association started to have Eid Milad un Nabi (PBUH) on a larger scale starting in 1977 with growth in the community.

This Eid Milad un Nabi (PBUH) was celebrated at the Four Seasons Hotel. The chief guest speaker was Hisham Badran. He had started to visit Regina for the youth and children, a dynamic personality to entertain the children with Islamic tradition and give an educational talk to them. The mayor of the city, Mr. Henry Baker, was invited as chief guest. Dr. David Russell, Vice-President of the Council of the Muslim Communities of Canada with his wife was invited.

A dinner was arranged in the Four Seasons Hotel. Because of the cultural nature of the event, a donation was received from the Multicultural Department of the province. A very good function was held successfully. The children also gave their presentation besides the guests and me as the president.

Announcement and Program for Eid Milad un Nabi 1977 Followed by Pictures of the Event

**THE ISLAMIC ASSOCIATION OF SASKATCHEWAN
REGINA**

PHONE

P O B 3572
Regina, Saskatchewan
Canada

وَاعْتَصِمُوا بِحَبْلِ اللهِ جَمِيعًا وَلَا تَفَرَّقُوا ۚ

'And hold together firmly to God's rope and do not
separate.'
The Quran 3:103

February 6, 1978

MESSAGE FROM THE PRESIDENT

By the Grace of God it is a great pleasure to know that we shall be
celebrating our Prophet Muhammad's (PBUH) Birthday on February 26, 1978 in
a very Islamic and dignified way, Insha-Allah. We shall be inviting civic
dignitaries and other guests. Br. Hisham Badran will be the chief speaker and
his topic will be "Prophet Muhammad (PBUH) as a Humanitarian", - a title most
appropriate for a mixed gathering of this age and time. Speakers from our
own community will also take part on important Islamic subjects. Please
take this opportunity to help the Association identify Islam and the Community
to other Canadian citizens by active participation. Please make an effort
to bring your friends, Muslims and Non-Muslims. Your interest in these
matters is of vital importance for the functioning and solidarity of the
Association.

I wish you all a very happy and enjoyable Eid-Milad-Un-Nabi and hope
to see you at the celebration.

Yours, Brother in Islam,

(Dr. N. Habib

THE ISLAMIC ASSOCIATION OF SASKATCHEWAN
REGINA

PHONE

POB 3572
Regina, Saskatchewan
Canada

وَاعْتَصِمُوا بِحَبْلِ اللّٰهِ جَمِيعًا وَلَا تَفَرَّقُوا

'And hold together firmly to God's rope and do not separate.'
The Quran 3:103

February 6, 1978

Dear Members,

    Aslamaulakam :

        It is with great sorrow that I have to mention the passing away of a prominent member of our Community, Dr. Ishrat Hussain on January 22, 1978. The burial took place at the Regina Memorial Gardens on Wednesday January 25, 1978 at 11.30 a.m. preceded by the Salat-Djinaza led by Dr. Habib. Quran recital and prayers were held at Riffat Hussain's residence on Sunday January 29, 1978.

        We all offer our deepest sympathies and condolence to his wife and three children and to his brother Riffat Hussain.

        Riffat Hussain wishes to convey through this news letter his appreciation and gratitude to all friends for their sympathy and comfort at that time of great sorrow.

Mawlid-An-Nabi

        The Executive Committee is pleased to inform you that the Department of Culture and Youth has co-sponsored the celebrations for Idd-Milad-un-Nabi this year by approving a grant towards the expenses. The celebrations this year are planned to be held on February 26, 1978 at the Four Seasons Palace Banquet Hall, 2401 Rothwell Street, Regina, between 11.00 a.m. to 4.00 p.m. with Luncheon served at 1.00 p.m. Arrangements are being made for prominent speakers on Islamic topics, invitations to guests and dignitaries from all walk of life. Participation by all members of the Muslim Community is very vital and very warm and sincere invitation is hereby extended to you and your friends, both Muslims and non-Muslims. To facilitate and finalise the seating and catering arrangements in particular, it is very important the precise number of guests attending, with a breakdown of adults and children, be obtained well in advance. You are requested to complete and return the attached form so as to reach us by February 15, 1978. Alternately please phone 545-7430 and leave the relevant information by February 16, 1978.

        Please note this is NOT A POTLUCK PARTY. Lunch, refreshments and Idd gifts to children will be served with compliments of the Islamic Association and courtesy and co-operation of Department of Culture and Youth.

/2....

- 2 -

A brief tentative programme is :

1. Commence: Recitation from Quran

2. Welcome and Introduction of Guests.

3. Speeches by chief guest speaker and other participants,
   film or slide show.

4. Lunch.

A detailed programme will be available.

Location of Four Seasons Palace: 2401 Rothwell Street, Regina.

Date: Sunday February 26, 1978

Time: 11.00 a.m. - 4.00 p.m.

Mawlid An-Nabi

(Prophet Muhammad's PBUH Birthday)

Dept of Culture and Youth and

the Islamic Association of Sask.
(Regina ch.)

Sponsored Event.

Please complete and return this form to reach by February 15, 1978

Name:_____ Address _____ Phone _____

Will attend: Adults _____   Children_____   Ages _____

Guests   Adults _____   Children_____   Ages _____

To: Secretary
336 Forsyth Crescent, Regina, S4R 5L5.

/3....

224

وَاعْتَصِمُوا بِحَبْلِ اللهِ جَمِيعًا وَلَا تَفَرَّقُوا

'And hold together firmly to God's rope and do not separate.'
The Quran 3:103

the ISLAMIC ASSOCIATION OF SASKATCHEWAN

REGINA

Mawlid An-Nabi (Prophet Muhammad's (PBUH) Birthday) Celebrations and Luncheon at the Four Seasons Palace, 2401 Rothwell St., Sunday, Feb. 26, 1978, 11:00 a.m. to 4:00 p.m.

Mawlid An-Nabi

PROPHET MUHAMMAD'S BIRTHDAY   pbuh

Programme :

11 am   Reception & Registration of Guests
in attendance :●nazan ●ismat ●ravida.

-

11 30   Recitation from Qur'an

-

Welcome from the President – naiyer habib

-

11 45   Nāat – zubair akhtar

-

Presentation by Islamic School students
1 shakeel   2 adnan

-

Sura Alaq – aftab ghani

-

12 15   Early history of Islam & Philosophy of Islam –
dr. david russel   president islamic association
saskatoon

12 30   -●● ●----- INTERMISSION – light refreshments

1 pm   Prophet Muhammad(peace be upon him) as
Humanitarian – imam hisham badran – croatian
islamic centre toronto

___

≈ SALAAM ≈

1 30   Reception of the Guest of Honour
        his worship the mayor – henry baker

~ **Luncheon** ~

A word from

- the mayor

- the president

Sponsored by :

Department of Culture and Youth

بسم الله الرحمن الرحيم

THE ISLAMIC ASSOCIATION OF SASKATCHEWAN
REGINA

P O B 3572
Regina, Saskatchewan

Executive Committee 1978

president   NAIYER HABIB
vice president   ANWAR QURESHI
secretary   AKRAM DIN
treasurer   SAJJAD MALIK

members   AFTAB GHANI

                   RIFFAT HUSSAIN

                   MEHDI ZAHEDI

February 26, 1978 at Four Seasons Hotel
Mayor Baker attends
Guest speaker: Hisham Badran

David Russell, Mrs. Russell, Anwar Qureshi, Naiyer Habib, Akram Din (secretary), Zubair Akhtar, Aftab Ghani, and Dr. M. Anwarul Haque (founding president) at head table

Mrs. David Russell, Anwar Qureshi (vice-president), Hisham Badran, Mayor Henry Baker, Naiyer Habib (president)

Mrs. D. Russell, Anwar Qureshi, Adnan Habib, Naiyer Habib, Hisham Badran, Akram Din (secretary), Zubair Akhtar, and Aftab Ghani at head table

Mayor Henry Baker with Chip, his sister, Arsalan, and Adnan Habib

The second largest Eid Milad un Nabi function was held at Empringham Palace on Montague Street on Sunday, February 11, 1979.

The main presenters here were the children and Hisham Badran was again the chief guest. He spent a few days in Regina with the children.

THE ISLAMIC ASSOCIATION OF SASKATCHEWAN
REGINA

P O B 3572
Regina, Saskatchewan
Canada

EXECUTIVE COMMITTEE – 1979

President		Naiyer Habib 308 Habkirk Drive	584-8578
Vice-President		Masood Hassan 7 Woodsworth Crescent	545-6460
Secretary		Aziza Sleightholm 1 Turgeon Crescent	586-4689
Treasurer		Mohammed Husain Khatri 3 - 4160 Rae Street	585-0675
Members	(i)	Masudul Alam Choudhary 1319 Wascana Street	525-5779
	(ii)	Nizar Rajabali 273 Wells Street	949-2518
	(iii)	Akram Din 336 Forsyth Crescent	545-7430

Mawlid An-Nabi

PROPHET MUHAMMAD'S BIRTHDAY   pbuh

Programme

232

Mawlid An-Nabî

PROPHET MUHAMMAD'S BIRTHDAY   pbuh

All members & guests are welcome

Programme   2:30 p.m. – 5:00p.m.

2:30 pm-
1. Reception & Registration of Guests

                    In attendence   *Ravida*Mutriba*Nazan
                         M C   Masood Hassan

3:00 pm-
2. Recitation from Quran *Asim Ghani
3. Welcome from the President *Naiyer Habib
4. Presentation by Islamic School students
    ☆ Sura Fatiha *Arsalan Habib *Nasreen Khatri
    ☆ Life of Prophet Muhammad pbuh * Andaleeb Qayyum
    ☆ Islamic Chorus * Group of students

5 **Prophet Muhammad** pbuh
  His life and teachings
         *Chief Guest

  Hisham Badran _ Field Director – Muslim World League, Mecca

6 **SALAAM** ☆ All please participate

☆ ☆ ☆ ☆ ☆ ☆ ☆ ☆ ☆ ☆ ☆ ☆ ☆
Social Hour before Dinner

233

Dinner: 5:30 – 7:30

Al-Empringham Hall

 advance reservations only

Greetings

May Allah guide us all in the right path and protect us from the evil. For your endeavours to uphold the banner of Islam, May Allah bestow His choicest blessings upon you all, Ameen.

"Truly Allah loves those who fight in His cause in battle array, as if they were a solid cemented structure." (Al-Qur'an: LXI V.4)

Abdul Qayyum   Arif Sethi   Aftab Ghani

Akram Din   Masood Hassan

Naiyer Habib, President

Hisham Badran, guest speaker

Andaleeb Qayyum

Arsalan Habib and Nasreen Khatri

Back row, left to right: Ali Sethi, Adnan Qayyum, Adnan Habib, Samiul Haque,
Aftab Ghani's son
Front row, left to right: Faisal Sethi, Arsalan Habib, Aftab Ghani's son, Arsalan
Ghani, Nasreen Khatri, Sabreena Haque

Naushaba Habib

Front row, left to right: Anwarul Haque, unidentified, Abdul
Qayyum, A. Majid Khatri, Arif Sethi, Aftab Ghani

Front, left to right: Arif Sethi, Aftab Ghani, (*behind* and *between* them on the
left) Razia Din and (*right*) Fareda Sethi, unidentified, Arsalan Ghani standing,
Ambreen Din next on the *right*
Four boys (*left to right*): Andaleeb Qayyum, unidentified, Samiul Haque, and
Adnan Habib

Subsequently, the Eid Milad un Nabi and other functions continued in the community hall as potlucks. A guest speaker would be invited, or a local speaker was arranged. The lunch and snacks were prepared by the ladies.

It should be noted that I made sure that the children attended the function especially to hear the speaker, and they participated. If they were found to be playing in the playground and the speaker was to begin the speech, I would go out and call them all in. That is noted to emphasize the importance of participation of the children in the society where the Muslims are in the minority and facing very different culture and religion of the majority.

Family Workshop: Children and Muslim Family by Dr. M. Sadiq (1990) at ICM on Montague Street

With my intent along with the enthusiasm of having acquired our new centre, we felt like expanding our horizon of learning and practicing what we wanted to learn and had learned. We arranged a two-day workshop. We invited Dr. M. Sadiq, an internationally renowned clinical psychologist with special interest in family for a two-day session. He was equally involved in the Muslim community serving the community and Islam.

There was active and good participation by the communities, men, women, and youth. Groups were arranged to follow up after, so that the learning was utilized by the communities.

That was the only workshop during our leadership. Speakers were invited from time to time on different occasions.

Opening with recitation of Qur'an

President Habib welcomes and opens the session

Dr. M. Sadiq in workshop

The participants

Discussions, questions, and answers

Dr. M. Anwarul Haque

Abdul Qayyum

Riazuddin Ahmed

Rasekh

Samina Ahmed Munirul Haque and Dr. M. Sadiq

Natasha Malik and Dr. M. Sadiq

Mosaic Festival: May 25-27, 1978 in Regina

This was a multicultural exhibit and socialization starting in 1977 in the city of Regina. Various members of the community from various countries and of various nationalities put their stalls in various buildings across the city. They had their cultural show, exhibit, and food. City bus was rotating from one place to the other with no charge. Individuals were required to purchase a Mosaic ticket for the season. The ticket was required to take the ride to the various pavilions. That lasted for two days. It was well-received and it continued. The Islamic Association participated in it. It had its first-time stall in the same building on Montague Street, which we purchased subsequently after twelve years of the first Mosaic. Unfortunately, there is no picture available of that Mosaic. The next Mosaic was held during the seventy-fifth anniversary of the city of Regina. The Islamic Association participated in this with enthusiasm and presented a very successful program. The documents and the pictures are included here. Unfortunately, the association could only participate in the first two Mosaic festivals.

We participated in May of 1978. This coincided with the seventy-fifth anniversary of our city. Our pavilion was called Islamic World Pavilion.

The Publicity

Our Program

The Islamic World **menu**

kabab	beef	3/$1·00	◊ 0·40	each
curry	beef-peas		◊ 0·75	plate
pakoray	bhajia snack vegetarian		◊ 0·50	plate
puree			◊ 0·35	each
rice	fried		◊ 0·30	plate
papad			◊ 0·30	each
gulab jaman	sweet	3/$1·00	◊ 0·35	each

islamic world special ..

rice, curry, kabab, pakoray, puree	◊ 2·50	plate

soft drinks ..

islamic delight aqua flowers & fruits	◊ 0·25
soft drink , coffee	◊ 0·25

Please ask for **TAKE AWAYS**

programme

5·30 pm	islamic chorus	main floor
6·00	film show	lower
6·20	adhan	main
6·30	cooking demonstration	lower
7·00	ethnic dress fashion show	main
8·00	mehndi	main
8·30	cooking demonstration	lower
9·00	film & slide show	

sat.

4·00 pm	ethnic dress fashion show	main

Our Invitation Card

THE ISLAMIC ASSOCIATION OF SASKATCHEWAN
REGINA

PHONE

P.O.B 3672
Regina, Saskatchewan
Canada

Invites

at the

ISLAMIC WORLD PAVILION

410 COLLEGE AVE

MAY 25,26,27 –1978

Fareda Sethi leading the chorus with the children

Fashion Show

Arif Sethi

Masood Hassan with his wife

Iranian Students

Group Cultural Fashion Show: Men and Women

Mehndi pre marriage function of Indo-pak custom

Naiyer Habib at the Islamic Stall

Left to right: Naushaba Habib, Mrs. Shamim Jamil, Anwar Qureshi, Aziza Sleighthom, Razia Din (sitting)

Naushaba Habib cooking

Ramadan and Eid

Ramadan

We were having potluck of tar at our houses on rotation. We were doing Sura Taraweeh by rotation and at our houses before any centre existed.

Eid Prayers and Functions

We held Eid prayers or Eid get-togethers in the basement of the Red Cross building at the corner of College Avenue and Broad Street. Before forming an association, we also performed Eid prayers in private homes. Eid prayer was also held in the Arts Department, and hall of the old campus of the University of Regina.

An Eid Function in the basement of the old Red Cross building, 2571 Broad Street, where functions took place for years.

Eid at Landmark Inn

We held an Eid function in the Landmark Inn at 4150 Albert Street in Regina in 1978 by family contribution. Eid gifts were presented to all children. It was very elegant. However, community attendance was small. We returned to the potluck function and held it at various places.

Qayyum family

Abdul and Qudsia Qayyum,
A.Majid and Mariam Khatri

Majid Khatri Family

Dr. Haque and Nilofer Haque facing
forward, Riazuddin looking sideways

Akram Din with Razia and
daughters, Samiul looking

Naushaba and Anwar Qureshi
with daughter of Anwar

Ali standing with Fareda Sethi sitting by Ali
Arif Sethi looking at us from a distance

Fareda Sethi's brother on the left,
Shahida with Masood
Arif Sethi front right

Talat Malik and her sister in the
middle

Mother of Anwar Qureshi in scarf, Mrs. and M. Hussain Khatri, with little Arsalan in the centre

Naushaba, Razia, Mrs. Juma, Adnan, Ali, Dr. Juma. Little girl by Naushaba—unidentified

Mrs. Juma, Adnan Habib, Ali Juma, Ali Sethi, Dr. Mehdi Juma, my little Arsalan Habib behind Juma

Naushaba searching for something!

Eid in Other Places

Subsequent Eid functions were held as potlucks in churches and community halls till we acquired our new ICM. Children made presentations. Gifts were distributed. At some functions, guest speakers were invited.

Eid in New ICM at Montague 1992 Event

The event took place in the new ICM offering prayers, snack after prayer, and then potluck dinner in which the community participated. It should be noted that we had not appointed any Imam. We participated in rotation to lead both Eid prayers.

We show here two Eid function pictures from the video clip. These were the only ones in my possession. Unfortunately, the quality is not good despite my efforts. One Eid is led by me and the other by Ayman Aboguddah. You will also note various members of the community—men and women.

Naiyer Habib leading Eid prayer   Community

Shahid, Dr. Haque, Munirul Haque

Ayman Aboguddah saying Eid Khutba

Khalid Afsar Naiyer Habib

Sajjad Malik with spoon,
Dr. Jafferey, Dr. Bhimji-*front*

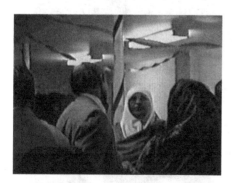

Naushaba talking to Sadeque Ahmed

At our house after the community
get-together

Eid Function 1998 in Community Hall

An elaborate Eid function was celebrated that year under the chairmanship of Dr. Abdul Jalil as the principal of the Islamic School. The entire community participated in a potluck in the community hall.

Children and youth made some presentations. Dr. Abdul Jalil delivered the welcome address. I addressed the community as the president. Entertainment was provided for the students by a magician within the parameters of Islamic criteria. Children received gifts.

This was my, along with my colleague's, last function with IAOS.

Pictures of the Celebration

Our Flag

Abdul Jalil, welcome address as principal of the school and secretary of IAOS

Kashif Ahmed reciting Qur'an

President Habib addressing the community

Children's Presentation

Children's presentation—a chorus

Children's game—supervised by Sr. Nasim Ahmed

Erum and Naushaba

Prayer

Eidul al-Adha (Feast of Sacrifice)

Prayers were offered as Eid. Some of us went to a farm, namely Dr. Haque and Dr. Habib with their children. Br. Mohammad Sadeque used to accompany us. As children grew up, we quit going to the farm whereas others (I do not recall names) continued.

Tri-community Get-Together

Abdul Qayyum initiated this in 1983. The objective was for the three communities to get together once a year on rotation at the three community centres to socialize and have other activities and discussions of mutual interest.

The first one was held in Saskatoon on Good Friday. The day was chosen for the ongoing program. Each community presented a program on behalf of their centres. Children's programs were a priority. Students of the Islamic School of each community presented their program. Children and the students were recognized. They received gifts. We had lunch, snack, etc. We all enjoyed ourselves.

It continued successfully for a few years, and then it died down in 2001 or 2002.

Bus ride to Swift Current

Dr. Jafferey on the bus

Masjid Al-Khair

Arrived at the destination

We in the basement of the Masjid where community functions used to be held

Prayers on the upper floor of the Masjid

Thank You to Ahmed Aboudheir, President of the Islamic Association of Saskatchewan, Regina 2004–2006

The charge of the association was handed over to the new board in 1998 with enthusiasm. The association faced a crisis in 1998, which continued till 2004. The founders and establishers of the association were surprised to see that the principles on which the association had been founded and established were being ultimately discarded. All steps were taken to ensure that they were no longer able to participate in the affairs of the association. They isolated themselves, noting their humiliation.

Ahmed Aboudheir was elected as the president of the association in 2004. He took decisive steps. In gatherings of Jumuah and Eid, publicly criticizing how these founders and establishers of the association were treated during that period. He recognized their service and restored their dignity by honoring them.

I thank him on our behalf. A community should respect individuals for who they are. I, during the terms of my presidency, always respectfully asked the advice of Dr. M. Anwarul Haque, the most senior of us and the founding president of the association.

An example of a plaque offered to me (with a copy of Qur'an and letter) is shown below.

Ahmed Aboudheir has a PhD in Industrial Systems Engineering from the Faculty of Engineering and Applied Science at the University of Regina, Saskatchewan. He is chief technology officer at HTC Purenergy in Regina. He has done research on many scientific subjects, contributing to the progress of the province, has published many scientific articles, and supervised PhD students.

Award: Centennial Commemorative Medal of the Government of Saskatchewan

He received the Government of Saskachewan Commemorative Medal for the centennial of Saskatchewan in April 2006. The Saskatchewan Centennial Medal is an official honor of the crown which recognizes individuals who have made significant contributions to the province, based on outstanding contribution for research and product development at HTC and on his leadership role in the community as the president of the Islamic Association of Saskatchewan, Regina.

He received other awards:

- NSERC Visiting Fellowship
- Post-Doctoral Fellowship

Naiyer Habib & Mahlaqa Naushaba Habib

On the occasion of	À l'occasion du
the Province of Saskatchewan's	100e anniversaire
100th anniversary	de la province de la Saskatchewan
in Confederation	dans la Confédération
the *Saskatchewan Centennial Medal*	la *Médaille du Centenaire de la Saskatchewan*
is presented to	est remise à

Ahmed Aboudheir

Premier
Premier ministre

Lieutenant Governor
Lieutenante-gouverneure

Charge of Documents to the President Elect 1998

These documents are lost as per my discussion with Dr. M. Anwarul Haque. This was officially communicated to the existing board in 2013, for the needful.

Oct 1998

Page I.   CHARGE: FROM N. HABIB To B. A. Haleem.

VERY IMPORTANT DOCUMENTS TO BE READ & UNDERSTOOD.

1. Islamic Centre Mosque 3273 Montefiore Street
   (a) Promissory note to CIT Nov 1, 1989 - original.
   (b) Trust Agreement - 1st Nov 1989 - original between CIT Foundation & IAOS, Regina Inc.
   (c) Promissory note - Redrawn copy - faxed document copy C Home Note 2 B. Nasr from Md. Ashraf
   (d) Draft agreement as (b)
   (e) (copy) Minutes General body May 1st '89 & 16 July '89
2. (a) Land title 3273 Montefiore Lot 14, 15, 16
      " Blvn (81) Laneview Centre 31 Oct 1989.
      Sign. Dan Madsen solicitor - Caveat
   (b) Certificate of Title Lot 14, 15, 16 Blvn 81
       Regina Sask. Plan F J 4373.
       — Canadian Islamic Trust Foundation (in owns).
       Certificate # 89 R 6281 7 fof 60 r 25 964
   (c) Survey Diagram copy x 4
3. (a) letter form Griffin, Morgan Madsen to Nasr Rull date Oct 5 1989.
   (b)   "   "   " Nov 16 '1989.
4. Old Constitution 1 (1971), 2, 3 & 4
5. (a) Regina Islamic Centre Mosque Inc Registration form drawn 16 18 82 Reg'n 20 8 82
   (b) i. Certificate of Incorporation of Regina Islamic Centre Mosque Inc (original)
      ii. Also attached Form 1 E seal of Incorporation (Rabbi)
      iii. Restriction of Activities Schedule 1

continued Next Page (2)

Naiyer Habib & Mahlaqa Naushaba Habib

274

Council of Muslim Communities of Canada

This was a vibrant Muslim Canadian national organization starting in the early 1970s. Various Muslim organizations were associated with it. It had various projects serving the Muslim communities. It used to have annual meetings rotating between east and west Canada. I used to attend these meetings fairly regularly.

Two of our youth, Andaleeb Qayyum and Adnan Habib, attended the First Youth Conference arranged by CMCC in Toronto.

A cover of its monthly magazine, *Islam Canada*, a list of Muslim organizations, its various projects with names of chairpersons for the projects, and names of the executives of CMCC of the year are attached here from the magazine. A photograph of long-term serving individuals also appears here.

They are all of historic importance.

Dr. Murray Hogben (Montreal), Salim Ganem (Edmonton), Vice Chairman, CMCC and Dr. Ahmad Fuad Sahin, Chairman CMCC. (February 1980).

See Salim Ganem in the *Early Muslims of Regina*.

VOLUME 3   NO. 1   SHA'BAN - RAMADAN, 1394 A.H.   SEPTEMBER - OCTOBER, 1974

ISLAM CANADA

 Council of Muslim Communities of Canada

THE COUNCIL OF MUSLIM COMMUNITIES OF CANADA

The Council of Muslim Communities of Canada (C.M.C.C.) is an expression of the natural desire of Muslim residents of Canada to work together for the common good. The Council was established by a unanimous vote of delegates from the Muslim Communities in Ontario and Quebec at the London Mosque on April 22, 1972. The Council succeeded and took over the work of the Ontario Council of Muslim Communities which had functioned since 1969. The London Meeting was followed by quarterly meetings of delegates from Muslim Communities in Montreal, Ottawa, Hamilton and Toronto. Various drafts of Constitutional proposals were circulated across Canada as well. Finally, on June 2, 1973, the Constitution of the Council was formally ratified

by the delegates from Cambridge, Edmonton, Hamilton, Montreal, Ottawa, Toronto and Windsor. Messages of endorsement and support were received from the Associations in Calgary, London, Regina, Saskatoon and Winnipeg.

The Preamble to the Constitution defines the rationale of the C.M.C.C. In these words, "We, the Muslim Communities of Canada, followers of the religion of Islam, intend to follow the Quranic injunction, 'Hold fast to the Covenant of Allah, and do not be divided', and resolve to combine our endeavours in the formation of the Council of Muslim Communities of Canada."

● Chairman: Dr. Ahmad Fuad Sahin,
R.R. 1, Niagara-on-the-Lake, Ont. (416) 262-4103
● Vice Chairman: M. Jomha,
9345 – 158 St., Edmonton, Alta. T5R 2C6 (403) 489-0879

● Treasurer: A.H. Shaikh,
43 Clifford Street, Hamilton, Ont. L8S 2Z7 (416) 528-2801
● Secretary: Q. Mahmud,
533 Foran, Aylmer, P.Q. J9H 6A3 (819) 684-1102

Council of Muslim Communities of Canada, P.O. Box 2364, Station 'D', Ottawa, Ontario K1P 5W5 — Telephone (819) 684-1102

MUSLIM COMMUNITY ORGANIZATIONS IN CANADA

Association of Islamic Community Gazi Husrev-Beg, P.O. Box 64, Postal Station "K", Toronto, Ontario M4P 2G1
Association des Etudiants Musulmans de Quebec, 2631 Port Royal, Quebec, P.Q. G1V 1A5, (418) 656-0126
B.C. Muslim Association, P.O. Box 34395, Stn. D., Vancouver, B.C., V6J 4P3, — President, Abdul H. Patel, (604) 224-9244
Brantford Muslim Association, 16 Applewood, Brantford, Ont. — President, Ebrahim Sayed, (519) 756-7698
Calgary Muslim Association, P.O. Box 1602, Calgary, Alta. T2P 2L7 — President, Ibrahim Rafih, (403) 243-7186
Cambridge Muslim Association, P.O. Box 2022, Cambridge (H), Ont. N3C 2V6 — President, Zubair Ahsan (519) 622-0349
Canadian Islamic Centre, 10205 – 111 Ave., Edmonton, Alta. (403) 422-0118 — President, M. Jomha, (403) 489-0879
Canadian Bosnian Muslim Association, 7071 Oakwood Dr., Niagara Falls, Ontario L2E 6S5
Canadian Islamic Cultural & Educational Foundation, 9014 – 90 Street, Edmonton, Alta. — President, S. Ganam, (403) 466-3495
Canadian Muslim Association, P.O. Box 641, Lac la Biche, Alta.
Croatian Islamic Centre, P.O. Box 244, Stn. N., Toronto, Ont. (416) 255-8338 — President, Kerim Reis, (416) 769-3045
Fatima Mosque, 2012 St. Dominique, Montreal, Quebec — President, A.R. El-Sumaiti, (514) 769-0396
Islamic Association of the Maritimes, P.O. Box 116, Dartmouth, N.S. — President, Naveed Akhtar, (902) 469-1014
Islamic Association of Saskatchewan, P.O. Box 3572, Regina, Sask. S4P 3L7 — President, Dr. Naiyer Habib, (306) 584-8578
Islamic Association of Saskatchewan, P.O. Box 330, P.O. 6, Saskatoon, Sask. — President, Dr. Z.H. Aivi, (306) 374-4293
Islamic Association of Sudbury, 961 Auger, Sudbury, Ont. B3A 4A7 — President, A.G. Zia, (705) 566-0560
Islamic Centre of Quebec, 2620 Laval Road, Ville St. Laurent, P.Q., (514) 331-1770 — President, Izhar Mirza
Islamic Centre of Toronto, 56 Boustead Avenue, Toronto, Ont. M6R 1Z5, (416) 769-7800 — President, Dr. M. Jinnah, (416) 278-7414
Islamic Foundation of Toronto, Inc., 182 Rhodes Ave., Toronto, Ont. (416) 465-2525 — President, Mohammad Nasir, (416) 445-2903
Islamic School of Ottawa, P.O. Box 2364, Station 'D', Ottawa, Ont., L2E 6S5 — President, Qasem Mehmud, (819) 684-1102
Islamic Society of Niagara Peninsula, 7075 Oakwood Drive, Niagara Falls, Ont. L2E 6S5 — (416) 356-1622
Islamic Society of Sault St. Marie, 780 Copper St., Sault St. Marie, Ont. — President, Ayub Hasan, (705) 949-5657
Kingston Islamic Society, International Centre, Queen's University, Kingston, Ont. — President, Dr. Hafiz ur Rehman, (613) 548-3731
London Mosque, 151 Church St. W., London, Ont. (519) 439-9451 — President, H. Hasan, (519) 434-5927
Malvern Muslim Association, 20A Eppleworth Drive, No. 212,Scarborough — Ameer, Inamullah Makki, (416) 261-4881
Manitoba Islamic Association, P.O. Box 1722, Winnipeg, Manitoba — President, Dr. H. Abu Zaid, (204) 269-9078
Millat Community Association, 203 Bayview Fairways Drive, Thornhill, Ontario L3T 2Z1 — President, M. Moinuddin, (416) 889-3501
Muslim Association of Hamilton, P.O. Box 201, Station A, Hamilton, Ont. — President, Mohammad El Farram, (416) 388-7776
Muslim Association of New Brunswick, P.O. Box 6373, Station 'A', St. John, N.B. E2L 4K8 — President, Khalil J. Malik
Muslim Society of Toronto, 564 Annette St., Toronto, Ontario — President, S.B. Kerim, (416) 244-4973
Muslim Society of Waterloo and Wellington Counties, 210 – 7 Glamis Road, Galt, Ontario — President, Zubair Ahsan, (519) 622-0349
N.W. Ontario Muslim Association, 448 North James, Thunder Bay, Ontario — President, M. Yasin Sharif, (705) 577-3612
Ontario Muslim Association, 73 Patricia Ave., Willowdale, Ontario M2M 1J1 — President, Ayube Ally, (416) 222-2794
Ottawa Muslim Association, 251 Northwestern Ave., Ottawa, Ont. (613) 722-0075 — President, Hussein B. Choudhry
Peel Islamic Association, 1 Mackay St. N., Bramalea, Ontario — President, Farouqui I. Baksh, (416) 456-1818
Sarnia Muslim Association, 1446 Sylvan Court, Sarnia, Ontario N7S 2K9, (519) 542-3656
St. John's Muslim Association, 140 Montague, St. John, Nfld. — President, M. Ahmed
Toronto and Region Islamic Congregation (TARIC), P.O. Box 66, Station U, Toronto, M8Z 1T0 — President, Haroon Salamat, (416) 822-4320
Windsor Islamic Association, 1320 Northwood St., Windsor, Ont., (519) 966-2355 — President, Dr. Ismail Peer

CMCC COMMITTEES & CHAIRPERSONS

Finance: A.H. Shaikh, 43 Clifford St., Hamilton, Ont. (416) 528-2801
Youth: Hani Hassan, 127 Camden Rd., London, Ont. (519) 434-5927
Ladies: Khatija Haffajee,
515 St. Laurent Blvd., Apt. 808, Ottawa, Ont. (613) 749-7138

Pub Relations: Ikram Makki 15 Andes Rd., Agincourt (416) 291-7811
Publications: M.S. Qaadri
2721 Bayview Ave., Willowdale, Ont. (416) 444-8697
Education: to be appointed — M.S. Qaadri to continue in the interim

CMCC PROJECTS & PROJECT MANAGERS

EDUCATION
• Islamic Textbook for Children:
Qasem Mahmud, 533 Foran St., Aylmer, Que. J9H 6A3, (819) 684-1102
• Parents Manual
M.S. Qaadri, 2721 Bayview Avenue, Willowdale, Ontario, (416) 444-8697
• Islamic Teachers Workshops
Ahmad Bhabe, 384 Limeridge Rd. W., Hamilton, Ont. L9C 2U5, (416) 389-2787
• Islamic Lecture Series
Izharuddin Mirza, 5715 Bellerive, Brossard, Quebec, (514) 676-8243
• Scholarships
Ghassan Attar-Hassan, 61 Woodfield Dr., Ottawa, Ontario K2G 3Y7, (613) 224-8837

YOUTH
• Camps
Hani Hassan, 127 Camden Rd., London, Ont. N5X 2K2
• Conferences
Munir El-Kassim, 1558 Allen Pl., No. 12, London, Ont. N5W 2V8, (519) 453-8288
• National Youth Exchange Programs
Sulaiman Khan, 1953 Marquis, Ottawa, Ont. (613) 741-0948
• International Youth Exchange Programs
Farouk El-Baroudi, 7570 Mirabeau Brossard, Montreal, P.Q., (514) 678-3461

PUBLIC RELATIONS
• (Muslim Survey)
Dr. Dawood Hamdani, 139 – 1075 Meadowlands Dr. E., Ottawa, Ont. K2C 3M7, (613) 224-1281

• Publicity for CMCC
Ikram Makki, 15 Andes Rd., Agincourt, Ont. (416) 291-7811
• Publicity for Conferences
Dr. M. Jomha, 9345-158 St., Edmonton, Alta. T5R 2C6 (403) 489-0879

PUBLICATIONS
• Islam Canada
Editor: M.S. Qaadri, 2721 Bayview Avenue, Willowdale, Ontario, (416) 444-8697
• Al-Quran Translation
Sayyd Abdul Khabyyr, 1882 St. Clare Rd., T.M.R., Montreal, P.Q., (514) 737-7823

PRESENTATION OF ISLAM
• Presentation of Islam to the Natives
Salim Ghanim, 9014 – 90 St., Edmonton, Alta., (403) 466-3495
• Islamic Textbook for High School Students
Dr. Murray Hogben, R.R. No. 3, Marshview Farm, Gananoque, Ont. (613) 382-2847
• Islamic Textbook for Elementary School Students — Mariam Bridgeman, 1127 King St. W., Hamilton, Ont., (416) 529-6713
• World Religions High School Course
• Television Programs
Dawood Akbar Ali, 3702 Twin Maple Dr., Mississauga, Ont. L4Y 3R5
• Interfaith Dialogue
To be appointed – Ikram Makki to continue in the interim

• Biases and Prejudices against Islam and Muslims – Khalil Baksh, 2 Acadia Bay, Winnipeg, Manitoba R3T 3H9, (204) 269-6928
• Muslim World Map
Akram Din, 336 Forsyth Cr., Regina, Sask.
• Travelling Exhibit
Ebrahim Sayed, 16 Applewood Dr., Brantford, Ont. (519) 756-7698

SPECIAL ASSIGNMENT
• Quranic Reciters

• Constitution
Dr. Hussein Abdul-Gawad, 2945 Southmore Dr. E., Ottawa, Ont., (613) 521-3751
• Al-Hajj
Ali Bazmi, 204 – 1535 Lakeshore Rd. E., Mississauga, Ont. L5E 2E2, (416) 274-9708
• Mosque Development
Mohammed Fazil, 5255 Dalcraft Cr., N.W. Calgary, Alta T3A 1N6, (403) 288-3922
• External Relations Director
Moin Muinuddin, 203 Bayview Fairways Dr., Thornhill, Ont. (416) 889-3501
• Government Liaison Officer
Moin Muinuddin, 203 Bayview Fairways Dr., Thornhill, Ont. (416) 889-3501
• Economic Co-operatives Consultant
Dr. Dawood Hamdani, 139 – 1075 Meadowlands Dr. E., Ottawa, Ont. K2C 3M7, (613) 224-1282

277

Regina Chapter

Canadian Council of Muslim Women
Regina, Saskatchewan
Chapter

1981

CCMW Canadian Council of Muslim Women
Le Conseil Canadien Des Femmes Musulmanes
—Regina Chapter—

In the name of God, Most Beneficent, Most Merciful

Introduction

Canadian Council of Muslim Women (CCMW) is an example of realization by the Muslim women to establish an organization to focus on recognition of their talent, social, cultural, religious, and political status in society at large.

As we turn the pages, it will show its evolution with time. CCMW and its chapters are well known across the nation. Their inputs are received and asked for on various issues from various sources.

CCMW of Regina chapter has dealt with all issues facing the Muslim women, joining other organizations as it is reflected in the presentation of this book.

Materials were collected and cited as much as could be available. So there is some that is lacking. Logo, letterhead, and brochure have been included, showing the thoughts and processes which went through in its evolution.

The reports show the activities, and how it grew historically and expanded to be part of other organizations and took on the tasks, which came along.

The women who were actively involved in running the organization from the beginning and later joining actively included Mahlaqa Naushaba Habib, Samina Ahmed, Rasheda Nawaz, Nilofer Haque, Zia Afsar, Nusrat Jalil, and Qudsia Qayyum.

Some pertinent information of the CCMW National organization is included from its website with due permission from Alia Hogben of the CCMW, National.

From: (http://ccmw.com/about-ccmw/)

Canadian Council of Muslim Women
Le conseil canadien des femmes musulmanes

The Canadian Council of Muslim Women is a national nonprofit organization established to assist Muslim women in participating effectively in Canadian society and to promote mutual understanding between Canadian Muslim women and women of other faiths.

About CCMW

"Women's organizations, working for women's equality, should be acknowledged as having a pivotal role in the strengthening of democratic societies."

The story of the Canadian Council of Muslim Women (CCMW) begins in 1982 when a group of dynamic and devoted Muslim women from across the country congregated in Winnipeg, Manitoba, led by the late founder of CCMW, Dr. Lila Fahlman. These women sought to mobilize their passion for social justice and faith in order to enrich their communities and work toward the common good of Canadian society.

This inaugural meeting led to the establishment of CCMW, a not-for-profit organization that works to provide equity, equality and empowerment for all Canadian Muslim women. For the past thirty years, its proud and accomplished roster of members has achieved and continues to achieve great milestones for Muslim women and Canada's multicultural landscape. As a highly diverse organization, CCMW is firmly committed to the overarching vision of improving the status of Muslim women to remain true to their Islamic heritage and Canadian identity.

Founder
Dr. Lila Fahlman (C.M, PhD)

"I believe in what I am doing, and I believe it should be done." A descendant of one of the earliest Muslim families to arrive in Canada, the late Dr. Fahlman was born in 1924 in Limerick, Saskatchewan. Her diverse upbringing served as a guiding force for the creation of CCMW. Lila was born to a Lebanese father and an English-American mother. As a socially engaged Muslim in the prairies, Lila was heavily involved in her local community including being an active member of the Girl Guides of Canada and serving as the Guard of Honour for the 1939 Royal Visit of Queen Elizabeth.

In 1982, Lila became the first woman in Canada to obtain her Ph.D in Educational Psychology from the University of Alberta. In 2001, she further made her mark on history by becoming the first Muslim woman to be awarded the Order of Canada for her service to the Muslim community, violence against women and interfaith dialogue.

In 2006, Lila passed away, but not without leaving her mark on Canadian history and setting the course for the future generations of Canadian Muslim women that will follow her. A celebrated author, educator, publisher, activist and Muslimah; CCMW continues to honor her memory each year through its work. This is inspired by her creative vision and the Lila Fahlman Scholarship provided to Canadian Muslim women each year at the annual fundraiser, Women Who Inspire.

Alia Hogben

Alia Hogben has been the executive director of the Canadian Council of Muslim Women, National for over a decade. She leads this organization on the following guiding principles. She is the recipient of a 2012 Order of Canada for her work in women's rights and promoting interfaith dialogue.

Maclean's magazine, in its annual 2014 Power List of people in Canada, ranks her 24th of the 50.

GUIDING PRINCIPLES

- We are guided by the Qur'anic message of God's Mercy and Justice, and of the equality of all persons, and that each person is directly answerable to God.
- We value a pluralistic society, and foster the goal of strength and diversity within a unifying vision and the values of Canada. Our identity of being Muslim women and of diverse ethnicity and race is integral to being Canadian.
- As Canadians, we abide by the Charter of Rights and Freedoms and the law of Canada.
- We believe in the universality of human rights, which means equality and social justice, with no restrictions or discrimination based on gender or race.
- We are vigilant in safeguarding and enhancing our identity and our rights to make informed choices amongst a variety of options.
- We acknowledge that CCMW is one voice amongst many who speak on behalf of Muslim women, and that there are others who may represent differing perspectives.
- We aim to be actively inclusive and accepting of diversity among ourselves, as Muslim women.

VISION

Maintain equality, equity and empowerment for all Canadian Muslim women.

VALUES

- To promote Muslim women's identity in the Canadian context.
- To assist Muslim women to gain an understanding of their rights, responsibilities and roles in Canadian society.
- To promote and encourage understanding and interfaith dialogue between Muslims and other faith communities.
- To contribute to Canadian society the knowledge, life experiences and ideas of Muslim women for the benefit of all.
- To strengthen the bonds of sisterhood among the Muslim communities and among Muslim individuals.
- To stimulate Islamic thinking and action among Muslim women in the Canadian setting.
- To acknowledge and respect the cultural differences among Canadian Muslim women, and to recognize and develop our common cultural heritage.
- To promote a better understanding of Islam and the Islamic way of life in the North American setting.
- To represent Canadian Muslim women at national and international forums.
- To encourage the organization and coordination of Muslim women's organizations across Canada.

Yet most importantly, reflecting the principles and spirit of the Canadian Charter of Rights of Freedoms, the Universal Declaration of Human Rights, the Convention on the Elimination of all Forms of Discrimination against Women (CEDAW), the Declaration on the Elimination of Violence against Women, and the International Convention on the Elimination of all Forms of Racial Discrimination.

Note: Most of the information (with some modification) was obtained from www.ccmw.com courtesy of Alia Hogben, the executive director of CCMW National.

The CCMW of Regina took important initiatives in getting together with people of other faiths, taking a very important role in participating in the affairs of the multicultural society and school board, and took a very effective role in dealing with the Bosnian crisis, particularly the rape of the women. These are reflected in the section of Canadian Council of Muslim Women – Regina, in this book.

Canadian Council of Muslim Women-Regina (CCMWR) History

Canadian Council of Muslim Women was established by an Edmonton educator's sister, Dr. Lila Fahlman. She was a woman representative on the Board of the Council of Muslim Communities of Canada, a national organization that looks after the interests of Muslims across Canada. She used to sit on the board and felt that she was not serving any useful purpose. She discussed this with the board, and was given the responsibility to organize Muslim women across Canada. She embarked on that project.

Sr. Lila Fahlman visited Regina in her province of birth at the residence of Mahlaqa Naushaba Habib, as noted below. A meeting of a few women was held with Dr. Lila Fahlman at the residence. The idea of establishing a chapter of the Canadian Council of Muslim women with its guiding principles as outlined by Dr. Fahlman was born.

Canadian Council of Muslim Women, Regina as a chapter of the national organization, was established in fall of 1981. The first meeting was held at the residence of Mrs. M. Naushaba Habib at 308 Habkirk Drive, Regina, Saskatchewan. The ladies were invited to attend the meeting. The objective of the council was discussed.

The chapter in Regina was established even before the national organization.

An election was held and the following were elected to the board of this newly formed Canadian Council of Muslim Women, Regina Chapter:

Mahlaqa Naushaba Habib, President

Fareda Sethi, Vice-President

Rasheda Nawaz, Secretary   Qudsia Qayyum, Treasurer

The first national meeting was held at the Manitoba Islamic Centre on April 24-25, 1982. Representatives from across Canada attended the meeting. Mahlaqa Naushaba Habib attended as a representative from Regina. Please refer to the *report of Canadian Council of Muslim Women Regina, Saskatchewan of 1981–1992* presented by Sister Naushaba Habib. Details are noted in it. All the activities of CCMW from 1983 to 1992 are included in this second report.

CCMW Regina Chapter, after being established in fall 1981, played a major role for Muslim women in Regina. It interacted with other women's groups in the province and participated in many activities.

It received praise from various organizations, and was recognized and respected by them. Besides playing various important roles, it played a very important role during the Bosnian crisis especially paying attention to the treatment of women in Bosnia. There was a demonstration, a rally, and media interviews. These problems were exposed by the media. Zia Afsar of CCMW and Kathleen Thompson of Women United played leading roles in the rally, along with others.

CCMW embarked on various fundraising projects, and ultimately, it established a scholarship at the University of Regina in the name of Canadian Council of Muslim Women Regina Chapter, to be awarded to students, particularly Muslim girls, and if not, it was available to any other deserving candidate as decided by the university. This initiative was taken by former Founding President

Mahlaqa Naushaba Habib. The University of Regina was very much appreciative of this contribution by the CCMW Regina Chapter.

Naushaba Habib finally left Regina in 2004, and the Canadian Council of Muslim Women by that time had achieved a very high profile during her presidency and other presidents, supported by all members of the organization. She moved with her husband to British Columbia.

Canadian Council of Muslim Women (CCMW)
Regina, Saskatchewan
Report 1981–1992

(Reflecting the History and Role Played by CCMW)
by
Sister Mahlaqa Naushaba Habib

In the name of Allah, Most Gracious and Most Merciful

Dear Sisters,

Asalam-O-Alaikum (peace and blessing be on you all),

I like to welcome you all to our group. Our President, Sr. Fatima Haleem could not come. She has been blessed with twin daughters. Please accept greetings from her as well. We like to thank you all for taking time to come here for our mutual interest. We will hope to work together, God Willing.

Sr. Zia Afsar will be chairing the meeting and has been active in calling this meeting. I thank her and everyone of our group for their effort in organizing this meeting.

I hope not to take much of your time. I shall briefly give you a historical background of our organization and let you know some activities we undertook or participated in.

Fortunately, we have continued to progress, though slowly, but surely by the grace of God.

IDEA:

Sr. Lila Fahlman was a woman representative on the board of the Council of Muslim Communities of Canada (CMCC). She felt that she had not been serving any useful purpose on the board. She discussed this with the board, and was given the responsibility to organize Muslim women across Canada.

Muslim Women's Group in Regina:

Sr. Lila, with her husband, visited Regina in fall 1981. The first meeting was held at my residence at 308 Habkirk Drive. After discussing the aims and objectives, the following office bearers were elected by consensus:

Sr. Naushaba Habib – President
Sr. Farida Sethi – Vice-President
Sr. Qudsia Qayyum – Treasurer
Sr. Rasheda Nawaz – Secretary

Formation of CCMW, National at the First National Meeting:

This was held in the Manitoba Islamic Centre, April 24–25, 1982. Representatives from across Canada attended the meeting. Naushaba Habib attended as a representative from Regina. The national organization was named *Canadian Council of Muslim Women (CCMW)*. Various projects were planned. The following office bearers were elected:

> Sr. Lila Fahlman – First President
> Sr. Leyla Shahin – Second President
> Sr. Tazul N. Ali – Secretary
> Sr. Talat Muinuddin – Assistant Secretary
> Sr. Raffina Ali – Assistant Secretary
> First project assigned to all chapters was Hijra Bazaar.

Second National Meeting:

This was held in Niagara on the Lake on August 16–17, 1982. Sr. Naushaba and Sr. Rasheda represented Regina. Representatives from across Canada gave their reports. Future plan of action was discussed.

Subsequent National Meetings:

Were held in Vancouver represented by Sr. Naushaba and Sr. Nilofer, in Edmonton and last attended in Toronto in April 1988 by Sr. Naushaba, Sr. Nilofer, and Perween (Najma).

Activities of CCMW, Regina 1983–1992

Other than social and religious activities, the local chapter did the following activities:

Hijra Bazaar: With city-wide open invitation on May 07, 1983 with great success. Just for your understanding, Hijra means migration. We relate this to the migration date of our Prophet (PBUH) to the city of Medina on command from God because of the torture of Muslims in Mecca. This event became a turning point for the spread of Islam. So Muslims celebrate this event from time to time.

Holiday International Market

Sponsored by the multicultural council on December 3, 1983, at the Centre of the Arts. This provided us good opportunities to meet people of other groups for knowing one another, but this project did not continue. Maybe all women's groups should do some kind of annual event of this nature.

Other Activities are as Follows:

International Christmas Craft Fair: (annual event) starting from 1987. Proceeds go to a charitable cause.

Other Ongoing Activities:

- Monthly meetings.
- Launched babysitting scheme for better parent relationship.
- Sick attendance—cards and flowers.
- Involved with youth program.

- Mosque: Support Mosque with fundraising as women's contribution.
- Gravel placement on parking lot of the Mosque.
- Working on project to make the parking lot of the Mosque paved as our contribution and project.
- Human Concern: Annually donating to Human Concern International for various projects—Bosnia, Somalia, and others.
- Self-Education: Religious education and others
- Other Community Contact: We made some attempt, but not very actively.

Today's get-together is an attempt on a larger scale.

I am very pleased to see you all here, which was my dream. I hope we can work together to understand one another in our multicultural country, Canada, with special projection on womens issues. Islam has very special status for women. Some culture elements and misrepresentation by media have portrayed the status of Muslim women badly.

As we go along, we will understand and we will help one another to contribute to our Canadian society for betterment of all.

Insha Allah (God Willing)
God Bless you all. God Bless Canada and the world. (Ameen)
Thank you very much.

H. Naushaba Habib

Sr. Mahlaqa Naushaba Habib, MA

A Period of Inactivity then Reactivation

There remained a period of no contact with CCMW, but the women's group continued its activities till the local chapter was reactivated by the visit of Sr. Talat Muinuddin in 1992. The meeting took place at the Islamic Centre and Mosque in Regina. The following were elected for the local chapter:

Sr. Fatima Halim, President
Sr. Naushaba Habib, Vice-President
Sr. Mariam Farooq, Secretary
Sr. Aisha Catikkas, Treasurer (later resigned)
Sr. Zia Afsar, Treasurer (new)

Canadian Council of Muslim Women (CCMW)
Regina, Saskatchewan
Report 1994–1995
(Reflecting the History and Role Played by CCMW)
by
Sister Mahlaqa Naushaba Habib

History:

The Regina Chapter of the CCMW was formed in 1981. There are currently 12 members. The annual membership fee is $10 per member. Elections were held on October 14 and since then there have been six meetings. The Regina Chapter is a separate but partial parallel organization to the Islamic Association of Saskatchewan, Regina. One member is elected to act as liaison person between the CCMW and the Islamic Association. The Regina Chapter utilizes the Mosque facilities in order to hold meetings and conduct workshops.

The Regina Chapter had the followings **goals** this year:

1. To increase youth involvement in the Mosque and to train the youth to take leadership positions within the Mosque
2. To educate sisters within the community on certain topics of interest
3. To network with other women's organizations in order to develop contacts and promote understanding of Muslim women's values

These goals were achieved with the following **activities**:

CCMW National Conference:

Two youth delegates were sent to the 1994 CCMW Conference in Hull, Quebec. These youth returned with positive comments on the conference. At the conference, the youth presented the Regina Chapter 1993–1994 Report. Attendance at this conference allowed the youth to develop networking and public speaking skills.

This year, the Regina Chapter has six delegates attending the 1994 CCMW Conference in Edmonton—four of whom are youth.

Workshops:

- Financial Management and Building workshop, November 1994
- Mother/Daughter Tea—January 1995

This tea was held on January 01, 1995. The purpose of the tea was to allow sisters the opportunity to meet one another and to address youth issues. The youth presented a skit on teen suicide. The skit was used as a catalyst to motivate discussion on youth issues and problems. This tea was a success with 45 sisters in attendance.

- Infant First Aid and CPR Course offered for free at the Mosque—March 1995
- Swimming

Arrangements have been made with the University Phys Ed Department to utilize their facilities. The cost is $3 per person and swim sessions are once a week. There is also a lifeguard hired to teach swimming to those who do not know how to swim.

These workshops were offered at no cost to the participants. This was possible by utilizing resources within the community. Members within the Islamic Association volunteered their time and expertise to offer the workshops on CPR and budgeting. Also, refreshments at the tea were donated by sisters in the community. All events were held at the Mosque (except swimmimg) so there was no cost associated with facility rental.

Programs:

- Display booth at the University of Regina **International Women's Day** celebrations. This allowed for the opportunity to network with other women's organizations, publicize the functions and contribution of the Regina chapter and to promote a positive image of Muslim women.
- Interfaith Council—Zia Afsar (President) attended an interfaith workshop in Davidson and spoke on women's rights in Islam. The workshop presenters were members of Jewish, First Nations

and Muslim groups. The audience was the local Interfaith Council in Davidson and other interested individuals.

- Seniors Class—Four members of the Regina chapter were panelists at Seniors Class in Islam offered at the University of Regina. The class is a general course on Islam. The panelists spoke on different issues concerning women in Islam, i.e. education, marriage, women's rights, etc. Two of the panelists were youth. The feedback from the class was positive and the Regina chapter has been invited to speak again in the future.
- Regina Council of Women—The chapter joined the council as a federate in January. The membership fee for this was $20 (yearly). Meetings are held on a monthly basis. The Regina chapter sends one representative to these meetings. The representative has been the President, Zia Afsar. Sister Zia also is the convener of the Standing Committee for Women and Employment for the council. The Regina chapter has also agreed to have the CCMW logo included on the Regina Council flag as a way of recognizing the Regina chapter's involvement with the council. Members have also attended the Centennial Tea and Founders' Banquet.
- Conference Prayer Service—Representative attended the prayer service held for success of the conference. A prayer (Dua) was read by a member of the Regina chapter. Prayers were also read by women from other faith groups.
- Community for Children Project: This project is funded by the United Way.
- Sister Nargis Bhimji represented the CCMW in many volunteer organizations. Some of these organizations include the Open Door Society, Immigrant and Visibile Minority Women's Organization against AIDS. In recognition of sister Nargis' efforts, the Regina chapter nominated her for the prestigious YWCA Woman of Distinction Award. This award is sponsored by the local YWCA as a way of recognizing an individual's contribution to volunteer work. This allowed the Regina chapter to recognize Sister Nargis' contribution and to publicize the contributions of Muslim women to the larger society.

These activities have helped to develop networking with other women's groups and to publicize the existence of the Regina chapter. Through these networks, the Regina chapter has been invited to participate in other important councils and activities. It is also suggested that the chapter be aware of local activities. The display booth at the International Women's Day celebration was organized by reading the paper, attending the celebrations and asking the organizers on the spot if the Regina chapter could have a booth. This resulted in positive feedback and results.

Because of this, the Regina chapter was listed in the Registry of Women's Groups at the Women's Center (University of Regina). From these contacts the chapter was invited to speak at the prayer service. The moral . . . networking pays off!

Also, it is important to recognize the contribution of members both within the organization and without. It is good for morale and it motivates others to get involved also.

Media:

- Press conference, March 1995
- The Chapter sent a representative to speak at a press conference organized by various religious groups. The purpose of the press conference was to protest expanded developing of gambling and casinos in Regina. The representatives were able to meet with the minister of sports and gaming—Joanne Crawford.
- Insights—Zia Afsar (president) was interviewed by the local cable TV show. She was invited to speak on Islam. The show received positive feedback by both Muslims and non-Muslims.

Presented by

M. Naushaba Habib

M. Naushaba Habib

Affiliation, Membership, and Participation in Various Organizations by CCMW, Regina

- Amnesty International Annual General Meeting.

- Breakthrough Fear of "The Other", hosted by CCMW Panelist Zeba Hashmi.

- Participation in World Religion Day.

- Canadian Cancer Society - Door-to-door fundraising campaign, Naushaba & Nargis.

- Canadian Institute for the Advancement of Women and National Organization of Immigrant and Visible Minority Women of Canada

- Immigrant Women of Saskatchewan

- Lions Club

- Member Regina Council of Women

- Multicultural Council of Saskatchewan

- Muslims for Peace & Justice

- Packing of eyeglasses by Lions Club—Sister Nargis

- Participated in Workshop and Recommendation on Access to Legal Services for Women Conducted by Saskatchewan Coalition Against Racism (SCAR)—attended by Naushaba.

- Peace Council

- Public Health Nursing—Informative meeting with following subjects discussed: Lecture on Islam by Nargis; Muslim Patients and Their Circumstances in Hospital, Nargis; Pamphlets on abortion, Muslim diet, and Ramadan distributed; Celebrated International Women's Day—hosted by Immigrant Women of Saskatchewan and CCMW; Lecture on Value of Women in Islam by Naushaba Habib.

- Regina City Hall—Peace Rally in February 2003 in Public Forum. Addressed by President Naushaba Habib.

Lecture by Mrs. Naushaba Habib on 01/15/2003 on Iraq War at City Hall:

Assalamualaikum, peace be upon you all.

I represent Canadian Council of Muslim Women. We stand with you against this war. I am going to summarize to you an article from Physicians for Global Survival (Canada) with my add-on comments.

"This organization is concerned with human health, well being and security. We assert that the plane attack on Iraq is inconsistent with International Law designed to protect vulnerable populations, is inhumane and is unthinkable because there are alternative ways to achieve any legitimate goals in this conflict." This is what Physicians for Global Survival is saying. They go on to say, "We are opposed to this war and therefore call on the Canadian government not to provide military or moral support for it." We at Canadian Council of Muslim Women fully agree with this.

"Contrary to International Law, human life is not being respected, be it for children or otherwise.

It is recognized that there is increasing awareness of the rights of the children and particularly the plight and rights of children in armed conflicts. The 1989 Convention on the Rights of the Child applies under all circumstances – peace or war. The child has a right to live, to a family, to adequate nutrition, to education, to health care and to play. Usually non-governmental organizations are called into action after a war has been waged when the lives of thousands of children have been lost. In this case, we look ahead to try to prevent this deliberate act.

This war will result in tens of hundreds of thousands of civilian casualties including the children. Civilians, likely half of them children, will be slaughtered in the internal conflict of Shia and Kurdis. We cannot accept this. The life of each child is precious. The lives of men and women in the armed forces matter too, whether US, UK or Iraqi.

Recent Canadian experience tells us that many will be incapacitated by the psychological aftermath of the horrors of armed conflict. We do not accept this unnecessary suffering. We are concerned that the lives of ordinary Canadians will be placed at greater risk of terrorism if our government participates in this planned war. Far from seeing this as a war to counter terrorism we see it as a war to provoke terrorism.

Violation of a country's sovereignty with pre-emptive war is frankly illegal under the UN Charter. Furthermore, President George Bush on December 10th started the threat that the US would consider the use of nuclear weapons against Iraq if Iraq uses chemical or biological weapons. Canada must not even contemplate giving support to such an act.

Additionally, the International Court of Justice advised in 1996 that use and threat of nuclear weapons is generally illegal. The strictest interpretation of threat in ICJ's advisory opinion included the threat to use nuclear weapons against a specific country under specific circumstances. In Afghanistan, US forces dropped thousands of cluster bombs dispersing hundreds of thousands of cluster bombs left there.

Cluster bombs have high failure rates and lay waiting for the touch of civilians, especially curious children, to trigger their explosion. It is highly probable that the US will use cluster bombs in Iraq.

It has humanitarian consequences. The efforts to remove Saddam Hussein through sanctions and the last war have already cost the lives of well over a million Iraqis. These efforts have also caused the destruction of civilians, civilian infrastructures, including water purification, sewage treatment, electrical and power generation.

The impact of the sanction contributes to damage to the social fabric through and increase in crime and family disruption. Together with direct effects on healthcare systems and punitive blocking of medical supplies and information technology, there is a high toll on physical and mental well being of Iraqis.

We cannot accept this and as health professionals, we strongly resist Canada's involvement in this contemplated war as indicated by the Physicians for Global Survival."

They further stated that they strongly resist Canada's involvement in this contemplated war. So do we.

There are various alternatives suggested by this organization to achieve the objective for which this war is being waged. We fully agree with these alternatives proposed by this organization:

- There is a UN inspection process, which should be supported, not undermined.
- The inspection process would also gain enormously in moral strength, form genuine moves on the part of the nuclear weapons states to follow through on their own promises to abolish nuclear weapons, to get rid of biological and chemical weapons and to support inspection and verification regimens to monitor these processors. Similarly, if it is demanded by a previous UN resolution to achieve a Middle East region free of nuclear, biological and chemical weapons, this should be supported.
- Sanctions affecting the basic needs of the Iraqi population and the economic development of Iraqi society should be discontinued.
- Convene a regional conference jointly by the UN and the organization of Islamic Conference to examine security and cooperation in the Middle East. After two appalling wars in Europe, there has been slow evolution of the European Union and the organization for security and cooperation in Europe. Peace in the Middle East would be no more miraculous than this.
- Nurture Democratic movements within Iraq. Democratic development cannot be imposed by outsiders or conferred

by war. Numerous examples of strenuous non-violent movement exist in many countries, e.g. Marcos, Soharto, military regimes in Latin America and communist governments in the eastern block were deposed without military intervention. Such non-violent movements can best be supported by both regional and international non-governmental organizations."

In the end, I would like to say: We must oppose this unwanted and unjustified war. We must not allow our government to participate. We pray for peaceful results for all conflicts. Ameen.

M. Naushaba Habib
President, Canadian Council of Muslim Women

- Regina Council of Women
- Regina Food Bank
- Regina Multi-Faith Forum
- Regina Open Door Society
- Representative to India-Canada Association of Saskatchewan Celebrating 55th Republic Day—Samina Ahmed.
- SCAR (Saskatchewan Coalition Against Racism)
- St. Pius School, Regina on Invitation. Lecture by Nargis, Islam and Eastern Culture
- Women United
- YWCA

These reports reflect the role played by CCMW and its history continued to evolve.

Canadian Council of Muslim Women (CCMW)
Regina, Saskatchewan
Report 2002–2003
by
Sister Mahlaqa Naushaba Habib

CCMW Regina Chapter's focus this year was on membership building.

Regular monthly meetings were held (excluding summer months). These monthly meetings were held in the homes of members to encourage a more relaxed and comfortable environment.

The meetings consisted of CCMW business, discussion of national organization, distributing pamphlets, display of CCMW books. We focused more on socializing, networking, and building relationships. In a way, this year has been a rebuilding year for the chapter. Some of the other activities were undertaken by members on an individual basis.

As of September 2003, our membership has increased to 17 (seventeen). Although it is a small number, it is a significant increase.

These are the following activities by CCMW this year:

1. Monthly meeting.
2. In every monthly meeting, money was raised from members for Souls Harbour Rescue Mission (soup kitchen) and food bank.
3. CCMW was involved in the Open Door Society, Immigrant Women of Saskatchewan, Regina Multi-Faith Forum, Peace Council, Amnesty International, SCAR, Muslims for Peace & Justice, and Lions Club. Representations were made by CCMW for interaction.

4. Sr. Nargis Bhimji gave a lecture on Islam to these organizations.
5. Naushaba Habib, President of CCMW Regina, was a guest speaker in Regina City Hall to address a Peace Rally in February 2003. Topic: *"Statement Opposing War on Iraq, its Consequences and Alternatives."*
6. Introduction of national organization to Luther College at University of Regina (Naushaba).
7. Workshop and recommendation on access to legal services for women in Saskatchewan by SCAR (Naushaba attended as representative).
8. One of our members gave an interview to Sun Community News regarding Islam and Muslims (Nargis Bhimji).
9. Fundraised for Canadian Cancer Society (Naushaba and Nargis).
10. CCMW also tried to show our presence on political scene and took opportunity to meet Sheila Copps and Paul Martin. (Naushaba and Nargis).
11. CCMW is a member of Regina Council of Women.
12. CCMW member Nargis Bhimji giving English classes for senior citizens at Open Door Society.
13. CCMW member (Nargis Bhimji) is a board member of Immigrant Women of Saskatchewan and represents CCMW.
14. Canadian Institute for the Advancement of Women, and National Organization of Immigrant and Visible Minority Women of Canada interviewed CCMW members on impact of post 9/11. Five members attended.
15. CCMW had a picnic of families and guests of members, which was well attended.

Allah accept our efforts
Respectfully submitted by

rf. Naushaba Habib

Naushaba Habib,
President, CCMW Regina Chapter
September 2003
ccmwregina@yahoo.ca

Canadian Council of Muslim Women (CCMW)
Regina, Saskatchewan
Report August–December 2003
by
Sister Mahlaqa Naushaba Habib

AUGUST:

August 28: A meeting was held at the Regina Multicultural Council of Saskatchewan office to discuss a presentation of a brief to the Rapporteur appointed by the government of Canada. The Rapporteur was charged with the mandate to study racism and its impact on the immigrant. Nargis represented the CCMW.

SEPTEMBER:

September 8: Amnesty International Annual General Meeting—represented by Nargis.

September 9: Regina Multi-Faith Forum—represented by Nargis.

September 10: A follow-up meeting was held at the Multicultural Council of Saskatcewan. Nargis prepared a brief of repertoire.

September 17: Regina Open Door Society held a meeting for the senior group of immigrants—represented by Nargis.

September 18: Regina Council of Women meeting at City Hall—represented by Nargis.

September 23: Nargis presented a brief on behalf of CCMW at request of Multicultural Council of Saskatchewan at the University of Regina Education Department, on *Racism and its Impact on Immigrants*. Several representatives came from Saskatchewan, Manitoba, and Alberta.

September 26: CCMW monthly meeting held at the residence of Naushaba.

OCTOBER:

October 1: Immigrant Women of Saskatchewan held a meeting at SGEU office from 10 to 1p.m.—represented by Nargis.

October 25: Immigrant Women of Saskatchewan held its Annual General Meeting. Nargis was elected as a board member.

October 25: Peace March for the occupation of Iraq—attended by Naushaba.

October 31: Protest—Campaign to stop secret trials in Canada—attended by Naushaba.

NOVEMBER:

November 7: Multicultural Council of Saskatchewan paid a tribute to thank the Hudson Bay Company (Zellers and Home Outfitters) for recognition of the holy month of Ramadan. Muslims for Peace & Justice awarded the Certificate of Recognition. Nargis gave a brief talk on the importance and significance of fasting by CCMW. Naushaba and Samina also attended.

November 12: Immigrant Women of Saskatchewan held a meeting—attended by Nargis.

November 13: The Regina Open Door Society invited CCMW member Nargis to attend a discussion group with a delegation from Paris, France, to study the situation of immigrants in Canada with the reference to how they are being treated by the mainstream society.

November 19: Naushaba Habib and Nargis Bhimji went to the Regina Food Bank where we donated a substantial amount of food items on behalf of CCMW. Same week both went to Souls Harbour Rescue Mission and donated coffee, sugar and milk powder. Prior to donation, CCMW toured both facilities.

DECEMBER:

December 7: CCMW held an Eid al–Fitr party at Regina Huda School where representatives of various organizations were invited by the CCMW. Function started with recitation of The Holy Qur'an by Sr. Moon Latif. Sr. Sheela Ahmed was the master of ceremonies. Naushaba Habib, the president, delivered the welcome address and gave a brief introduction to the national organization and Regina chapter. Award of Recognition was given to Ms. Doreen Hamilton for her longtime support to CCMW, Regina from 1992. Sr. Bhimji was given Award of Recognition for participation in and representing CCMW at various organizations. Samina Ahmed introduced the chief guest, Doreen Hamilton, MLA and Cabinet Minister who brought greetings from the premier. Ms. Sharon Brice represented the mayor. Various representatives of the organizations were introduced. Zeba Hashmi explained the significance of Eid Al–Fitr. Closing remarks by Nusrat Jalil and supplication by Nargis Bhimji followed. Following this, refreshment was served.

December 10: Amnesty International Regina Chapter held a potluck supper at the Unitarian Centre. Naushaba and Nargis represented CCMW Regina.

December 12: The Regina Open Door Society held their Christmas party for new immigrants. Nargis was invited and she prepared 70 containers of a variety of candies for the children.

December 15: CTV held an editorial board luncheon meeting to discuss Muslims and Islam focus on news issues affecting the Muslim community and how these issues are covered by the Regina CTV news cast. Muslims for Peace & Justice, Huda School and CCMW-Regina participated.

Naushaba Habib, President of CCMW, gave an introduction of the national organization and Regina chapter. Zeba Hashmi and Zarqa Nawaz, CCMW members, gave their input. The MPJ and Huda School represented their views.

December 15: Nargis Bhimji and Samina Ahmed attended a Christmas lunch hosted by Regina Council of Women for CCMWR.

Canadian Council of Muslim Women (CCMW)
Regina, Saskatchewan
Report August–January 2004
by
Sister Mahlaqa Naushaba Habib

January 16: We visited a Bosnian Muslim lady whose son passed away, for condolence. We joined others to recite Qur'an and join in her sorrow. We presented a fruit basket.

January 18: World Religion Day . . . Our member represented CCMW. We attended the celebration where prayer was offered by all groups for world peace.

January 21: Multiple Sclerosis Society recognized Sr. Nargis Bhimji (who represents CCMW) as well as Dr. R. Bhimji as volunteers.

January 24: We co-sponsored family night get-together with new and old families in Regina, especially to welcome refugee families.

January 25: CCMW sent a representative to India-Canada Association of Saskatchewan celebrating 55th Republic Day of India on invitation. Sr. Samina Ahmed attended the function.

Canadian Council of Muslim Women (CCMW)
Regina, Saskatchewan
Report February–April 2004
by
Sister Mahlaqa Naushaba Habib

February 4: First partnership meeting held with Immigrant Women of Saskatchewan for International Women's Day to be held on March 6, 2004.

February 9: Participation in Amnesty International meeting—Sr. Nargis represented.

February 13: CCMW monthly meeting at Sr. Yasmin's residence.

February 23: Informative meeting with public health nursing staff:

- Lecture on Islam by Sr. Nargis Bhimji
- *Muslim Patients and Their Circumstances in Hospital*—Sr. Nargis
- Pamphlets on abortion, Muslim diet, and Ramadan

February 24: Planning meeting with Immigrant Women of Saskatchewan for International Women's Day.

March Publication: *"When Cultures Differ"* By Naushaba Habib *Briarpatch News Magazine* Vol 33 No. 2 March 2004 Pages 22–23

March 6: Celebrated International Women's Day—hosted by Immigrant Women of Sskatchewan and CCMW Regina: Lecture on *"Value of Women in Islam"* By Naushaba Habib.

March 8: *Islam and Eastern Culture* Lecture by Sr. Nargis at St. Pius School, Regina—On Invitation.

March 12: CCMW Regina Election:
President—Mrs. M. Naushaba Habib
Secretary—Mrs. Samina Ahmed
Treasurer—Mrs. Nusrat Jalil

April 3: Represented in "Sears Canada Passage to India and Postcard Collection" —a multicultural event—Sr. Nargis

April 5: Participated in the meeting of Immigrant Women of Saskatchewan—Rep. Sr. Nargis

April ?: Participation in Regina Council of Women meeting—Rep. Samina Ahmed

April 21: Packing of eyeglasses by Lions Club—Sr. Nargis represented CCMW to help in packing.

April 23: CCMW Regina monthly meeting

Canadian Council of Muslim Women (CCMW)
Regina, Saskatchewan
Report May 2004
by
Sister Mahlaqa Naushaba Habib

May 4: Participated in Fundraising dinner of Multi-Faith

May 8: Zeba Hashmi represented as panelist on behalf of CCMW Regina on the topic of *"Breaking through Fear of 'the other,'"* hosted by Initiatives of Change

May 10: CCCMW Regina finally completed a long-awaited Project: "Canadian Council of Muslim Women—Regina Entrance Scholarship" of $5000 for Muslim girls at $800 per year. See attached letter.

May 21: CCMW Meeting
Submitted by

M. Naushaba Habib, MA
President CCMW Regina Chapter
June 12, '04

A Letter from CCMW, National

December 12, 2003

CANADIAN COUNCIL OF MUSLIM WOMEN
CHAPTER PRESIDENT and/or REPRESENTATIVE

Dear Sisters:

Assalamu Alaikum.
We hope this email finds you well

The national board would like to inform you of some changes at the national office. MashaAllah, we have been fortunate in being granted funds by the federal government to increase the work of CCMW, such as projects and the strengthening of our chapters. To work on these tasks the board has made changes which we think will enhance our capacity to accomplish our Strategic Plan, which was shared with you at the 2003 Annual General Meeting in Montreal.

Andreea Muscurel is the Administrative Assistant.
Andreea will assist the board to become more effective and organized.

Razia Jaffer is the President of the board.

Alia Hogben will be the Executive Director.

Noreen Majeed has joined the board.

As to the rest of the board members, **Iman Zebian** will continue to coordinate the website so as to increase its use by the chapters and the board and participate in other projects.

Najet Hassan is the treasurer, **Humera Ibrahim** will continue to be the chapters' contact, the Recording Secretary for the board and participate in other projects.

Nuzhat Jafri will lead on the project of media relations and training, represent us on the employment project with Women Working with Immigrant Women, Toronto, and lead on our Strategic Planning sessions with the chapters at the Regional meetings to be held in 2004.

Solmaz Sahin will continue to provide her guidance, support and experience, while **Nina Karachi Khaled** will decrease her load for a period of time to concentrate on her growing family.

The board has set dates for the Regional meetings with the chapters and further information regarding the agenda will be forwarded in January, 2004.

Regional Meetings Dates are:

> **Vancouver - April 2/04**   **Toronto - April 23/04**
> **Halifax - May 28/ 04**   **Calgary - June 11/04**
> **Montreal - June 25/04**

Would the Chapter Presidents please inform their members about these dates? Thank you.

Please also note the dates of the board meetings, and as always, you are welcome to attend. The board will provide accommodation, meals and reimburse half the travel costs. Please contact us if you wish to come.

Board Meetings Dates are:

Jan. 23/04; March 26/04; May 7/04; July 16/04

The Reports of the Forum and the AGM will be completed by mid-January, Insha Allah, and will be forwarded to you to share with all members.

Thank you and please do not hesitate to contact us,

Yours truly,

Humera Ibrahim, Nuzhat Jafri, Razia Jaffer, Najet Hassan, Nina Karachi-Khaled, Noreen Majeed, Solmaz Sahin and Iman Zebian.

Andreea Muscurel and Alia Hogben

CCMW Establishes Scholarship at the University of Regina

The Process

Mrs. M. Naushaba Habib, MA (Karachi)

9227 Wascana Mews
Regina, SK, S4V 2W3
Tel: 306-584-8578

April 29, 2004

I, Mrs. Mahlaqa Naushaba Habib of Regina have advanced a sum of five thousand Canadian Dollars to the Canadian Council of Muslim Women, Regina (CCMWR) to establish Canadian Council of Muslim Women –Regina Entrance Scholarship Education Fund at the University of Regina.

CCMWR will transfer its investment reference GIC PLUS 7632-8065265-01 at TD Canada Bank to me. This will become my property (or of my heir). However, the Bonus Interest on this investment earned at maturity on March 25, 2006 will be divided into 36 parts (36 months of investment). I shall keep the 23 parts and will pay 13(a period of investment that remained in the name of CCMWR before transfer to me) parts to CCMWR.

M. Naushaba Habib

Signature
Mrs. M. Naushaba Habib
President, CCMW, Regina

Witness Signature

CCMW Canadian Council of Muslim Women
Le Conseil Canadien Des Femmes Musulmanes
Regina Chapter---

In the name of God, Most Beneficent, Most Merciful

We the undersigned have received a sum of five thousand Canadian dollars from Mrs. Mahlaqa Naushaba Habib of Regina to pay for the Canadian Council of Muslim Women—Regina Entrance Scholarship Education Fund at the University of Regina.

We authorize the TD Canada bank to transfer the investment of Canadian Council of Muslim Women, Regina reference GIC Plus 7632-8065265-01 to Mrs. Mahlaqa Naushaba Habib. This will be her property. The Canadian Council of Muslim Women, Regina, its present board members or future board members or members will have no claim on it whatsoever.

As agreed between the two parties, the bonus interest incurred on this investment at the maturity on March 25, 2006 will be divided into 36 parts (representing 36 months of investment). Mrs. Mahlaqa Naushaba Habib will keep twenty-three parts for herself and will give thirteen parts (representing the period of this investment in the name of the council (March 25, '03 to April 30, 2004) to the Canadian Council of Muslim Women, Regina.

Signing authorities on behalf of Canadian Council of Muslim Women, Regina:

1. Mrs. Mahlaqa Naushaba Habib
   President
2. Mrs. Samina Ahmed
   Secretary
3. Mrs. Nusrat Jalil
   Treasurer
4. Uroos Hasani
   Chairperson Social Committee

Mrs. Mahlaqa Naushaba Habib _____

Dated: April 30, 2004 at the City of Regina, Saskatchewan

Naiyer Habib & Mahlaqa Naushaba Habib

CCMW Canadian Council of Muslim Women
Le Conseil Canadien Des Femmes Musulmanes
---Regina Chapter---

In the name of God, Most Beneficent, Most Merciful

Oct. 23, '04

Mr. J.G. Jacob,
Branch Manager,
Lakeview Plaza, TD Canada Trust 4240 Albert Street
Regina, SK

Dear Sir/Madam:

Re: GIC Transferable

I regret to write this letter but I have been asked by the Board of the CCMW, Regina. We had a GIC Plus 7632-8065265-01 in the name of CCMWR. Our treasurer, Nusrat Jalil went to check if this could be transferred. She was told that it was not possible. Then I went. I checked at the Teller. Teller introduced me to a lady. We had discussion in the office. I was told that it could not be transferred. I do not know the name. What I wanted to do is to give money to CCMWR in exchange of the GIC to be transferred to my name. They wanted to establish scholarship at the U of R. They could not cash this. So we went to lawyer. Sherri Shiels of your branch did research. She confirmed with the lawyer that it was possible to do so. So it was done.

We are concerned that the people who answered 'no' should have explored all possibilities as Sherri did, before answering no. We did not expect this from the high standard bank of Canada TD trust. This would have prevented our waste of time and lawyer's fee of $88.71. It may be reasonable for the bank to refund this amount. This is to bring to your attention for managing the bank better.

I am moving to BC. If you wish to reply to this, you may send to me or contact the new President, Mrs. Samina Ahmed 306 789 0416 at 2254 Mahony Crescent E, S4V 1B5. Thank you for your attention.

Yours truly,

[signature]

Mrs. M. N. Habib
President—Past
9227 Wascana Mews, Regina, SK, S4V 2W3
584 8578 till 27 Oct. '04
Enc: copy of letter from Sherri Shiels

Naiyer Habib & Mahlaqa Naushaba Habib

CANADIAN COUNCIL OF MUSLIM WOMEN – REGINA ENTRANCE SCHOLARSHIP

The Canadian Council of Muslim Women Regina Chapter is an affiliate of the national CCMW non-profit voluntary organization started in 1982 to assist Muslim women participating effectively in Canadian society and to promote mutual understanding between Canadian Muslim women and women of other faiths. As an initiative to support and promote post-secondary education within the Regina Chapter community, an annually funded entrance scholarship has been established in 2004 to encourage students to begin their university studies at the University of Regina.

DONOR   Canadian Council of Muslim Women – Regina.

FUNDING $5,000 to be received by the University Relations Office in May 2004.
- At the time of approval of the Terms of Reference, the donor wishes to establish an annual award of $800 for a six year period, years 2005, 2006, 2007, 2008, 2009 and 2010.
- In year 2010, the scholarship will be presented for a combined value of $800 plus any residual funds in the trust account.
- The award funding is open to receive additional donations from the Canadian Council of Muslim Women – Regina Chapter membership.

AWARD $800 in support of tuition, course and semester based fees.
- Annually. Fall semester. Commencing in Fall 2005.
- Student who has received other awards is eligible.

ELIGIBILITY   The scholarship will be presented annually to a University of Regina entering student who meets the following criteria:
- University of Regina scholarship entrance average of 80%, based on early conditional average which consists of five courses from the approved subject areas common to all faculties for admission to the University of Regina;
- registered in 12 or more credit hours of study in the semester the scholarship is paid out;
- financial need will be considered;
- preference to an entering female Muslim student or male Muslim student, if no application is received from a Muslim student, the award is open to any student who has met the other eligibility criteria;
- demonstrate through application in writing, not to exceed 250 words, highlights of volunteerism within the Muslim community and their familiarity with the Muslim faith.

APPLICATION   Must be submitted by April 30th.
- Applications are available from the:
  - Student Awards and Financial Aid Office, Riddell Centre, Room 229
  - or on the web, see www.uregina.ca/awards.
- Return completed application to:
  - Student Awards and Financial Aid Office.

SELECTION   University of Regina Undergraduate Scholarship Committee.
- The University of Regina Student Awards and Financial Aid Office shall notify a representative of the Canadian Council Of Muslim Women Regina and the student recipient, in writing, each year the scholarship is presented.

NOTES   (1) If, in the opinion of the University, it should become no longer practical or possible to use this funding for the specified purpose, (for example, if a program to which it relates is restructured or discontinued), the University will seek the written consent of the donor to redirect the gift to a new purpose. The support provided by the gift will continue to be clearly identified with the name of **Canadian Council of Muslim Women-Regina Entrance Scholarship.**
(2) Continued receipt of the award is conditional upon the student's compliance with all of the terms, conditions, guidelines and regulations as set out in the University Calendar from time to time. The University may suspend or cancel the award at any time if the recipient has committed any misconduct (academic or otherwise) as described in the University's Calendar.
(3) The **Canadian Council of Muslim Women-Regina Entrance Scholarship** amount will be presented in accordance with these Terms Of Reference or until such time the donor organization wishes to increase funding support.

_____   May 10/04
Signature: Representative Canadian Council of Muslim Women-Regina   Date

_____   May 12/04
Signature: Betty St. Onge, Assistant Registrar, Student Awards & Financial Aid   Date

February 12, 2004

Mrs. Naushaba Habib, President
Canadian Council of Muslim Women-Regina Chapter
C/o Medical Office Wing
3rd Floor
1440 – 14th Avenue Regina, SK S4P 0W5

Dear Mrs. Habib:

Thank you to Samira Ahmad, Nusrat Jalil and you for meeting with me on Friday, January 23, 2004 to discuss the terms of reference criteria for a new scholarship funded by the Canadian Council of Muslim Women, Regina Chapter.

The Terms Of Reference have now been prepared and, hopefully, reflect the wishes of your organization. The Assistant Registrar, Student Awards and Financial Aid, has assisted in the preparation of the Terms Of Reference. Therefore, I would ask that you review the Terms Of Reference as attached and let me know if your concur with the criteria as prepared for the **Canadian Council of Muslim Women – Regina Entrance Scholarship.** Please telephone me once you have completed this task so that we may prepare formal copies for approval signature.

The scholarship will be presented for the first time in fall 2005 to a University of Regina student who has successfully met the admission requirements to enter the University of Regina as well as other criteria as cited under ELIGBILITY. As discussed, the donation amount of $5,000 will be held in an interest earning account for the time the scholarship is active.

The University of Regina recognizes our donors to scholarship initiatives and the recipients annually in the May and October Convocation Programs. As well, a complete listing of undergraduate awards can be viewed on the University of Regina home page, www.uregina.ca/awards and in our annual University of Regina Undergraduate Awards booklet.

A gift of scholarship enriches the lives of our entering students in so many ways. Once again, thank you for choosing to create this most precious gift of scholarship through your CCMW chapter.

I look forward to hearing from you should you have any questions, my direct telephone number is 585-4446 or by e-mail, darlene.freitag@uregina.ca.

Sincerely,

Darlene Freitag
Development Manager, University Relations

Enclosure   Terms Of Reference:
                Canadian Council of Muslim Women-Regina Entrance Scholarship
                Education

Cc: Betty St. Onge, Assistant Registrar, Student Awards and Financial Aid

Mrs. M. Naushaba Habib, MA (Karachi)

9227 Wascana Mews
Regina, SK, S4V 2W3   Tele: (306) 584-8578
In the Name of Allah, Most Gracious, Most Kind

                                                      Oct. 23, '04

Sr. Zeba Hashmi,
MPJ General Secretary

Assalamo Alaikum WRB

We are able to establish Scholarship program by the grace of Allah
(SWT) as detailed in the attached document.

We request its circulation and urge people to donate to maintain
this scholarship indefinitely, Insha Allah. Ms. Darlene A. Freitag,
Development Manager, University Relations Campaign Office,
Univ. of Regina 306-585-4446 may be contacted to donate to the
Scholarship fund established by the Canadian Council of Muslim
Women, Regina Chapter.

Your sister in Islam,

M. Naushaba Habib

M. Naushaba Habib,
President, CCMW, Regina

A letter to CCMW, national representative for circulation for donation to this project:

Mrs. M.Naushaba Habib, MA(Karachi)

9227 Wascana Mews
Regina, SK. S4V 2W53   Tele: (306) 584 8578

In the Name of Allah, Most Gracious, Most Kind

19-Oct-04

Dear Sister Rabia
Assalamo Alaikum WRB

We are able to establish Scholarship program by the grace of Allah (SWT) as detailed in the attached document.

We request its circulation and urge people to donate to maintain this scholarship indefinitely, Insha Allah. Ms. Darlene A. Freitag, Development Manager, University Relations Campaign Office, Univ. of Regina 306 585 4446 may be contacted to donate to the Scholarship fund established by the Canadian Council of Muslim Women, Regina Chapter.

Your Sister in Islam,

M. Naushaba Habib
M.Naushaba Habib,
President, CCMW,Regina

CCMWR Joins Immigrant Women of
Saskatchewan on Invitation
CCMW Canadian Council of Muslim Women
Le Conseil Canadien Des Femmes Musulmanes
—Regina Chapter—

December 22, 2003

Nelu Sachdev
Program Officer
Immigrant Women of Sask. Regina Chapter
2248 Lorne Street Regina Sask S4P 2M7

Dear Nelu,

I received your letter. I appreciate your praise for CCMW. Our organization has small number of members and volunteers. We also have limited resources as to finance. We will be happy to join your organization and work with you as long as you understand our limitation. We will be happy to support the program on women's health. So with that understanding if you wish us to join, please confirm.

I am enclosing the letter of support for official use addressed to the President.

Yours truly,

M. Naushaba Habib

M. Naushaba Habib,
President, Canadian Council of Muslim Women, Regina Chapter
E-mail: mnaushaba@yahoo.com
cc. Rosetta Khalideen

CCMW Canadian Council of Muslim Women
Le Conseil Canadien Des Femmes Musulmanes
—Regina Chapter—

December 22, 2003

Rosetta Khalideen
President
Immigrant Women of Sask.
Regina Chapter.
2248 Lorne Street
Regina Sask S4P 2M7

Dear Ms. Khalideen,

This is to confirm that Canadian Council of Muslim Women, Regina will be pleased to join the partnership and support the forum on Women's Health.

We will also join you in fulfilling the requirements.

Yours truly,

M. Naushaba Habib,
President
Canadian Council of Muslim Women, Regina Chapter

CCMW Joins Shared Values Group of Regina School Board and Sends Representative Nargis Bhimji

THE BOARD OF EDUCATION OF THE
REGINA SCHOOL DIVISION
NO. 4 OF SASKATCHEWAN

August 29, 1997

J.A. Burnett Education Centre
1600 4th Ave., Regina, Sask., S4R 8C8

Ph: (306) 791-8200
Fax: (306) 352-2898

Mrs. Naushaba Habib
9227 Wascana Mews
Regina, SK
S4V 2W3

Dear Mrs. Habib:

Re: **Shared Values Forum - September 24, 1997**

You are invited to take part in a Shared Values Forum to be held on

Wednesday, September 24, 1997,
from 5:00 to 8:00 p.m., (supper provided)
at the J.A. Burnett Education Centre
1600 - 4th Avenue, Regina.

The Regina Board of Education believes that shared values unite our school community around basic fundamental beliefs that give direction to what we teach, both inside and outside the classroom. This forum is being held to provide information about shared values in Regina Public Schools and to receive your suggestions about communicating and emphasizing those values within our school communities.

The four categories of shared values were developed from a Values Forum held in 1995, and from the work of a community advisory committee and a staff working committee. The shared values are those that the committees saw as common among all cultural, spiritual and ethnic groups in our community.

The goals of this forum are to share and discuss the shared values we have identified to date and to receive your ideas and suggestions about how we can work with the community to communicate and teach those values.

Enclosed is a copy of the Shared Values document and an agenda for the forum. Displays will be available that will include curricula material, student/teacher demonstrations and examples of how shared values have been applied in the classroom and across the system.

A buffet supper that includes vegetarian and chicken dishes will be provided.

Your participation is important to us. We hope you will be able to join us. **Please RSVP to Myrna Scott at 791-8225, by September 15, 1997.**

Sincerely

Larry Huber

L.J. Huber
Director of Education

Encls.

Shared Values Forum Agenda
September 24, 1997
at the J.A. Burnett Education Centre
1600 - 4th Avenue, Regina

5:00 p.m.   Welcome
                 - Registration
                 - Information Kit

5:00- 5:45 p.m. Visit displays around the building, including student/teacher demonstrations

5:45-6:15 p.m.   Supper

6:15 p.m.   Opening Remarks
                 1. Advisory Committee Panel Discussion
                     Chair: Dr. George Baxter

                 2. Steering Committee
                 •   Video - Values in Action
                 •   History, process of shared values

                 3. Instructions to small groups

6:45 p.m.   Discussion Groups
                 (Facilitators and Recorders will be provided.)

                 • Assessment of value statements: Positive? Missing? Cautions?

                 • How can the community contribute to the programs?
                   community awareness?

7:30 p.m.   Plenary Session
                 •   Share ideas
                 •   Closing Remarks
                 •   Evaluation/Interest sheets

8:00 p.m.   Adjourn

NOTE: Summaries of group ideas and suggestions will be mailed to participants.
                 Parking available at rear of building.

CCMW - Regina Chapter
November 1996–October 1997
PART OF THE REPORT SHOWING SHARED VALUES

We have three members who sit on the Shared Values Forum which provides input into curriculum development with the school board members.

We have also participated in the Night March and Walk for Breast Cancer.

We have members who volunteer their time at the Open Door Society, Women's Shelter, and act as mentors to high school students interested in science and technology.

CCMW Report: Presented at Annual General Meeting, London, Ontario Oct. 9/97

The Regina Multicultural Council

welcomes you to

Saturday, December 3, 1983
Saskatchewan Centre of the Arts

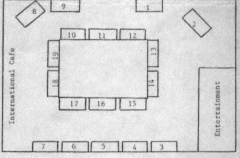

1. Scandinavian Club of Regina
2. Philippine Cultural Society
3. Canadian Italian Club
4. Philippine Association of Sask.
5. Kodaly Hungarian Dancers of Regina
6. Regina Open Door Society Inc.
7. Canadian Council of of Muslim Women
8. Regina Friendship Centre
9. Assoc. of United Ukrainian Canadians

10. Daughters of P lope, Ariabs
11. German Canadia Society Harmo
12. Polish Canadia Cultural Club
13. St. David's We Society
14. Regina Chapter Sweet Adelines
15. Regina Highla Dance Assoc.
16. Ukrainian Cana
17. Committee
18. India Canada of Sask. Inc.
19. Beth Jacob Synagogue

The Regina Multicultural Council gratefully acknowledges the following for their support:

Saskatchewan Culture & Recreation; Saskatchewan Centre of the Arts; CKTV; CK Radio; CJME; CFMQ; CBC; Regina Sunday News; Regina Real Estate Review; W.A.Printworks Ltd.; Phoenix Dancers - Chinese Cultural Society; Royal Scottish Country Dancers; Y's Men's Christmas Tree Regina Police Service; Regina Women's Guide and Holiday Market volunteers.

Islamic School with CCMW
in
Multicultural Event

Naseem Ahmed with children

← Naushaba

This group is from another event, but was here in the album
Back: Ziad Malik, Junaid and Azam Hussain, Munirul Haque, Natasha Hussain;
Front: Farzana, Natasha Malik, Raza Hasni, Faisal Sethi, Arsalan Habib

CCMW in Multicultural Event

Shahla Qayyum, Yasmin Habib, Nilofer Haque,
(face unidentified) Rasheda Nawaz

Front to back: Rasheda Nawaz, Samina Ahmed, and Naushaba Habib
Saleena Ahmed on a chair, (*next*) mother of Naiyer Habib on a
chair in sweater and white head cover

Left to right: Najma, Saleena, Rasheda, Mayor Larry Schneider

Left to right: Saleena Ahmed, Azra Iqbal, Mayor Larry Schneider

Left to right: Naushaba, Rasheda, and Makhani's mother

INTERNATIONAL
CRAFT
FAIR

ADMISSION IS FREE

November 12, 13, 14, 1992

YWCA

1940 McIntyre Street

You won't want to miss this wonderful opportunity to start crossing names off your Christmas list with some of the most unique gift items available. At the same time, you'll be supporting the efforts of many organizations working for the betterment of the world we live in.

Special international food is also available to tempt your taste buds.

What better way to say a Merry Christmas that extends around the world.

Hours: Thurs. & Fri., Nov. 12 & 13   -11:00 a.m. to 8:00 p.m.
Sat., Nov. 14   - 9:00 a.m. to 3:00 p.m.

A project coordinated by the International Cooperation Committee and supported by CUSO, Common Ground, UNICEF, the Saskatchewan Council for International Cooperation, Canada Save the Children, the YWCA Shelter for Women, Third World Imports, Self-Help Crafts, Immigrant Women of Saskatchewan, Canadian Council of Muslim Women, and Soroptomist International.

For more information, please contact your YWCA at 525-2141

Garage Sale

Fundraising for CCMW 1996

Left to right: Erum Afsar, Amina Afsar, Natasha Malik,
Naushaba Habib, Arsalan Habib

Celebration of Eid Festival

Muslim women celebrate Eid get-together with others- Regina ,Saskatchewan,Canada.

Feb.25th1996

Muslim women group(Canadian council of Muslim Women)celebrated Eid get-together with various women groups as special occasion at the Islamic Centre and Mosque in Regina.This was received with great enthusiasm.

Eram Afsar(Youth member and Secretary) introduced the guests and the speakers . Sr.Zia Afsar, the president welcomed the guests and outlined the status of dignity , equality,and complimentary role as recognised by Islam expressing pleasure that it is now being recognised by the modern society.

Sr.Naushaba Habib,the Vice President gave introductory talk on Ramadan and Eid. Brochures were also distributed.

Joanne Crofford,Hon.Minister for Status of Women(Govt.Of Saskatchewan) was the guest of honour. She welcomed the effort of such get- together and emphasised the need for all women group to work together.

Doreen Hasmilton,MLA a frequent visitor to Muslim women group recollected the role of the Muslim Women in being instrumental to form Women United at Regina at the time of Bosnia Crisis.This group remains active in Regina for common forum

Sr.Samina Ahmed gave vote of thanks to all. Function ended with exchange of greetings and excellent snack. Special gift was given to the minister and flowers to all guests.

End

EID GET TOGETHER

February 25, 1996
Islamic Center / Mosque

(Master of Ceremonies - Erum Afsar)

PROGRAM

2:00-2:05	Welcome	Erum Afsar
2:05-2:15	Recitation of Al-Quran and Opening Remarks	Zia Afsar
2:15-2:20	Introduction of Guests	Zia Afsar
2:20-2:30	The Significance of Eid	Naushaba Habib
2:30-2:35	Address by Councillor Linda McKay	
2:35-2:40	Introduction of the Guest of Honour	Erum Afsar
2:40-2:50	Address by Hon. Joanne Crofford	
2:50-3:00	Closing Remarks	Samina Ahmed

- Refreshments -

Welcome by Erum Afsar

Good afternoon Assalam-o-Alaikum (PBU)

My name is Erum Afsar. I am the secretary of the Regina chapter of the CCMW. On behalf of the CCMW and the Muslim women of Regina, I welcome all of you to the Islamic Centre of Regina or as referred to in Arabic, Mosque.

You have been invited to celebrate Eid al-Fitr with us (Festival of the fast breaking). The past week, Muslims all around the world gathered together in Mosques, community centres and homes to celebrate the end of a month of fasting—Ramadan. During this time when Muslims meet each other, they greet each other saying "Eid Mubarak. I extend these Eid greetings to you and wish all of you an Eid Mubarak."

Muslims in Regina celebrated Eid here in this Islamic Centre as they have for the past few years. We gathered for the traditional Eid prayer in the morning, and in the evening for a potluck supper. This Islamic Centre is central to the Muslim community throughout the year. We gather to pray. Together, we teach our children Islam, learn Arabic (the language that the Qur'an is written in) and socialize.

I call on Sister Zia Afsar, President of the CCMW Regina chapter who will recite a verse from the Qur'an, the religious text of Muslim.

Recitation of Al-Qur'an and Opening Remarks by Zia Afsar

Honourable Minister, distinguished guests, and members of the Muslim community, Asallam-O-Aalikam, Peace be upon you all.

أَخِيهِ مَيْتًا فَكَرِهْتُمُوهُ وَٱتَّقُواْ ٱللَّهَ إِنَّ ٱللَّهَ تَوَّابٌ رَّحِيمٌ (١٢) يَٰٓأَيُّهَا ٱلنَّاسُ إِنَّا خَلَقْنَٰكُم مِّن ذَكَرٍ وَأُنثَىٰ وَجَعَلْنَٰكُمْ شُعُوبًا وَقَبَآئِلَ لِتَعَارَفُوٓاْ إِنَّ أَكْرَمَكُمْ عِندَ ٱللَّهِ أَتْقَىٰكُمْ إِنَّ ٱللَّهَ عَلِيمٌ خَبِيرٌ (١٣) ﴿۞﴾ قَالَتِ ٱلْأَعْرَابُ ءَامَنَّا قُل لَّمْ تُؤْمِنُواْ وَلَٰكِن قُولُوٓاْ أَسْلَمْنَا وَلَمَّا

49:11(part of)–14(Part of)

Human dignity and equality are the fundamental principles of Islam, which we Muslims believe is the revealed religion of God brought to mankind by a series of prophets including Ibraheem,

Moses, Jesus and Mohammed (Peace and blessings of God be on all of them). Yet this message of equality and particularly the aspect of the rights of women seems to be least understood in many societies of the world.

Many of us who came from other parts of the world are grateful that the Islamic principal of equality is guaranteed in the Canadian Charter of Rights. Muslim women always read about Abu-Hanifa, an 8th century Muslim Jurist who decreed that in every Islamic town a woman should be appointed as a judge, officially responsible for keeping a check on the aspect of women's rights. Abu-Hanifa would have been pleased to witness that Canada and its provinces indeed have implemented this important principal through the ministries for the status of women.

Brothers and sisters in humanity, while progress has been made toward enhancing women's rights in Canada, many more societal barriers still need to be brought down. The United Nations' 4th World Conference on Women in Beijing has demonstrated that the women of the world have the same struggles, same issues, and same problems. More than 50,000 women gathered in Beijing to raise their collective voices. These women came from all corners of the globe and from very different backgrounds. They had the same agenda; to discuss their common issues. In this context, we Muslim women have to struggle a bit harder. We have to change the image of Muslim women; the image that we are veiled, crushed and silent and perhaps inferior human beings. The best way to correct this stereotyping is to educate the people. Muslims came to Regina near the turn of the century with the arrival in 1903 of Mohammad Ali Ta Haynee and Saeed Amin Ganem of Lebanese background. Dr. Lila Fahlman, daughter of Saeed Ganem and the founder of Canadian Council of Women was born in Saskatchewan 71 years ago. She lives in Edmonton now. Twenty-five years ago, Muslim women worked side by side with Muslim men to form the Islamic Association of Saskatchewan, Regina. Muslim women have also contributed significantly to our society. We work as volunteers in women's shelters, hospitals, Open Door Society, Immigrant Women's Organization, MLAR to name a few. Muslim women are also beginning to enter into politics. Her Worship the Mayor of Davidson is a Canadian Muslim woman. Fatima Houda

Pepin, a Muslim lady from Morocco was elected as a member of the Quebec National Assembly in the last election. We hope by the next millennium we will see more Muslim women participating in the local and provincial political scenes. We work hard as mothers to keep our youth drug and alcohol free. We volunteer in various organizations to help and enhance the life of our fellow Canadians. My sisters in humanity, we women have come a long way, but we still have far to go. Let's build bridges of friendship and understanding and walk together to achieve more than we ever have. I like to take this opportunity to introduce the guests. Please identify yourself as I call out your name. Please hold the applause till the end (guest list attached).

I also like to introduce the board members of the Islamic Association of Saskatchewan, Regina (board member's names called out).

Thank you for your attention.

Yours truly,

Zia Afsar

Significance of Eid by Mahlaqa Naushaba Habib

Dear Brothers and Sisters in Humanity, Eid Mubarak.

Alhamdulillah. All praise is due to Allah and to Allah do we seek help and forgiveness from the evils caused by our own wrongdoings. I bear witness that there is no power other than Allah and that Muhammad is His Messenger.

At the conclusion of the month of Ramadhan, muslims all over the world celebrate Eid ul Fitr. Eid ul Fitr celebrates the completion of the month of fasting for the sake of Allah.

The ceremony of Eid ul Fitr starts early in the morning with worship service on the 1st of Shawwal of the Islamic Lunar Calendar. This service is generally held in a large open place usually in a Mosque and is attended by the Muslim community. After prayer, a short sermon is delivered and then the people greet each other. The family and friends exchange greetings and gifts.

Fasting is one of the pillars of Islam and is a mechanism whereby a Muslim is able to put Allah first in every aspect of her life. During Ramadhan, abstaining from food, water and sex from sunrise to sunset provides a context within which you can try to establish Allah's presence in your life as the fast is extended to abstaining from all kinds of lusts, hypocrisy, lies and dishonesty.

Fasting allows Muslims to feel very close to other human beings and the rest of creation. More forgiving and accepting of co-workers. More liable to overlook weakness and petty jealousies.

The spirit of Eid is the spirit of peace and forgiveness and as such we forget all grudges and ill-feeling towards other human beings and hope that Allah's presence will persist until the next Ramadhan comes.

Allah bless us all. Ameen.

M. Naushaba Habib

M.Naushaba Habib,

Past President, CCMW,Regina

Regina, January 30th 1999
"EID GET TOGETHER"
We invited various interfaiths to celebrate and understand Eid and Islam with us.
This took place at our Mosque. As well various members of Parliament were there too

Hon. Doreen Hamilton and Samina Ahmed

Naushaba with guests

Guest representatives

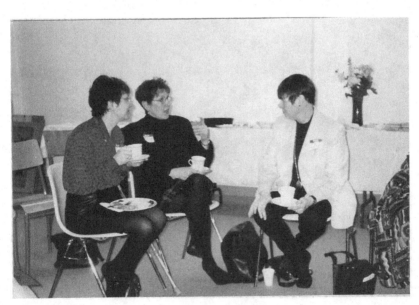

Eid at Huda School, Canadian Council of Muslim Women 2003

Opening: Sheela Ahmed   MC: L. Moon reciting Qur'an

Address by the President, Sister Naushaba Habib of CCMW

Honorable Minister Doreen Hamilton, City Councillor Sharon Bryce SNB, and distinguished guests and members of the Muslim community, Assalam-O-Alaikum (peace be upon you all).

Indeed, it is my honor and pleasure to welcome you here today. You have been invited to celebrate Eid al-Fitr with us (festival of fast breaking and thanksgiving). This past week, Muslims all around the world celebrated the completion of Ramadan, a month of fasting adhering to the tenets of Islam. To celebrate this, Muslims meet each other saying Eid Mubarak. I extend this Eid greeting to you and wish all of you an Eid Mubarak.

We are encouraged by you participating and we hope to continue such interaction in future.

Now, I will give you a brief introduction to Canadian Council of Muslim Women. Sister Dr. Lila Fahlman was a woman representative on the board of the Council of Muslim Communities of Canada. She felt that she was not serving any useful purpose on the board for the women. She discussed this with the board, and was given the responsibility to organize the Muslim women in Canada. Twenty years ago, she travelled to each city across Canada beginning in St. John, Newfoundland and ending in Vancouver. She visited and talked with Muslim women in each community. The goal was to bring these women together into a national body.

In April of 1982, Muslim women representatives from each city met in Winnipeg where we founded the Canadian Council of Muslim Women. I represented Regina. Chapters were established in various cities. The Canadian Council of Muslim Women is a national non-profit organization established to assist Muslim women in participating effectively in Canadian society and to promote mutual understanding between Canadian Muslim women and women of other faiths.

The national organization is geared toward organizing and strengthening our bond as women in Islam at the community and national levels. Muslim women must strive to achieve a balance between divergent cultures, traditions, family values, and religious beliefs. As women, we experience many of the same difficulties as other Canadian women of different religious backgrounds. At the same time, pride in our own values should also be developed through a strong organization through which we can improve our lives as women and more importantly as Muslims. We are proud of the fact that CCMW had its 20th anniversary last year.

It is quite an achievement for a small volunteer organization not only to have survived but also lived up to the vision created 20 years ago. It has provided a voice for Muslim women and demonstrated that Islam is a woman-positive faith and it has brought Muslim women into the mainstream of society. It has done so through conferences, newsletters, networking, initiation of projects, holding regional meetings and publications.

We also have an active chapter in Regina. It was formed in 1981 even before the national organization. Our membership is small, but we are actively participating in various organizations and expanding. We have extended ourselves outside the Muslim community. We initiated the formation of Women United in Regina at the time of the Bosnian war, which was an exciting experience to get to know one another and work together from whatever background we have culturally or religiously.

In the larger Regina community, we have contacts with Regina Council of Women, Immigrant Women of Saskatchewan, Open

Door Society, Amnesty International, Multicultural Society, Lions Club, SCAR and SCR, and others.

We raised funds for the Canadian Cancer Society, Souls Harbour Rescue Mission, Women's Shelter, and Food Bank. We hope we can work together and develop mutual understanding to enrich our Canadian society.

Eid Mubarak to you all, God bless us all. Amen. Thank you for your attention.

M. Naushaba Habib

Mrs. Mahlaqa Naushaba Habib
President, CCMW, Regina

Zeba Hashmi

Samina Ahmed

Presentation to Honourable Doreen Hamilton
by the president

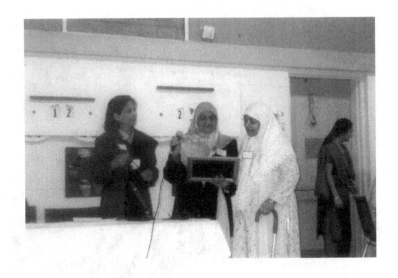

Presentation to Nargis Bhimji by President Naushaba Habib
and Samina Ahmed

Nargis Bhimji

Welcome Naiyer Habib, President of Muslims for Peace & Justice

Nusrat Jalil, Treasurer

Welcome To A Presentation
On

The Contribution of Women in the Development of Muslim Society During The Life of The Holy Prophet PBUH and The Rightly Guided Caliphs In' ISLAM

Dr. Riffat Hassan
Head Of Religious Studies
University of Louisville, Kentucky USA

Cathedral Neighbourhood Center
2900-13ᵗʰ Avenue
Regina
February 20ᵗʰ 1999
7:00pm Sharp

Sponsored By Muslim Women of Regina and Canadian Council of Muslim Women-Regina Chapter

Left to right: Erum, Samina, Naushaba

Left to Right: Dr. Riffat Hassan, Erum, Samina

Dr. Riffat Hassan

National Meeting of CCMW with
Regina's Representation

Nargis
Bhimji

Zia

Samina

Anwar
Qureshi

International Women's Day

Honourable Doreen Hamilton

Naushaba Habib, President of CCMW

Mona Aboguddah in the center

CCMW Takes a Stand in Bosnian Crisis

CCMW took a leading role joining Women United, appeared in media, held a rally and protest raising the issues to the public, government and media.

The Bosnian crisis was an ethnic conflict after the collapse of Yugoslavia. In the words of Hartmann (*Crimes of War*): "The conflict in Bosnia-Herzegovina, which began in April 1992 and ended in November 1995, has come to be seen as the model for wars of ethnic cleansing throughout the world. This was the most violent event Europe experienced since World War II."

Women were raped in front of their husbands, brothers, and children.

In a statement on 23 September 2008 to the United Nations, Dr. Haris Silajdžić, as head of the Bosnia and Herzegovina delegation to the United Nations 63rd Session of the General Assembly, said that "according to ICRC data, 200,000 people were killed, 12,000 of them children; up to 50,000 women were raped, and 2.2 million were forced to flee their homes.

CCMW, Regina took a leading role against the rape of women in the Bosnian Crisis. They took part in a rally, took a political stand, and had media interviews. Various women's organizations and others joined CCMW, Regina wholeheartedly.

All media in Regina overwhelmingly and sincerely supported their cause. This included *Leader-Post*, CKCK, STV (CKCK and STV are now Global TV), and CBC. This is reflected here in their interviews and news cast. These are presented here as a courtesy from them without which, this book would not have been complete.

JOIN US IN PROTEST!
JOIN US IN PROTEST!

JOIN US IN PROTEST!

"STOP MASS RAPE
OF
BOSNIAN WOMEN!"

TUESDAY, FEBRUARY 23, 1993
11:30 A.M.YWCA LOBBY

12:00 P.M.Noon-hour Demonstration

YWCA to Victoria Park

Everyone Welcome

Our Goals Are:

1. Stop Genocide and Ethnic Cleansing

2. Close ALL RAPE CAMPS

3. Provide Assistance to trauma victims and child resulting from rapes

Sponsored by:
Women United*, Regina

For More Information Contact:
YWCA of Regina - 525-2141

Free Childcare for the March provided at the YWCA

*Participants: SAC, YWCA of Regina, Council of Muslim Women, Regina Council of Women, Croation Council of Women, Multicultural Assoc, United Church, U of R Women's Centre and others

S T O P MASS RAPE
OF
BOSNIAN WOMEN

Join World-wide Protest

12 International Women's Groups launch campaign to have RAPE RECOGNIZED AS WAR CRIME & HUMAN RIGHTS VIOLATION.

Campaign Focus:
• United Nations Human Rights Commission: "Recognize Rape as Violation of Human Rights" (February, 1993)
• International Commission on the Status of Women: "Strengthen proposed 'Declaration on Elimination of Violence Against Women' " (March, 1993)
• All countries urged to implement Provisions of 4th Geneva Convention, recognizing rape as war crime.

Regina women join international outcry:

1. **STOP** Ethnic Cleansing and Genocide
2. **CLOSE** all RAPE CAMPS
3. **ASSIST** trauma victims and children resulting from rapes
4. **DECLARE** rape war crime and human rights violation (via United Nations)
5. **BRING** perpetrators to **JUSTICE** in International Court of Law

Sponsored by: "Women United" Regina
Regina Participants include: YWCA, Council of Muslim Women, Croatian Council of Women, Regina Council of Women, United Church, Roman Catholic Archdiocese, Saskatchewan Action Committee on the Status of Women, Multicultural Association, Women's Secretariat UoR Women's Centre and others

Therefore, we invite the media to a press conference at the above mentioned place and date to introduce our action group and to request the media help in raising the public's awareness about the

rape crimes and other war atrocities in the former republics of Yugoslavia,particularly Bosnia-Herzegovina.

.Zia Afsar   761-2435   .Katleen Thompson   584-1255

.Lyda Fuller   525-2141   .Widy Davis   352-3301

"WOMEN UNITED REGINA"

On the afternoon of February 7, 1993 women from Regina organizations, including the United Church, the Caribbean Association, the Multicultural Association, the Croation Community, Saskatchewan Action Committee, the Saskatchewan Women's Secretariat, the YWCA, the Regina Council of Women, the University of Regina Women's Centre, Amnesty International, Immigrant Women of Saskatchewan, Regina Open Door Society, University of Regina Faculty Association and the Regina Peace Council, gathered at the invitation of the Canadian Council of Muslim Women, Regina Chapter, to discuss what we in Regina can do to address the continuing violence in the former Yugoslavia, and in particular, to end the rape of women there - - the majority of whom are Bosnian Muslim women - - rape that has now been confirmed by the UN and the European Community.

Women's groups in Regina, across Canada and in other nations are gearing up to join forces in a fast and forceful letter-writing campaign. This will give women and men from many ethnic, religious and political backgrounds a common voice. A list of those who should receive these letters, as well as a suggested form letter will be available. You are asked to contact Zia Afsar of Women United at 761-2435 for this information.

Our Regina collective asks you and your group to join us in calling for action by our federal government and the United Nations on the following issues:

1. To take action to stop the genocide and ethnic cleansing in Bosnia.
2. The UN take immediate action against war crimes, rape and other human rights violations in Bosnia-Herzegovina.
3. Immediately close all the detention and "rape camps".
4. To bring the perpetrators of these crimes to justice before an International Criminal Tribunal.
5. To provide assistance, financial and volunteer personnel, to work with the trauma victims, including raped women and the children resulting from the rapes.

In support of an internationally designated day of action, a demonstration will be held on Tuesday, February 23, 1993. Women, men and children are asked to gather at the YWCA at 11:30 a.m. to march around Victoria Park to express our concern for immediate action from our government and the United Nations against the use of rape as a military weapon of terrorism and ethnic cleansing in former Yugoslavia. Please contact any sister organization you may be involved in to ask for their support.

Please join this grassroots protest against the crime of terrorism and cruelty against women and children.

NOTE - Please make as many copies of the attached petition as you need.(try for at least 500 signatures from your organization, church, or group and check with your area M.P If they are willing to present the petition to the parliament. If not please mail it to Regina United 3273 Montague Street, Regina, Saskatchewan S4S 1Z8, by March 15th 1993.)

CCMW Canadian Council of Muslim Women
Le Conseil Canadien Des Femmes Musulmanes
—Regina Chapter—

In the name of God, Most Beneficent, Most Merciful

February 11, 1993

From
Mrs. M. Naushaba Habib, President of CCMW
Canadian Council of Muslim Woman, Regina

To
Talat Muinuddin
President Canadian Council of Muslim Woman, National

Dear Sister Talat,

Assalam-o-Alaikum, just to let you know that Canadian Council of Muslim Woman of Regina hosted a meeting on February 07, 1993, with our sister organization of different groups.

The main agenda was what is happening in Bosnia with our Muslim sisters and other women. We have adopted the following action plan:

1. Rape to be declared a war crime and human rights violation.
2. Close down the rape camps.
3. Bring the perpetrator of the crime to justice.
4. We are most interested to know what our national organization is doing.

Kindly let us know at the earliest.

We would like our sister organizations to do the same. Please forward a copy of this letter to other organizations in Canada.

Thank you, *Wassalam*

H. Naushaba Habib

Naushaba Habib
President

March 08, 1993
Women United
3273 Montague Street
Regina, Sask. Canada S4S 1Z8

CCMW Canadian Council of Muslim Women
Le Conseil Canadien Des Femmes Musulmanes
—Regina Chapter—

In the name of God, Most Beneficent, Most Merciful

February 11, 1993

Mr. Boutras Boutras–Gali
Secretary General, United Nations
866 U.N. Plazas
New York, New York, USA 10017

Dear Sir,

We, the Women United, request the United Nations to earnestly attend to the following issues:

1. Take action to stop the genocide and ethnic cleansing in Bosnia.
2. Take immediate action against war crimes, rape, and other human rights violations in Bosnia-Herzegovina.
3. Immediately close all the detention and rape camps.
4. To bring the perpetrators of these crimes to justice before an international criminal tribunal.
5. To provide assistance, financial and volunteer personnel, to work with the trauma victims, including raped women and the children resulting from the rapes.

Yours truly,

Lyda Fuller
M. Naushaba Habib
Representing

- Women United
- Sask Action Committee on Status of Women, Regina
- Regina Council of Women
- Jewish Women's Organization (Regina)
- Canadian Council of Muslim Women - Regina
- YWCA University of Regina Women's Centre
- United Church
- Croatian Community of Regina
- Regina Peace Council
- Amnesty International (Regina)
- Regina Multicultural Association
- Immigrant Women of Saskatchewan (Regina)
- Caribbean Association Regina

cc:

Mrs. Hillary Rodham Clinton
Right Honourable Brian Mulroney, Prime Minister
Hon. Barbara McDougall, Secretary of State for External Affairs
Hon. Audrey McLaughlin, Leader of Opposition (NDP), Ottawa
Hon. Jean Chretien, Leader of Liberal Party, Ottawa

PETITION

TO THE HONOURABLE HOUSE OF COMMONS OF CANADA,
IN PARLIAMENT ASSEMBLED

The petition of the undersigned residents of Canada who now avail themselves of their ancient and undoubted right thus to present a grievance common to your Petitioners in the certain assurance that your honourable House will therefore provide a remedy.

HUMBLY SHEWETH

WHEREAS, the current conflict in Bosnia-Herzegovina has resulted in loss of thousands of innocent lives, uprooting of hundreds of thousands of civilians from their ancestral homes, and atrocities like ethnic cleansing,

WHEREAS, informed European Community and UN sources have estimated tens of thousands of Muslim women who have been repeatedly raped by their Serbian captors in what are now being described as "Rape Camps" in the Serbian occupied areas of Bosnia-Herzegovina,

WHEREAS, while rape is considered a war crime under the Geneva Convention, no one has ever been prosecuted for it, and

WHEREAS, the governments of the most civilized and powerful nations of the world, like the United States, Britain, France and Canada, and international institutions like the UN have not taken any action against such crimes being committed against women and children.

WHEREFORE the undersigned, your Petitioners, humbly pray and call upon the Government of Canada to put pressure on the UN to;

1) Take action and stop the genocide and ethnic cleansing in Bosnia-Herzegovina.
2) Take immediate action against war crimes of rape and other human rights violations in Bosnia-Herzegovina.
3) Immediately close all the detention and "rape camps."
4) Bring the perpetrators of these crimes to justice before an international criminal tribunal.
5) Provide assistance, financial aid and volunteer personnel, to work with the trauma victims, including raped women and the children resulting from the rapes.

AND as in duty bound your Petitioners will ever prays.

SIGNATURES   ADDRESSES

_____   _____

_____   _____

_____   _____

_____   _____

_____   _____

_____   _____

_____   _____

_____   _____

_____   _____

BOSNIAN CRISIS
CCMW, REGINA CHAPTER NEWS

In January, Regina chapter invited local women's organizations to join hands and raise a strong collective voice against the violence toward women in Bosnia-Herzegovina. Sixteen such organizations joined us and an ad hoc group called Women United was formed. We developed an action plan consisting of:

(a) To write letters to our respective sister organizations in other cities to raise a voice against the atrocities in Bosnia.
(b) To write letters to the secretary general of the United Nations and other concerned heads of states to take immediate action and declare rape as a war crime, stop rape camps, and ethnic cleansing.
(c) To have a petition-signing campaign.
(d) To hold a protest rally on February 23 in Regina.

In Regina, Women United gathered approximately 1100 signatures, and petitions containing these signatures were forwarded to local MPs.

On February 23, a rally was held in downtown Victoria Park. About two hundred people turned out to brave the minus 28-degree temperature and took part in the protest march. A member of CCMW Regina and a Bosnian Muslim sister from Saskatoon addressed the rally. Speakers denounced the violence in Bosnia and demanded immediate action from Canada and the United Nations.

Media coverage was excellent and representatives of CCMW Regina chapter and others were interviewed by CBC Regina, STV, CKCK, local newspaper (*Leader-Post*), and radio station and covered the protest march.

YWCA of Regina invited our representative to their annual Woman of Distinction dinner to recognize our chapter's efforts toward elimination of violence against women.

We pray to Allah (SWT) to help us in our efforts toward enhancing the quality of life for Muslim women.

Media and CCMW with Others
(Published as a courtesy of *CKCK*, Regina)

Zia Afsar, Lydia Fuller, Samina Ahmed

Naushaba Habib

Together they formed what they call Women United. It is an action group to raise the awareness of women's issues. The move is in response to the report from the former Republic of Yugoslavia that women are being raped systematically by the tens of thousands.

ERIC LONGLEY: Reports saying that the rape is being used as a military weapon in the former Yugoslavian Republic has sent shock waves around the world. The rape crimes are part of what is being called virtuous ethnic cleansing. Reports say insofar as Serbian soldiers are being ordered to rape Muslim women so they would bear Serbian children.

SABREENA HAQUE: Between 20,000 and 50,000 women, most of them Muslims, are being raped.

ERIC LONGLEY: In Regina, the situation has prompted an unprecedented coalition of a dozen women's groups, churches and other organizations spearheaded by the Canadian Council of Muslim Women.

SABREENA HAQUE: We are here to get together with other women to do something about it. These are all Muslim sisters; they are suffering in Bosnia right now.

ERIC LONGLEY: They are called Women United and they are using a common voice to raise the awareness of the plight of Bosnian women. Their plan of action includes demonstrations, petitions and letter writing to put pressure on the Canadian government and international institutions like the United Nations. Organizers say similar movements are taking place around the world.

LYDIA FULLER (YWCA): The women of Regina are joining our voices with those of the world community and speaking out against rape and ethnic cleansing in Bosnia-Herzegovinia.

ERIC LONGLEY: Women United's first step will be a march on downtown Regina planned for next Tuesday. It will not be their last. The group then formed a group of long standing committee in the city to meet whatever serious issues like the war crimes in Bosnia need to be addressed. Eric Longley, CKCK news.

STV NEWS: Bosnia (Courtesy of Global TV)

There is a new action group here in Regina made up of over a dozen women's organizations. The group is putting action in Bosnia-Herzegovina where recent reports indicate at least 20,000 Muslim women have been raped.

Sabreena Haque is part of the Women United. She said the European Community report also says soldiers are being ordered to rape the women as part of an ethnic cleansing campaign.

SABREENA HAQUE: They have been ordered to rape the Muslim women. They said, "We were told to rape so that our morale will be higher. We will fight better if we rape the women". Rape is also being used as a threat so that they go away from the community. They are threatening the women by saying they will rape them so these women will right away leave their home. Rape is also a way, if it happens, they won't want to return to their community.

REPORTER: The group is also planning a letter writing campaign, petitions and demonstrations to protest the event in Bosnia. Demonstrations will be held on Tuesday. A coalition of women's groups from Regina, called Women United, held the protest today, where 100 people took part in the march to raise awareness about the plight of women in the former Yugoslavia.

KATHLEEN THOMPSON (Women United): We think if we work here locally to put pressure on our government and working across the country we can put pressure on the federal government, and people are doing this in other countries, the international community may have a voice so that rape is recognized as a war crime.

ZIA AFSAR (CCMW): It is unusual. It is gang rape and it is a deliberate policy of the government, and commanders are ordering the men and their soldiers to gang rape the women.

CBC News Bosnian Crisis presented courtesy of CBC:

HOLLY PRESTON: United Nations is suspending relief operations to most parts of Bosnia. The UN Commission of Refugees says Bosnian leaders are not allowing the organization to do its work. The announcement comes one day after Ottawa says it is sending 1200 peacekeepers to the outskirts. Meanwhile, a number of Regina groups have joined forces to protest violence against women in former Yugoslavia.

In Zagreb last September, when she learned the alleged atrocities, a Saskatoon woman, Marina Begic, who is trying to find her parents, read to us from the local newspaper detailing one woman's story of rape.

WOMAN: ...and she could not believe. She found a soldier, 'that is my dad and you are beating my dad, but they said, "Oh we are not just beating him, and now we are going to rape you, and she was screaming and asking why they are doing that, and they said well you have to be proud because you are Muslim and will be carrying a Serbian child.

HOLLY PRESTON: The stories like these have prompted pressure to pay attention to the abuse of Bosnian women. Zia Afsar represents the Canadian Council of Muslim Women, Regina chapter and Kathleen Thompson is with Women United, Regina. Thank you both for coming in. What is the extent of these crimes in Bosnia?

ZIA AFSAR: Probably you know of recent reports from the European Community suggesting that rape is being used as a military weapon. And they back up their claim—rape is used to terrorize the women or demoralize them and it is a deliberate policy for the rape. The second thing is that Serb soldiers and commanders, they are ordering their men to rape Bosnian women and using rape as to leave their homes and community and keep them until the baby is born or pregnancy is too advanced for an abortion.

HOLLY PRESTON: Kathleen, the numbers are almost impossible to believe. Can we believe that this is not wartime propaganda?

KATHLEEN THOMPSON: It is truly horrendous, the atrocities that are happening, and we can't believe that these numbers are true, but the number of reports we are hearing and the European researchers have been there and the researches of the UN and the information we hear and the personal story from the woman of Saskatoon we hear allow us to know that it is true and is happening.

HOLLY PRESTON: Tell me about the women you represent here and what you are trying to do?

KATHLEEN THOMPSON: It is has been quite overwhelming what is happening locally as a result of this. A number of local women's groups came together last week on behalf of the Canadian Council of Muslim Women, and that was the first organizational meeting last week. It was overwhelming the people who came, people from the Saskatchewan Provincial Secretariat, government, church groups. And what we decided to do is to join together to form a group to raise awareness about what is happening right now. Between the groups, we have a lot of talent and skills; we can cover a large amount of area and will continue to maintain relations. So we have an ongoing group here in the city.

HOLLY PRESTON: What do you think that you might need to be successful, especially since the UN has been unable to come any closer to stopping the conflict, or what kind of outside pressure to help these women?

KATHLEEN THOMPSON: Well I think the public is aware what is happening. If we join our hands nationally and internationally and put pressure on the United Nations, then I am sure something will come out.

HOLLY PRESTON: You would like to see rape treated as a war crime.

KATHLEEN THOMPSON: Definitely. That is what needs to be done, would need to be done. We are not just working locally; also nationally a lot is going on. We are having a demonstration on Tuesday and across the country, people are working - internationally as well, and we need to work with the international community so that the UN will recognize rape as a war crime.

HOLLY PRESTON: How can people get involved on Tuesday?

KATHLEEN THOMPSON: They can contact our group, Women United, through the Islamic Centre, or the women's centre at the University or Saskatchewan Action Committee on the Status of Women.

HOLLY PRESTON: Thank you.

Some Snapshots of Media-Bosnian Crisis

CCMW (National) Position Statement on Sharia (Muslim Law)

December 2003

CANADIAN COUNCIL OF MUSLIM WOMEN:

POSITION STATEMENT ON THE PROPOSED IMPLEMENTATION OF MUSLIM LAW [SHARIA] IN CANADA

As the proposed implementation of Muslim law [Sharia] has been a recent development and we have just heard about it via the media, we, the Canadian Council of Muslim Women, have more questions than answers regarding the proposed implementation of Muslim law [Sharia] in matters of family law and contracts.

We are trying to contact the members involved in the newly formed Islamic Institute of Civil Justice to obtain further information on their proposal:

1. CCMW's position is that we, as Canadian Muslim women, prefer to live under Canadian laws, governed by the Charter of Rights and Freedoms which safeguard our human rights. We acknowledge that this is not a perfect system but also know that if changes are needed there are mechanisms which allow for these changes, and this flexibility in the law is important to families of men, women and children. For us, it is important that there be safeguards to ensure the correct application of the values of the Charter, rather than adopting a set of traditional rules.

   A recent example of the flexibility and change has been the granting of joint/shared custody to both parents, as mothers and fathers are seen as necessary for children's healthy development.

   CCMW is concerned about the introduction of Sharia. It is a complex system and it is interpreted differentially in different countries and we question how, why and by whom it will be implemented in Canada.

In deference to their religious beliefs, some Canadian Muslim women may be persuaded to use the Sharia option, rather than seeking protection under the law of the land.

2. We are seeking an understanding of the laws of Canada and the provinces, regarding arbitration and its role within the legal system, and secondly about the newly formed Islamic Institute of Civil Justice itself.

   As to Canadian laws, we understand the desire to have community input into settling issues. We are aware that there are many informal mediation bodies functioning in Muslim and non-Muslim settings; however, mediation is very different from a binding arbitrated settlement.

   We need further clarification regarding protection and safeguards in the Canadian federal and provincial systems to ensure that any arbitration agreements do not result in unfair or unjust settlements for Muslim women.

   For example, what will be the process/formal mechanism and criteria, at the Canadian courts which use Canadian laws and the Charter to evaluate that these agreements adhere to the law of the land?

   Will this really save the courts' time or will it slow the process and create a "two tier" system of legal recourse for Canadian Muslim women?

   Other questions are about the binding nature of the arbitrated agreements, about the legal representation for women at these meetings and the role of the courts. Will the courts merely "rubber stamp" an arbitrated agreement, or will they ensure that the agreements are fair to both parties? Examples are that a woman may agree to a low financial agreement to obtain a divorce and then may find herself destitute, as in the famous Indian case of Shahbano, or may agree to her husband taking a second wife.

3. As to the Islamic Institute of Civil Justice, or any other body which assumes the role of arbiters, questions arise regarding their role, their powers and their training in a very complex, variant system of law.

CCMW is concerned about the competence of individuals who will serve as Islamic jurists in applying Sharia in the Canadian context.

Sharia, or more accurately Muslim law, is not divine, as argued by some. It is based on divine text, the Qur'an, but it was interpreted a few centuries after the death of the Prophet Mohammad, by jurists in different countries, who themselves insisted that these were only interpretations. It is a vast, complex judicial system, with many schools of thought and with adaptations to local customs.

For example, some countries where Muslim law is applied, such as Tunisia, have interpreted the law as limiting marriage to monogamy, while others, like Pakistan, allow polygamy if the first wife consents.

Also, there are some interpretations and practices which adversely affect women. For example in some schools of jurisprudence, inheritance favours males; a husband can divorce his wife without legal recourse; financial support for wives can be for a limited period of time; alimony is questionable; division of property can be against the woman; and child custody can be given to fathers, according to the age of the child. How and who will ensure that these are not the interpretations which are used by the arbiters?

4. As with any Law, it is problematic to apply some aspects and not consider the "totality" of the system, nor its context or its underpinning principles.

We acknowledge the well-meaning intentions of some to reflect the sensitivities of Canadian Muslims, and for their need to have a presence and some power in society to ensure their interests are met.

However, the introduction of a Sharia council may not solve the problem, and in fact may exacerbate the issues for families. There is ongoing debate amongst Muslims about the static or evolving nature of the jurisprudence and its adaptation to the realities of today's world.

For example, some argue that Muslim inheritance law, though it provides for a greater share to men, is fairer to women because a woman keeps her monies and does not have to contribute toward the expenses of the household, which is seen as the sole responsibility of the male. This may be practiced in some countries such as Saudi Arabia, but the reality of most families is that both partners share in the maintenance and the costs of their household, and few women would think that the burden should be borne only by the husband. This reality makes the inheritance law of greater share to men a questionable practice.

Muslim law is not monolithic or simple or applied consistently across the world and so we seriously question how it will be applied here in Canada and why is it needed here when the law of the land tries to be fair and just and is not contrary to the principles of the Qur'an.

CCMW would like Canadian Muslim women to live under Canadian law with its emphasis on equality and justice which are the cornerstones of Islam and should be the basis of any Muslim law anywhere.

Thank you.

CTV Invitation:
Naushaba Habib Attends on Behalf of CCMW

CTV Television Inc.

216 - 1ª Ave. N.
Saskatoon, Saskatchewan
Canada S7K 3W3

Tel 306.665.8600
Fax 306.665.0450

Thank you for attending our third Editorial Board Luncheon Meeting!

The meeting will focus on news issues affecting the Muslim community, and how these issues are covered by the Regina CTV news cast. The following individuals have planned to attend:

Dr. Ayman Aboguddah – Cardiologist ; President of Huda School (Public and Islamic education)

Mr. Kashif Ahmed – University Student and Communication Director of Muslims for Peace and Justice (MPJ)

Mr. Riaz Ahmed – City Planner / Director or Public Relations for MPJ

Dr. Naiyer Habib – Cardiologist; Former Head of Cardiology for Regina Health District; Former President of the Islamic Association of Saskatchewan (Regina); President of MPJ

Mrs. M. Naushaba Habib – MA (Political Science); President of Canadian Council of Muslim Women (Regina Chapter)

Dr. Samiul Haque – Child Psychiatrist

Zeba Hashmi – Homemaker and Secretary of MPJ; Bilingual Medical Office Administration Certification

Zarqa Nawaz – Journalist and Film Maker

Carl Worth - News Director - CTV Regina

Dale Neufeld - News Director - CTV Saskatoon / Prince Albert

Brian Zawacki - Director of Community Relations

Angela Loewen - Human Resources Specialist (Saskatchewan)

Geoff Bradley - Creative / Promotions Manager (Saskatchewan)

Wade Moffatt - Sales Manager - CTV Regina / Yorkton

Tara Robinson - News Anchor - CTV Regina

Manfred Joehnck - News Anchor - CTV Regina

Nelson Bird – Video Journalist; Host of Indigenous Circle

We want critical feedback on CTV Regina's news stories and interviews. We would like you to consider the following discussion questions:

1. How do our news stories cover issues affecting the Muslim community? Give specific examples.

2. Comment on how Muslim people are presented in the news.

3. What issues are being ignored? Give specific examples.

4. What news program do you watch all the time? If it's not CTV, explain why you prefer it.

5. Describe what you like about our station's approach.

6. What suggestions do you have about how we could improve our ability to serve your community?

A DIVISION OF
Bell Globemedia

CCMW Publications

- ➢ *Briarpatch* Magazine—Mahlaqa Naushaba Habib as Courtesy of *Briarpatch* Magazine, Andrew Loewen

- ➢ *Muslim Veil in North America*: as a courtesy of Editors Homa Hoodfar and Sajida Sultana Alvi
  - Zia Afsar
  - Naushaba Habib

Voices of the Sisters

A look at the special barriers that First Nations Women and Women of Colour face to full participation in our communities, workplaces and society in general.

Naiyer Habib & Mahlaqa Naushaba Habib

WHEN CULTURES DIFFER

A glimpse into the experiences of an immigrant Canadian family.

by M. Naushaba Habib

photo: Debra Brin

My family immigrated to Canada in 1973 and our links are to India and Pakistan. We left both of these countries because of discrimination. In India, Muslims faced discrimination from a predominately Hindu population, and Indian Muslims who moved to Pakistan faced discrimination as immigrants.

Our first stop on the way to Canada was the United States. My husband had come for medical training and I was pregnant with my first child.

The primary barrier we faced was ignorance and continues to be ignorance. Most of the people around us did not know anything about our faith, or if they thought they did it was often a mistaken understanding. We avoided activities which were contrary to our cultural or religious upbringing.

Accommodation

When we first arrived, access to food was a problem. We eat *Halaal* food, animals slaughtered in a special religious way. Pork, pork products and alcohol are forbidden for Muslims. Because of the lack of food suitable for our eating, we remained vegetarian for a while. Subsequently, we arranged to slaughter cow, lamb and chicken on farms. Now *Halaal* food is available in many grocery stores. Hotels arrange for our kind of food when we invite people for marriages and other events.

When we started to receive invitation from our local friends and neighbours we did not know how to tell them about our food requirements. We thought we would be imposing on them. Therefore, we would go and eat whatever was suitable for us to eat. One day a family invited us for a meal and served only foods containing pork. Therefore, we could not eat. When the hosts found out, they were very embarrassed and we felt guilty for not telling them. Because of this experience we have decided to let our hosts know and we request that they not bother with any special preparation. In spite of this request, people go out of their way to make sure that there is some food for us. Thus, it was a process of learning to be frank and cordial.

When we arrived here we were welcomed by the larger society and participated in social and community gatherings, but we did not have a place to offer

History of the Muslims of Regina, Saskatchewan, and Their Organizations

congregational worship. Churches were generous to offer their places without hesitation when approached. Now there are Mosques in every city, from small houses to palatial buildings.

When we first arrived here, and until lately, children were allowed to leave classes for our holidays but were marked absent. The children are no longer marked absent, and schools are even providing a place and allowing the children to pray at the required times. Employers now allow their Muslim employees to go to offer prayer; the Muslim employees compensate by working for the total hours they are expected to work. Workers generally have to use their annual holidays to celebrate our religious holidays, except in Ontario. We are appreciative of these accommodations.

Racism

My children faced racial discrimination in schools. Our home and car were vandalized and I faced taunts over my head scarf; I was walking one time in the downtown area and a youth poked my head from behind and ran away. Another time I was walking in the park in my neighborhood and a boy called me "Hebrew lady" and tried to hide. I went to him and told him, "I am a Muslim lady." It was gratifying that a white woman came to me and told me, looking at my traditional dress, "You look different and nice. Do not change yourself." It was encouraging for me to be reminded that there are kind people! I also have a fond memory of our first landlady when we lived in the USA. Jackie was a registered nurse and was like a mother to us. She even took time off work to attend to me during my pregnancy, and to my child when he became very sick.

Muslim Community

Over time my family became involved with the Muslim community. I was, and am, President of the Regina Chapter of the Canadian Council of Muslim Women and my husband was President of the Islamic Association for many years. We established Muslims for Peace and Justice after the 9/11 incident in order to address misunderstandings about Islam and Muslims, and to deal with the ensuing rise in discrimination. My children were active with the Muslim youth and were also involved in the society at large.

I started an Islamic school in my home to teach religion to the children and did so for a number of years. The school started with nine children of different age groups. By the time we acquired our own centre or Mosque, the number of children had grown to 30. The Mosque now provides religious study.

Some of the Muslim families felt the need for a full time Muslim school and Regina Huda School was

started in 1999 with 20 students. Two years later it became an associate school with the Public School Board. Saskatchewan School Board curriculum is followed and taught by five certified non-Muslim teachers. Three Muslim teachers teach Islam and Arabic. The school has 85 children from pre-kindergarten to Grade 8. These families are originally from 15 different countries. The school maintains a very high standard and has excellent facilities. There is a plan to eventually include high school.

We are active in university programs for Islamic discussion, folk festivals, work related functions, and in interfaith and intercultural activities. My children, now grown up, were involved with us, and continue to be active in the Muslim community and in society at large.

Prior to 9-11, I believed that Muslims were gaining greater acceptance by the mainstream society. After 9-11, I became apprehensive for the future of my family and my country, Canada. While I see the rise of all kinds of bigotry, at the same time I am reassured to see many of my sister and brother Canadians outside my faith group standing up for us.

Ignorance is the biggest disease of the human being. I believe that the best way to overcome something is to face the problem head on and deal with it. We have to develop understanding and respect for one another to live and progress as individuals, as society and as a nation. We are created by God as one.

As God says in the Holy Quraa'n: "O mankind, We have created you from a single male and female and made you into nations and tribes so that you may know each other. The most honorable in the sight of God are surely the Righteous."

M. Naushaba Habib is an immigrant citizen of Canada with a Master's degree in Political Science. She is a homemaker, medical office manager, community volunteer worker and a founding member and the President of Canadian Council of Muslim Women, Regina Chapter.

congregational worship. Churches were generous to offer their places without hesitation when approached. Now there are Mosques in every city, from small houses to palatial buildings.

When we first arrived here, and until lately, children were allowed to leave classes for our holidays but were marked absent. The children are no longer marked absent, and schools are even providing a place and allowing the children to pray at the required times. Employers now allow their Muslim employees to go to offer prayer; the Muslim employees compensate by working for the total hours they are expected to work. Workers generally have to use their annual holidays to celebrate our religious holidays, except in Ontario. We are appreciative of these accommodations.

Racism

My children faced racial discrimination in schools. Our home and car were vandalized and I faced taunts over my head scarf; I was walking one time in the downtown area and a youth poked my head from behind and ran away. Another time I was walking in the park in my neighborhood and a boy called me "Hebrew lady" and tried to hide. I went to him and told him, "I am a Muslim lady." It was gratifying that a white woman came to me and told me, looking at my traditional dress, "You look different and nice. Do not change yourself." It was encouraging for me to be reminded that there are kind people! I also have a fond memory of our first landlady when we lived in the USA. Jackie was a registered nurse and was like a mother to us. She even took time off work to attend to me during my pregnancy, and to my child when he became very sick.

Muslim Community

Over time my family became involved with the Muslim community. I was, and am, President of the Regina Chapter of the Canadian Council of Muslim Women and my husband was President of the Islamic Association for many years. We established Muslims for Peace and Justice after the 9/11 incident in order to address misunderstandings about Islam and Muslims, and to deal with the ensuing rise in discrimination. My children were active with the Muslim youth and were also involved in the society at large.

I started an Islamic school in my home to teach religion to the children and did so for a number of years. The school started with nine children of different age groups. By the time we acquired our own centre or Mosque, the number of children had grown to 30. The Mosque now provides religious study.

Some of the Muslim families felt the need for a full time Muslim school and Regina Huda School was started in 1999 with 20 students. Two years later it became an associate school with the Public School Board. Saskatchewan School Board curriculum is followed and taught by five certified non-Muslim teachers. Three Muslim teachers teach Islam and Arabic. The school has 85 children from pre-kindergarten to Grade 8. These families are originally from 15 different countries. The school maintains a very high standard and has excellent facilities. There is a plan to eventually include high school.

We are active in university programs for Islamic discussion, folk festivals, work related functions, and in interfaith and intercultural activities. My children, now grown up, were involved with us, and continue to be active in the Muslim community and in society at large.

Prior to 9-11, I believed that Muslims were gaining greater acceptance by the mainstream society. After 9-11, I became apprehensive for the future of my family and my country, Canada. While I see the rise of all kinds of bigotry, at the same time I am reassured to see many of my sister and brother Canadians outside my faith group standing up for us.

Ignorance is the biggest disease of the human being. I believe that the best way to overcome something is to face the problem head on and deal with it. We have to develop understanding and respect for one another to live and progress as individuals, as society and as a nation. We are created by God as one.

As God says in the Holy Quraa'n: "O mankind, We have created you from a single male and female and made you into nations and tribes so that you may know each other. The most honorable in the sight of God are surely the Righteous."

M. Naushaba Habib is an immigrant citizen of Canada with a Master's degree in Political Science. She is a homemaker, medical office manager, community volunteer worker and a founding member and the President of Canadian Council of Muslim Women, Regina Chapter.

The Muslim Veil in North America

Issues and Debates

EDITED BY

Sajida Sultana Alvi, Homa Hoodfar, and Sheila McDonough

PART 1

Veiling Practices in Everyday Life in Canada

CHAPTER 4

VOICES OF MUSLIM WOMEN

Voices of Muslim Women

Statements of 7 women in the book about their personal view on *Hijabs.*

Here statements of Zia Afsar and Naushaba Habib are noted from CCMW Regina chapter in the book.

Printed here as a courtesy of editors: Sajida Sultana Alvi, and Homa Hoodfar and authors

Statement 5: Zia Afsar

I started wearing a *Hijab* when I was in my forties. I was not influenced or pressured by my family to do so. It was my own independent decision, which I discussed with my family before starting to wear it. I am a religious person, and after the study of the available Islamic literature, I concluded that wearing a *Hijab* is essential to portray my Muslim identity.

At that time we lived in a small town where most of the people knew me personally. My wearing of a *Hijab* did not make any difference in my daily interaction with people. I was involved in many volunteer organizations and I continued doing so without any strange looks or remarks from anybody.

Shortly after that, we moved to a big city with a bigger Muslim community. I was received very well by the Mosque community, especially by sisters with an Arab background. But the sisters of my own ethnic background (Indo-Pak subcontinent) were hesitant in welcoming me in their social circle. Perhaps they thought that either I was too religious or too backward. It took them awhile to invite me to their social and cultural gatherings. There were only a couple of ladies from my ethnic background who wore the *Hijab*.

As I had always done volunteering in community organizations, I wanted to get involved in this city too. That was an uphill battle. I had to struggle hard to make a place for me in the society at large. Communities where there are not many *Hijab*-wearing ladies, have the perception that *Hijaibis* are not educated and that they are oppressed by the male members of their respective families, and that they wear a *Hijab* because they are forced to. That was not the case with me. I have a Master of Physics from a Canadian university. I am an outgoing, outspoken person, and wearing a head covering did not change me as a person at all. I kept trying and proved that I am neither uneducated nor oppressed. Gradually I changed the perception of people with whom I interacted as a neighbor, as a volunteer or as a citizen. I stayed in that city for six years and eventually I became a sought-for volunteer. I gained respect as an individual who believes in freedom of choice and respect for individuality.

We moved again to a small town where I am the only *Hijab*-wearing woman. Now I know how to handle the challenge. People talked to me slowly as if I did not understand English, or else they used hand gestures to make me understand the conversation. Once when I was standing in a checkout lineup, an Oriental man came up to me, who could speak English with much difficulty, and asked me if I could speak English. On my affirmation, he asked me a question, and was surprised to hear me replying in English.

Sometimes I laugh, other times I feel angry. Why is there so much emphasis on women's dress? If the dress does not fit the norms of society, then the woman is considered to be uneducated and oppressed. I have noticed that in big cosmopolitan cities, where the population is diverse in ethnicity, people accept *Hijab*-wearing women more easily than they do in smaller, less diverse towns. Now that the *Hijab* has become part of my personality, I usually forget that I am different from other women.

Statement 6: Naushaba Habib

I had never thought about the *Hijab* seriously until we went for *hajj* in 1988. We were an average Muslim family from an Islamic point of view. Neither I, nor my friends, who now wear the *Hijab*, used to take it seriously. We did cover our heads at Islamic gatherings, and I covered mine in the Islamic School where I was teaching. But it was only after going on *hajj* that I consciously decided to wear the *Hijab* regularly.

The pilgrimage convinced me that I should observe my Islamic duty of wearing the *Hijab*. My general idea was that a Muslim, especially one returning from *hajj*, should be as perfect as possible. I tried to accept this responsibility.

I did not face any problems related to my job. I had done my master's degree in political science. I remained a mother and wife until my children were grown up. I then started to manage the medical office of my husband, a job I still do. One day when I was walking downtown in Regina, a teenage boy struck me on the head with his hand. On another occasion, when I was walking in the neighborhood, some children shouted "Hebrew lady." I stopped and told them I was Muslim and not Hebrew and they ran away. I find that when I go shopping, or fill the car with gas by myself, people look at me curiously and whisper to one another.

I also had some good experiences. A lady patient of my husband remarked that I looked good, and looked different. She advised that I should not change. When I travel, especially in a long skirt, coat and *Hijab*, people seem to respect me. Perhaps this is a sign of better education and status among travelers.

I sympathize with Muslim sisters who have to work, and who feel inhibited about wearing the *Hijab*. This situation may be improved by educating the public at large to understand the religious concerns of Muslim women better. Some sisters may opt to wear the *Hijab* only in family and Muslim gatherings, and pray to God to make it easy for them.

Muslim men, who criticize Muslim sisters for not wearing the *Hijab,* should understand the problems faced by the women, and help ease the difficulties instead of just being critical.

Farewell to Zia Afsar 1997

Front: Shaheen Talat, Naushaba Habib, Zia Afsar, Nasreen Aftab, Ismat Saleem
Back: unidentified, Erum Afsar, Samina Ahmed

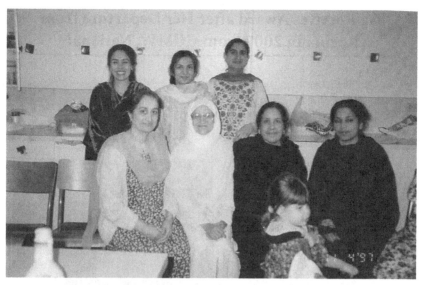

Front: Talat, Zia Afsar, Naseem Ahmed, Saleena Ahmed;
Back: Rizwana Rahman, Ghazala Ahmed, Sumera Ali

Sitting: Nusrat Jalil, Zia Afsar, Uroose Hasni, Nasreen Aftab

Zia Receives Award after Her Departure from Regina in 2007 from CCMW, National

CANADIAN MUSLIM
WOMEN WHO INSPIRE

ZIA AFSAR **is a tireless advocate of women's rights.**

Her activism began at an early age. As a young woman in the 1960s in Pakistan, she raised a constitutional challenge for women to be granted admission into engineering institutions. Her advocacy received national media attention, and as a result, in the years to follow, young women in Pakistan have been able to study engineering.

Zia strongly believes in and encourages women to seek equality through education and financial independence. She herself has a master's degree in nuclear physics, and her two daughters, inspired by their mother, are trained in engineering and law.

Zia promotes understanding and respect for diversity both within Muslim communities and the broader Canadian society. While living in Saskatchewan, she helped build bridges between Muslim and non-Muslim women's groups by spear-heading the creation of an umbrella organization, Women United. It provided a forum for coordinating action on women's issues at provincial, national and international levels. Zia also firmly believes that diversity is the basic characteristic of humanity as recognized in the Quran. This has led her to promote, in her personal and professional life, the concept of unity within diversity, one which is central to Canada's multicultural ethos.

She volunteers with a variety of Muslim and larger civil society organizations, including women's or immigrant centres and an old people's home. As such, she continues to do what she's accomplished all her life: to break down stereotypes of Muslim women that her colleagues may have held and to show by example through her personal achievements that Muslim women can achieve whatever they set out to do.

INSPIRING
INSPIRING
MUSLIMS
INSPIRING
MUSLIMS
MUSLIMS
CANADIANS
CANADIANS
INSPIRING

Canadian Council of Muslim Women
Conseil canadien des femmes musulmanes

Picnic at Wascana Lake

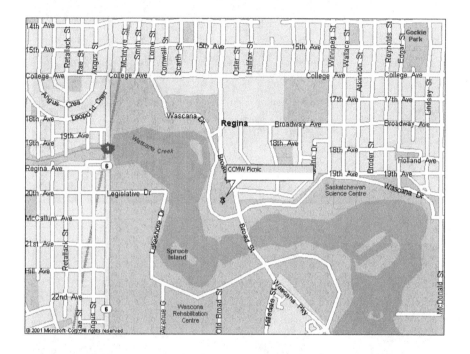

Executives of the

Canadian Council of Muslim Women

Invites

to join them for a
Family Picnic
ON
JULY 10, 2004 (12:30 p.m. sharp)

At

ECHO LAKE
Weather permitting!
Please bring a little extra food to share with your friends.
CCMW will provide paper plates & cutlery.

For more information, please contact any of the social
committee members.

Uroose Hasanie	*584-9804*	*Tracy (Abdou) Shier 596-7052*
Naushaba Habib	*584-8578*	*Yasmin Zia 522-0229*

We look forward to your participation

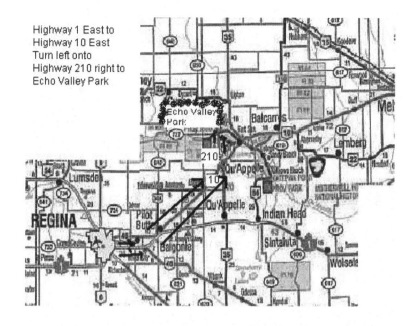

Highway 1 East to
Highway 10 East
Turn left onto
Highway 210 right to
Echo Valley Park

In the Name of God, Most Kind, Most Merciful

History of Muslims for Peace & Justice

2001–2005

Naiyer and Mahlaqa Naushaba Habib

Introduction

Muslims for Peace & Justice was founded after the event of 9/11. It was established to deal with the expected impact of 9/11 on Muslims. Who did this disaster has remained controversial. Who to blame and who not to blame is a question, which has not been resolved. The website is full with such information.

I heard this news when I was parking my car in the parking lot of my medical office in Regina General Hospital. This shattered me. I called my wife immediately. At that time, I had stepped down from the leadership of the Islamic Association of Saskatchewan, being involved since 1977 to 1998. I served as president for multiple terms and as a director on the board occasionally. My wife also served on its board. I perceived that the Islamic Association of Saskatchewan did not take any active part. I felt that this was going to have a serious impact on the Muslims in the West. Not being involved in the leadership of the Islamic Association, I was at a loss what to do.

I was in the Masjid offering Friday Prayer on September 14, 2001. My mind was bogged with the incident. I came out of the Masjid after the prayer was over, and I saw Ejaz Ahmed coming out from the Masjid after me. He had also served as a president of the Islamic Association. We got close to each other to have some discussion. Meanwhile, Abdul Jalil, the former secretary of the Islamic Association also came out. The three of us looked at the issue and felt that something needed to be done, as the Islamic Association was not taking any part. The *Leader-Post* interviewed me, Ejaz Ahmed and the Imam of the Masjid on September 13, 2001. This has been incorporated in the history of Muslims for Peace & Justice. We decided to invite a few people from the community who had worked with us and also were old timers in Regina.

We scheduled a meeting at the residence of Ejaz Ahmed on in the evening of September14, 2001. We all agreed that an organization had to be formed. Subsequently, a meeting was called at the university, and we felt that Ejaz Ahmed should chair this meeting. The media was also invited. This led to the formation of

Muslims for Peace & Justice (MPJ). The next meeting was held at my residence. The board was elected unanimously. The purpose and objectives were defined and how to pursue them.

As it appears in the history of Muslims for Peace & Justice, the Muslims for Peace & Justice took exemplary steps in dealing with the impact on Muslims. We sent representatives to schools, churches, and elsewhere. We were also represented in the Interfaith organization, which was formed on the initiation of the Islamic Association led by Riazuddin Ahmed at the time of the Iraq first war. We represented Islam to various communities and public. We also started two days of conference every year. We dealt with any media onslaught, any political or Islamophobic matters. These are noted in the Activities of the MPJ.

I felt strongly that we should leave a history of Muslims for Peace & Justice for the coming generations to see what we achieved with our limited resources as to finance and as to personnel. It proved that it is the quality that matters rather than quantity. Our commitment to the community's cause was no less than our commitment to family and profession. In our work, we never took any matter casually. With such individuals, we limited the authorities to look after this important organization to them as trustee to minimize infiltration that would hamper the effort. Seventy-five percent of the vote for trustee was required to fill a vacancy of a trustee. I was of the opinion to have unanimous vote to fill such vacancy.

We were all people of similar or same thinking. This led to smooth, cooperative and very productive outcome from this organization. Allah bless those who worked for it and who have taken the responsibility to carry on the task. I retired from the Muslims for Peace & Justice in February 2005. The chairmanship was given to Riazuddin Ahmed with his board, which appears in the history of Muslims for Peace & Justice in the minutes of the annual general meeting of February 2005 of the trustees.

History of Muslims for Peace & Justice Formation

September 11, 2001: Disaster occurred.

Muslims became targets across the world. Victimization started immediately.

Muslim leaders received the jolt and had to stand up for the defense of Muslims.

September 13, 2001, Thursday—*Leader-Post* published the interview of Dr. Ejaz Ahmed and Dr. Naiyer Habib, former presidents of the Islamic Association of Saskatchewan, Regina, and that of Hafiz Ilyas of the *Masjid.*

Leader Post

ty Editor: David Ramsay

Thursday, September 13, 2001

ThirdPage

Phone: 565-8300

ISLAMIC REACTION

Local Muslims condemn violence

By PAMELA COWAN and JANEL WHITE
of The Leader-Post

The sleep of a University of Regina professor was tormented Tuesday night as live TV images of the deadly terrorist attacks on New York and Washington continued to rerun in his mind.

"I still can't believe this has happened," said Dr. Ejaz Ahmed. "When I saw it on TV, it seemed like a movie, but this is reality.

"I think this is the most terrible event of the century. I had lots of difficulty sleeping."

Those responsible for the carnage should be punished, Ahmed said, but he hopes the U.S. waits until they have conclusive evidence before responding.

"If innocent people get killed, it won't serve the purpose and the retaliation will be a disaster," Ahmed said.

TV coverage of Muslim leaders expressing fear on Tuesday night temporarily panicked Ahmed.

"I feel pretty secure in Canada as compared to the U.S. because the U.S. is a superpower and you can make lots of enemies, no matter if you do the right or the wrong thing," he said.

In 1995 and 1996, Ahmed served as president of the Regina branch of the Islamic Association of Saskatchewan. He estimates there are between 300 and 400 Muslim families in Regina.

Regina cardiologist Dr. Naiyer Habib called Tuesday "the saddest day of my life."

"To see this barbaric act on innocent people was most unexpected — I just couldn't watch the news last night," he said.

"We are quite concerned that these kinds of things are spreading instead of stopping ... whoever has done it has

done it out of frustration because their goal or ideology could not be achieved. Not everybody can be ideal, but if people are fair and honest in dealing with things, it creates friendship and avoids these kinds of problems."

No matter who is responsible for the barbaric acts, Habib hopes an entire community does not pay the price for the actions of a smaller group.

"This is a time of prayer and consolation, he said.

Priest Hafeez Ilyas of Regina's Islamic Association was busy answering calls and scheduling prayers dedicated to the tragedy.

Special prayers were held at the Islamic mosque Tuesday evening and more are planned for Friday.

Ilyas has received over 20 calls from Regina residents. But most of the calls he's answering aren't about prayer services.

"People keep calling here — just calling to make sure we are safe and the prayer place is safe," he said.

Ilyas said there is a concern that his ethnic group will be targeted.

But Regina residents have been showing their concern for his well-being.

"Some of the people come in and ask if we are getting a hard time," said Ilyas.

Three of Ilyas' neighbours, that have seen him and his family in traditional dress, have already told him to be careful because "they're worried we might be harmed."

Ilyas is grateful for the concern, but said there is nothing he can do.

"We are all human beings and are related to each other, but we are not part of it (the terrorism). But we are feeling bad," Ilyas said.

"All we can do is pray and we've done that."

September 14, 2001, Friday

Ejaz Ahmed and Naiyer Habib talked to each other in the compound of the Islamic Centre and Mosque at Montague Avenue regarding the September 11, 2001 events with worries. They called Abdul Jalil as he came out of the Mosque. They perceived that the Islamic Association was not playing an appropriate leadership role for the Muslims of Regina. They decided to do something. They met at the residence of Ejaz Ahmed, 11358 Wascana Meadows, that evening.

Subsequently, another meeting was called and attended by the invitees. The meeting was held at the residence of Ejaz Ahmed. It was attended by: Ayman Aboguddah, Ejaz Ahmed, Riazuddin Ahmed, Naiyer Habib, Anwarul Haque, Abdul Jalil, Abdul Qayyum, and Fashat Wasty. It was finalized to form the organization of Muslims for Peace & Justice.

November 4, 2001, Sunday

Subsequently, a meeting was held on Sunday, November 4, 2001, in the University of Regina Union Centre. It was chaired by Ejaz Ahmed. There was also a press conference. Media coverage was provided by *STV* and *Leader-Post*.

The objective of the Muslims for Peace & Justice (MPJ) was finalized as follows:

Objective 1.   Respond to peace and justice issues through different media interviews, columns, and write-ups in various provincial and national media.

Objective 2.   Interact with Interfaith and other peace and justice groups in Saskatchewan, for better understanding and harmonious relationships between Muslims and other citizens.

Objective 3.   Provide lawful help and support where Muslims are falsely accused and/or receive unfair treatment from the public and/or government agencies.

Objective 4.   Serve as a bridge of understanding to Muslim world affairs.

Objective 5.   Educate and inform the Muslims and the Canadian community about the basic religious principles, peaceful co-existence, and universal humanistic values of Islam.

The meeting was attended by:

- Prof. Ejaz Ahmed
- Prof. Ejaz Ahmed
- Dr. Naiyer Habib
- Riazuddin Ahmed
- Abdul Qayyum
- Arif Sethi
- Dr. M. Anwarul Haque
- Prof. Abbas Hasanie
- Zeba Hashmi
- Kashif Ahmed
- Samina Ahmed
- Prof. Syed Rizvi
- Dr. Fashat Wasty
- Feroze Naqvi
- Naushaba Habib
- Qudsia Qayyum
- Dr. Samiul Haque
- Dr. Abdul Jalil
- Nusrat Jalil
- Prof. Abdella Abdou
- Zarqa Nawaz
- Aijaz Hussain
- Faeeza Moolla

Meeting Invitation

Place: University of Regina
            Union Centre Room # 286
Date: November 4th 2001
Time: 3:00 PM to 5 PM

Purpose: To show support to a recently formed Muslim
            organization in Saskatchewan called **Muslims for Peace
            & Justice** and to assist in finalizing the objectives of the
            group, and the identification of some key actions to be
            undertaken on the short and long term basis to achieve
            the objectives.

Proposed Agenda:

1. Meeting Opens with Recitation from the   3:00 PM
   Qur'an
2. Opening Remarks and Background (Also   3:05 PM
   Q&A)—Ejaz Ahmed
3. Asr Prayers   3:30 PM
4. Review of draft objectives and   3:40 PM
   identification of key actions (Facilitator:
   Riazuddin Ahmed)
5. Other Business   4:25 PM
6. Wrap–Up and Dua   4: 45 PM
7. Refreshments / Networking   Until 5:15 PM

Note: See introduction and draft objectives following.

Introduction

Some Muslims (noted below) in Saskatchewan felt the need for a contemporary organization that would act as a facilitator and liaison with the community at large, media, government, Islamic and other faith groups. This initiative has been undertaken by the following persons after a brief discussion among Naiyer Habib, Ejaz Ahmed and Abdul Jalil on Sept 14, 2001, in the premises of ICM of IAOS after Friday Prayer. Thereafter a meeting was called at the residence of Ejaz Ahmed immediately that evening.

The following were present at the Residence of Ejaz Ahmed on September 14:

Dr. S. E. Ahmed, Regina, SK,
Dr. Abdul Jalil, Regina, SK
Dr. Naiyer Habib, Regina, SK
Mr. Riazuddin Ahmed, Regina, SK
Dr. M. Anwarul Haque, Regina, SK
Mr. A. Qayyum, Regina, SK
Dr. Fashat Wasty
Dr. Ayman Aboguddah

The name of the organization has been agreed to be:

Muslims for Peace & Justice

The following **draft objectives** of the group have been formulated:

Objectives:

1. Inform the media about the Islamic perspective on recent issues (like the attacks on the WTC, bombing of Afghanistan,) and public affairs through different media interviews, columns and write-ups to various provincial and national media.

2. Interact with people of different faith groups in the city and the province for better understanding and harmonious relationships between Muslims and other citizens.

3. Provide lawful help and support where Muslims are falsely accused and/or receive unfair treatment from the public and/or government agencies.

4. Serve as a bridge of understanding to Muslim world affairs.

5. Educate and inform the Muslims and the Canadian Community at large about the basic religious principles, peaceful co-existence, and universal humanistic values of Islam.

6. Re-enforce the sense that Muslims are an essential part of the Canadian Mosaic.

Minutes of the Meeting

Muslims for Peace & Justice Organizational
Formation November 4, 2001
MINUTES

A larger meeting was called today.

This meeting was organized on Sunday, November 4, 2001 in the University of Regina Union Centre to present and discuss the Purpose and Objectives of the newly formed Muslims for Peace & Justice [MPJ] organization in Saskatchewan. Twenty-one Muslims and Muslimahs attended the meeting:

- Prof. Ejaz Ahmed
- Dr. Naiyer Habib
- Riazuddin Ahmed
- Abdul Qayyum
- Arif Sethi
- Dr. M. Anwarul Haque
- Prof. Abbas Hasanie
- Zeba Hashmi
- Kashif Ahmed
- Samina Ahmed
- Prof. Syed Rizvi

- Dr. Fashat Wasty
- Feroze Naqvi
- Naushaba Habib
- Qudsia Qayyum
- Faeeza Molla
- Dr. Samiul Haque
- Dr. Abdul Jalil
- Nusrat Jalil
- Prof. Abdella Abdou
- Zarqa Nawaz
- Aijaz Hussain

Professor Ejaz Ahmed chaired the meeting. He explained the purpose of the newly formed group—To be a voice for peaceful Islam, to provide outreach & advocacy activities between Muslims and the larger Canadian community, and to defend Islam and Muslims against any harmful stereotyping, and to inform the media about Islam and Muslims.

Three past-presidents of the Islamic Association of Saskatchewan, Regina (Dr. M. Anwarul Haque, Dr. Naiyer Habib, and Br. Abdul Qayyum) provided their experiences and the history of organizing the Muslim community on a permanent basis since 1969.

After Asr prayer the group reconvened again to review and approve the draft objectives of Muslims for Peace & Justice, and to identify some actions for achieving these objectives.

The previously circulated draft objectives were reviewed and accepted with some minor changes, and a number of "Actions" were identified for each objective as follows:

Objective 1. Respond to peace and justice issues through different media interviews, columns, and write-ups in various provincial and national media.

Suggested Actions:

1.1. Very graciously point out to the media (Print, Radio, and TV) the truth whenever you hear of something that goes against our belief. For example, offensive talk show comments, or biased editorials.

On the other hand, if you hear something positive, logical and reasonable, pay that source of media a compliment.

Would this group be willing to attend a peace rally?

1.2. Create a group of members for media watch.

1.3. Issue statement that the guilty party should be brought to justice.

1.4. Identify peace and justice issues that are of immediate interest to Muslims:

Organize seminars/conferences on these issues. Prepare us to understand issues and how to present them to the public at large, i.e. workshops for ourselves.

Objective 2. Interact with Interfaith and other peace and justice groups in Saskatchewan, and other provinces for better understanding and harmonious relationships between Muslims and other citizens.

Suggested Actions:

2.1. Organize interfaith group actions.

2.2. Invite people of other faiths to social receptions at Eid etc. and provide social exposure and interaction. Occasional speaker/talk may be useful from time to time.

2.3. Raise some funds for food bank, organize other help for poor children in the Canadian community. We should involve ourselves in charitable activities in the community at large.

2.4. Organize annual MPJ conferences

Objective 3. Provide lawful help and support where Muslims are falsely accused and/or receive unfair treatment from the public and/or government agencies.

Suggested Actions:

3.1. Organize workshop on the legal rights of a Canadian citizen, and/or a legal visitor and how they will be affected under the new Terrorism Act under discussion—urgently.

Make people aware of any Legal Aid available to the persons under investigation.

Establish an ad-hoc committee to be contacted in case of any unnecessary detention/harassment by security agencies. Committee should compile a list of such cases and report to the members of parliament, attorney general, and the prime minister's office of any misuse of power by security agencies.

3.2. Create a fund, and contact local lawyers who are willing to help in incidents of misuse of power by the security agencies, and who can approach courts for speedy trial and justice.

3.3. Identify cases or situations where a member of the Muslim community has been detained or is being harassed; and then take actions to support such person(s).

3.4. Make a representation to the federal government expressing the Muslim community's deep concern about the possibility of misuse of the proposed Anti-Terror Law.

3.5 Monitor the affairs of the Muslims in Saskatchewan and/or Canada if treated unfairly, contact media to show how their rights are being violated.

3.6. Immediately study the proposed Anti-Terror Law to be passed and advise government on our views and suggestions.

3.7 Participate in matters of making laws and other actions by the government that may affect Muslims as part of the Canadian mosaic.

Objective 4. Serve as a bridge of understanding to Muslim world affairs.

Suggested Actions:

4.1. Organize symposiums and workshops with the help of other peace and justice, and human rights groups to focus on the injustices being faced by Muslims and other people of the world at the hands of superpowers, regional powers and powerful Western business interests.

4.2. Invite MPs of different federal parties in Saskatchewan to explain their party's and own position on issues of war, peace, justice and human rights in Muslim hot spots internationally.

Objective 5. Educate and inform the Muslims and the Canadian community about the basic religious principles, peaceful co-existence, and universal humanistic values of Islam.

Suggested Actions:

5.1. Organize discussion forums/workshops on important Islamic subjects by Islamic scholars (traditional and progressive) to learn about issues like persecution of women in Muslim countries, misunderstanding of the concept of Jihad, living as a minority in a Western society, etc. Hold supper gatherings on such occasions to raise funds to defer costs of such events. Have some fun too.

5.2 Create a speakers roster for responding to requests from other faith or peace and justice groups to speak on Islam—human rights, women's rights, Jihad, slavery in Islam, practice of concubine by Muslims, polygamy, etc.

Objective 6. Emphasize that Muslims are an integral part of the Canadian Mosaic and support the safety and security measures for peaceful living as part of the Canadian community.

Suggested Actions:

6.1. Make sure that the safety and security measures are not misused and misapplied against the Muslims in Regina, and Canada. Network with the legal and human rights groups to deal with this issue.

Other Comments and Suggestions:

- Focus on objectives and issues and do not get bogged down by the past
- Be firm about what you believe in and stick to it
- Be straightforward and keep it simple
- There is a difference between unlawful and unjust
- There can be unjust law. Example—deporting someone or detaining. We will have to stand against such law-making
- Circulate to all Muslims these objectives and invite to a larger meeting for input.

Some important questions raised and answers:

Q.1: Is this group going to compete with the existing Islamic Association?

A: No. The Muslim community has various needs and interests. The board of the Islamic Association is focused on arranging services for the spiritual and the *Qur'an* and Hadith teaching for adults and children. Some community members felt the need and started a fulltime Islamic elementary school, called the Huda School. All those present here are full members of the Islamic Association and support the Huda School also.

There is a strong need felt for outreach, advocacy work, media relations, and contact with government leaders on issues important to the Muslim community. Muslims for Peace & Justice organization will service this need.

Q.2: Are you going to register this organization?

A: If and when the supporters of this initiative feel the need
for such formal organization, we will consider the issue and
with consultation with the supporters will make the final
decision. In the short term, we do not feel the need. We
wish to implement actions to achieve the objectives with
your help.

Recording secretary: Riazuddin Ahmed

The work of the MPJ was started. Members shared their
responsibilities.

The involved people were all initiators who attended the meeting
of November 4, 2001.

June 2, 2002, at the residence of Dr. Naiyer Habib, 9227 Wascana
Mews, a board was elected unanimously and was charged to carry
on the work of the MPJ and to develop a constitution. The elected
board members were:

President: Dr. Naiyer Habib
Vice-President: Dr. Mansoor Haq
Secretary: Sr. Zeba Hashmi
Treasurer: Br. Arif Sethi
Community Relations Director: Br. Riazuddin Ahmed

MPJ Meeting June 2, 2002

The above meeting of the MPJ group was held at Dr. Naiyer
Habib's residence, 9227 Wascana Mews. The following members
were present:

> Dr. Amer, Dr. Ayman Aboguddah, Mr. Abdul Qayyum, Mrs.
> Qudsia Qayyum, Dr. M. Anwarul Haque, Mr. A. Jalil, Mrs.
> Nusrat Jalil, Mr. Arif Sethi, Dr. Bhimji, Mrs. Nargis Bhimji,
> Prof. Dr. Ejaz Ahmed, Dr. Naiyer Habib, Mrs. Naushaba
> Habib, Dr. Wasty, Mrs. Zeba Hashmi, Dr. Mansoor Haq,
> Mrs. Kulsoom Haq, Mr. Faisal Sethi, Mr. Riazuddin Ahmed,

Mrs. Zarqa Nawaz, Mr. Munirul Haque, Dr. Samad Malik, Mr. Kashif Ahmed, Shahid Rehman, and Sheela Rehman.

Minutes MPJ Meeting, June 2, 2002

The above meeting of the MPJ group was held at Dr. Naiyer Habib's residence, 9227 Wascana Mews. The following members were present:

Dr. Amer, Dr. Ayman Aboguddah, Mr. Abdul Qayyum, Mrs. Qudsia Qayyum, Dr. M. Anwarul Haque, Mr. A. Jalil, Mrs. Nusrat Jalil, Mr. Arif Sethi, Dr. Bhimji, Mrs. Nargis Bhimji, Prof. Dr. Ejaz Ahmed, Dr. Naiyer Habib, Mrs. Naushaba Habib, Dr. Wasty, Mrs. Zeba Hashmi, Dr. Mansoor Haq, Mrs. Kulsoom Haq, Mr. Faisal Sethi, Mr. Riazuddin Ahmed, Mrs. Zarqa Nawaz, Mr. Munirul Haque, Dr. Samad Malik, Mr. Kashif Ahmed, and Shahid Rehman.

Agenda:

The agenda of the meeting was to elect office bearers for the MPJ group. Previously, the group had requested Mr. Abdul Qayyum to suggest some alternative structures for the group.

Based on the emailed recommendations of Abdul Qayyum and the discussions in the meeting it was moved by Riazuddin Ahmed, seconded by Anwarul Haque that:

We elect an interim board for the MPJ group composed of five members as follows: Chair, Vice-Chair, Secretary, Treasurer, and Community Liaison member. The motion was carried.

On the basis of this motion the following MPJ board members were elected unopposed in the meeting:

1.	Chair	Dr. Naiyer Habib
2.	Vice-Chair	Dr. Mansoor Haq
3.	Secretary	Mrs. Zeba Hashmi

4.   Treasurer   Mr. Arif Sethi

5.   Community Liaison Mr. Riazuddin Ahmed

The board was authorized to appoint working committees from among the MPJ members. The meeting closed after the elections.

Minutes recorded by Riazuddin Ahmed.

Subsequently, Kashif Ahmed was included as Communications Director by the board.

Sr. Tracy (Abdou) Shier was elected vice-president in the general meeting of MPJ held on March 23, 2003.

February 12, 2004, founding members and trustees were finalized and constitution was approved by the trustee members. New election was held, and the following directors were elected:

President: Dr. Naiyer Habib
Vice-President: Sr. Tracy (Abdou) Shier
General Secretary: Sr. Zeba Hashmi
Treasurer: Sr. Qudsia Qayyum
Board Members: Kashif Ahmed, Dr. Samiul Haque, Dr. Amr Henni

All activities carried out by MPJ are available at its Website: www.mpjsask.org

Only those participants who agreed to be included as founding members and trustees were included in the final list noted here:

Founders of Muslims for Peace & Justice Year 2001		
Last Name	**First Name**	**Signature**
Aboguddah	Ayman	
Ahmed	Ejaz	
Ahmed	Riaz	
Ahmed	Samina	
Ahmed	Kashif	
Ahmed	Sheela	
Bhimji	Nargis	
Bhimji	Raza	
Habib	Naiyer	
Habib	Naushaba	
Haque	Anwarul	
Haque	Samiul	
Hashmi	Zeba	
Hassanie	Abbas	
Hassanie	Uroose	
Hussain	Aijaz	
Jalil	Abdu	
Jalil	Nusrat	
Nawaz	Zarqa	
Qayyum	Abdul	
Qayyum	Qudsia	
Sethi	Arif	
Rehman	Shahid	
Wasty	Fashat	
The names are here of those who a greed to be included as founder		March 15, 2004

Founders of Muslims for Peace & Justice

The founders are listed in the previous pages under Minutes MPJ Meeting, June 2, 2002. Some initiated the organization perceiving its need. They were the three—Ejaz Ahmed, Naiyer Habib, and Abdul Jalil. Others joined Muslims for Peace & Justice over the course of time recognizing its importance. These individuals were of similar views and had the immense abilities to work together and to agree to disagree. Having experienced the hijacking of an organization with open or semi-open membership, they were given the ultimate power of decision-making in the Constitution of this organization, available with the board.

Initiators of Idea:

➤ Naiyer Habib

➤ Ejaz Ahmed

➤ Abdul Jalil

The list of the Founders signed by the president and the secretary is in the file of the Board of the MPJ.

I pay respect to the Founders wholeheartedly for joining to establish the much needed organization and to work together tirelessly to achieve its goals. Our work became exemplary despite our limited resources.

Objectives of MPJ

Objective 1. Respond to peace and justice issues through different media interviews, columns, and write-ups in various provincial and national media.

Objective 2. Interact with Interfaith and other peace and justice groups in Saskatchewan, for better understanding and harmonious relationships between Muslims and other citizens.

Objective 3. Provide lawful help and support where Muslims are falsely accused and/or receive unfair treatment from the Public and/or government agencies.

Objective 4. Serve as a bridge of understanding to Muslim world affairs.

Objective 5. Educate and inform the Muslims, and the Canadian community about the basic religious principles, peaceful co-existence, and universal humanistic values of Islam.

Strategic Planning 2005

In the Name of Allah, the Most Compassionate, the Most Merciful MPJ always followed a plan and acted according to the need and as dictated by the situation since its inception. Now the constitution was finalized. This was developed taking into consideration the experience generated by working in the community with community organizations. With finalization of the constitution, the strategy for 2005 was established as a base to follow. It is noted below:

—FOR THE YEAR 2005—

The MPJ board of directors has compiled a strategic plan in order to improve the overall effectiveness of the organization. This plan is presented to the MPJ trustees for approval.

Administration

The MPJ board has completed the application for MPJ to receive non-profit status from the government. Alhamdolilah, we are pleased to report that MPJ was granted non-profit registered status from the government of Saskatchewan in February 2005. As such, MPJ is now a legally incorporated entity.

The MPJ board will be adopting guidelines and procedures to make the operations of the organization more efficient and effective, in accordance with the Constitution. Such guidelines and procedures will be shared with the MPJ trustees in order to reinforce transparency and accountability.

Organizational Functions

1. Membership
2. Finances

3. Education and Community Relations
4. Media Relations and Communications
5. Anti-Defamation and Anti-Discrimination

1. Membership

   The MPJ board has set a goal of registering 30 new MPJ members (both general and associate) for the year 2005.

   This goal will be pursued through the following proposed activities:

   ➢ Holding information meetings about MPJ in Saskatchewan cities with concentrations of Muslims, such as Regina, Saskatoon and Moose Jaw, respectively
   ➢ Mailing out MPJ information kits to Muslims across Saskatchewan
   ➢ Advertising MPJ activities across Saskatchewan through mailings, direct contacts and electronic communication

2. Finances

   Evidently, MPJ's finances are largely coming from membership dues and donations. The MPJ board plans to coordinate monthly pre-authorized deposits with our bank, enabling the organization to receive funds from our membership and donors who wish to make pre-authorized donations on a monthly basis. This will ensure a steady cash flow to carry out MPJ's mandate and activities.

   Furthermore, successful Muslim businesses in Saskatchewan have become known to MPJ. It is possible that MPJ can approach such businesses for funding purposes.

   MPJ's bookkeeping will be audited yearly by a chartered accountant for presentation at the Annual Trustees Meeting.

3. Education and Community Relations

The MPJ board plans to continue with its widespread educational activities and community outreach work. In particular, the MPJ board wants to increase cooperation with other organizations and further disseminate accurate information when it comes to issues surrounding Islam and the Muslim community.

This will be accomplished through:

➢ Delivering presentations on Islam to the public
➢ Building coalitions with Canadian organizations that have similar interests
➢ Solidifying existing coalitions with Canadian organizations through cooperation in political activity and social justice issues
➢ Working within the Muslim community to increase membership and support for MPJ
➢ Working with other Muslim organizations in the province on issues of interest
➢ Working with elected and public officials on issues important to the Muslim community
➢ Holding workshops and seminars to inform Saskatchewan Muslims about their rights, and empower them to be effective activists and contributors
➢ Holding MPJ Annual Conferences on issues of contemporary importance to Muslims

4. Media Relations and Communications

MPJ has been very successful in its media relation's efforts up-to-date. We have developed a good relationship with media outlets such as the Leader-Post, CBC, and CTV News. The year 2004 saw many more articles published by MPJ in Saskatchewan newspapers, and more news coverage of our work.

The MPJ board plans to further its media relations and communications work for 2005. In particular, we propose to:

> Increase the monitoring of radio and broadcast news in the province (2004 saw a substantial increase in anti-Muslim rhetoric in broadcast news)
> Continue publishing more articles on Muslim perspectives, especially on issues that concern all Canadians
> Develop good relationships with other media outlets in the province, such as CJME/CKOM Radio and Global TV
> Publish advertisements in Saskatchewan newspapers

5. Anti-Defamation and Anti-Discrimination

MPJ has been very successful in challenging anti-Muslim defamation, especially in the Saskatchewan broadcast media. MPJ has been able to give full responses to prejudicial and bigoted views.

We have not had any discrimination cases reported to MPJ from Saskatchewan Muslims. This is a very positive indication.

In these areas, we plan to:

> Continue to firmly challenge those who make defamatory and malicious statements against the Muslim community
> Continue to disseminate accurate information about Islam and Muslims to foster a correct understanding of the Islamic faith and beliefs
> Work with other organizations in opposing anti-Muslim views, racism, and defamation
> Examine alternative options in addressing defamation that crosses into the realm of hate propaganda, which is illegal under Canadian law
> Provide anti-discrimination services for Saskatchewan

Constitution

In this constitution, kept secured by the board, authority was given to trustees who formed the general body to approve or disapprove any matter related to MPJ. One is referred to the board for knowing its detail.

The constitution of Muslims for Peace & Justice, giving powers to the trustees was the key to run the organization by people of similar views and not allow it to be hijacked by infiltrators of very different views just by numbers. It has the requirement of 75 percent of trustees for inclusion of a new trustee although I was of the opinion of unanimous acceptance. Following such criteria of membership and of how to run such an organization, it is an example for those who want to maintain an organization of people with similar views without letting others hijack the organization. This organization flourished.

I always say that a democracy can be worse than a dictatorship, where rights of minorities are run over by the like or dislike of the majority. This occurred with the founders and establishers of the Islamic Association between the periods of 1998–2004.

MPJ standardized its logo, developed its letterhead, and published an informative brochure for general circulation.

Logo Designed by Tracy (Abdou) Shier

MPJ Saskatchewan Muslim Voice on Public Affairs

Muslims for Peace & Justice
P.O. Box 28044
Regina, SK S4N 7L1
Tel: 1-866-284-5910
URL: http://mpjregina.tripod.com

Brochures

ACHIEVEMENTS

❖ Improved the coverage of Islam and Muslims in the Saskatchewan media

❖ Delivered over 50 presentations on Islam throughout Saskatchewan (2001-2004)

❖ Built coalitions with many organizations on issues of interest

❖ Held successful annual conferences featuring dynamic speakers and hundreds of participants

❖ Successfully responded to incidents of anti-Muslim defamation

❖ Successfully lobbied elected officials on issues of concern to Saskatchewan Muslims

❖ Trained Muslims to be effective activists through workshops & seminars

** Check our website for more updates of our achievements **

SUPPORT OUR WORK

Muslims for Peace & Justice (MPJ) needs your financial support to continue with its work for the Muslim community of Saskatchewan. Our mandate heavily depends on your cooperation and support. We are working tirelessly towards making Saskatchewan Muslims more visible on issues of public affairs.

Various categories of membership are available, including for non-Muslims. Please become a member of MPJ and donate generously.

Muslims for Peace & Justice

P.O. Box 28044
Regina, Saskatchewan S4N 7L1
Tel: (306) 535-0155

info@mpjsask.org
www.mpjsask.org
In the Name of God, Most Compassionate, Most Merciful

MUSLIMS FOR PEACE & JUSTICE

"Saskatchewan Muslim Voice on Public Affairs"

MPJ'S VISION

To establish a vibrant Saskatchewan Muslim community that will enrich Canadian society by promoting the Islamic values of peace and justice.

MISSION STATEMENT

"To promote and articulate Muslim interests and work for the integration of the Muslim community in Saskatchewan as part of mainstream Canadian society".

The scope of this mission includes, but is not limited to, the following:

1. Communicating with and informing the public about the Muslim perspective on peace & justice issues that are important to Muslims and on Canadian public affairs

2. Interacting with other faith groups, communities and organizations to create better understanding and develop a harmonious relationship between Canadian Muslims and other citizens of Canada.

3. Educating and informing Muslims and other Canadians about the basic religious principles, peaceful co-existence, universal humanistic and social values of Islam

4. Serving as a bridge of understanding to the status of Muslim affairs

5. Promoting and facilitating the integration of Muslims in Canadian society and supporting safety and security measures for peaceful living in Canada that are within the law.

A CONSISTENT AND RELIABLE SOURCE

MPJ has successfully published articles in leading Saskatchewan newspapers. Major network television and radio stations have interviewed MPJ spokespersons. In addition, MPJ officials have presented analysis of Canadian policy to journalists and other opinion-makers.

The organization's efforts are not limited to the news media. MPJ also strives to promote an accurate image of Islam in all public spheres.

BUILDING BRIDGES

MPJ works diligently with other Canadian organizations across the varied social and political spectrum in addressing issues involving civil and human rights, social justice, civic participation, and interfaith dialogue.

MPJ ACTIVITIES

❖ Educating about Islam & Muslims

❖ Providing speakers and literature on Islam

❖ Annual Conferences

❖ Workshops

❖ Media Relations

❖ Building coalitions

❖ Anti-Defamation

❖ Grassroots outreach

448

Communication with Community: Historic Letters

Muslims for Peace & Justice
P.O.Box 28044
Regina, SK
S4N 7L1
E-Mail: muslims4peace@yahoo.ca
In the Name of Allah, Most Kind, Most Merciful

Re: Muslims for Peace & Justice

Asalamo Alaikum WRB,

I have the pleasure of introducing to you the Muslims for Peace & Justice [MPJ] organization in Regina. MPJ is an organization formed by some members of the Muslim community of Regina shortly after September 11, 2001 to educate and inform the general public about the religion of Islam and Muslims, to foster better relationships as well as mutual understanding by appropriate communication

Our active involvement in the main stream of Western Society while maintaining Islam and our Muslim Identity as well as Dignity is very essential.

We left our home for one reason or the other. We made the West our home. We have to be participating actively in the affairs of the government and society as a whole.

Your ongoing suggestions and attendance in its various functions and activities are of vital importance. Since most of our conferences are open to all, it is important that you attend these conferences and meetings with active participation to show our strength.

Kindly note the objective and some of the activities on this website that it has offered. Various members of the board have continued to do letter writing campaign to media and politicians regarding 9/11 and Palestine with some publication by media and fair response from politicians.

I highly appreciate the efforts of Kashif Ahmed for making the website.

KINDLY SEND YOUR EMAIL ADDRESSES to <u>muslims4peace@ yahoo.ca</u>
OF ANY ONE YOU KNOW SO THAT WE MAY PUT THEM ON MPJ MAILING LIST.

Wassalaam

Dr. Naiyer Habib,
President

Naiyer Habib	M. Mansoor Haq	Zeba Hashmi	Arif Sethi	Riazuddin Ahmed
President	Vice-President	Secretary	Treasurer	Public Relations
306 766 6999	306 949 7165	306 790 9789	306 586 9049	306 789 0416

Muslims for Peace & Justice
P.O.Box 28044
Regina, SK
S4N 7L1
E-Mail: muslims4peace@yahoo.ca

In the Name of Allah, Most Kind, Most Mercifull

From: Muslims for Peace & Justice
To: The Muslim Community of Regina,

Salaam

AS the 'War on Terrorism' progresses onwards, Muslims residing in Canada have to deal with allegations and half-truths against Islam and Muslim in newspapers, magazines, TV, and radio. These media biases impugn Islam and Muslims. Whether they are done ignorantly or on purpose, we Muslims are obliged to defend our faith. We must defend our faith for deen and for dunya, so that we can live a secure and peaceful life with our fellow Canadians without being harassed in Canada.

FOLLOWING September 11th, many establishments have yearned to learn more about Islam and Muslims in order to have a better understanding. MPJ directors and members have lectured at many sessions. MPJ is also involved in the Multi-Faith Forum which is also essential for us in order to have dialogue of understanding with other faiths. Imagine if we did not represent ourselves at inter-faith events or failed to fulfill a request on explaining Islam; a void for the representation of Islam would be left and all those allegations perpetuated against our faith would be deemed true.

MUSLIMS need to be more informed concerning their rights. To address that, MPJ organized an information session on the 'anti-terror bill'.

MUSLIMS for Peace & Justice has embarked on a sustained campaign of media relations, public/government relations, and anti-discrimination work. We have sent many Press Releases pertaining to major Islamic events and issues concerning Canadian Muslims. If you have been reading the Leader-Post for the last year, you will have noticed that many articles on Ramadan, Eid, and Letters have been published as a result of continuous MPJ relations with Saskatchewan Media. Insha Allah, you will see more of our work in the media.

MPJ has also been supporting peace demonstrations which have been organized by the Regina Peace Council. MPJ has demonstrated against the War in Afghanistan and has been demonstrating against the impending War on Iraq. MPJ continues to be active in making the government of Saskatchewan and Canada aware of our just stance concerning political situations ranging from unnecessary deportations to unjustified wars.

MPJ has organized Eid events and our Annual Conference to which important government officials and key community leaders attended and participated. We were also extremely pleased by the attendance of many from the Muslim community. These events have been covered by Global TV, CTV News, Regina Leader-Post and CBC news. MPJ continues to communicate with the media and public officials for the purpose of advocating for Saskatchewan Muslims.

MPJ has devoted much time, effort, and money to improve our relations with the general public, media, and government in Saskatchewan and in Canada but now **we need your help**. If you wish for us to continue with our advocacy work to defend the Muslim community in Saskatchewan and promote the true image of Islam, please support us. Please donate whatever amount you can. Cheques can be made to 'Muslims for Peace & Justice' and given to the following MPJ Executives:

President - Dr. Naiyer Habib
Secretary- Sr. Zeba Hashmi
Acting Treasurer - Br. Kashif Ahmed
Community Relations – Br. Riaz Ahmed

Cheques can also be mailed to our address:

Muslims for Peace & Justice
P.O. Box 28044
Regina, SK
S4N 7L1

May Allah (SWT) bless you and give us all guidance toward what is right (Amen).

Please pledge an amount today: (Please make cheques out to 'Muslims for Peace & Justice')

_____ \$50 _____\$75 _____ \$100 _____ (other)

Your name: _____

Muslims for Peace & Justice
P.O.Box 28044
Regina, SK
S4N 7L1
E-Mail: muslims4peace@yahoo.ca
In the Name of Allah, Most Kind, Most Merciful

In the Name of Allah, Most Kind, Most Merciful

Asalamo Alaikum WRB,

Dear Br and Sister in Islam,

MPJ is on its way of progress, *Masha Allah.*

Your encouragement was, is and will be very helpful. Your name appears as core members/supporters. It is requested that we should formalize our membership/ support list.

Therefore the board considers you to be members of MPJ unless you advise us otherwise. We have to go long way.

We ask for annual membership dues of $50 to $100 each. Your suggestion for it is most welcome. Any generous donation is most welcome and is requested to support the work. A sum of approximately $2,500 was spent for October 12 for a day-long successful conference.

We ask if you would contribute any. Dr. Jamal Badawi is likely to come in Feb'03 as speaker.

With your support we intend to hold CONFERENCE 2003 Insha Allah in early fall as well. We hope to initiate a once every two months event. Insha Allah.

You may make a check payable to Muslims for Peace & Justice. You may hand over the check to any board member or mail to P.O. Box. Please go to http//:mpjregina.tripod.com.

Since MPJ is an advocacy group we may not get tax exemption. There is no tax exemption or rebate for any donation to MPJ. We have assigned to prepare constitution to a committee. The work is not complete yet.

We have received some comment from couple of members regarding emailing. Your suggestion as to emailing that you receive is most welcome. I have asked the board of directors to indicate on the e mail if the email is on behalf of MPJ to indicate so and if personal to indicate so, if it is being emailed to MPJ listing. We like to keep you informed of events that affect us nationally and internationally.

Please Visit www.islamicity.com and become a member to support it.

Therefore any email that will be emailed to you on behalf of MPJ will have such note "From MPJ" Sd. President, V. President, Secretary, Public Relation and Treasurer otherwise it will be all personal.

My email will always be on behalf of MPJ.

I shall be away from 27th Dec '02 to Jan 28 '03

Wassalaam

Thank you,

Dr. Naiyer Habib, President, MPJ

Election

Elections were held according to the constitution.
Nomination and ballot papers that we used are presented here.

Muslims for Peace & Justice
P.O. Box 28044, Regina, SK S4N 7L1. Tel: (306) 535-0155
Email: muslims4peace@yahoo.ca Website: www.mpjsask.org

In the name of God, Most kind, Most Merciful
Nomination for Board of Directors 2005-2006

Deadline February 12th'2005

                                       President

Name: **Yes I agree to be nominated**

Signature: **Date:**

Proposer: **Signature:**   **Date**

Seconder: **Signature:**   **Date**

                                         Vice-President

Name: **Yes I agree to be nominated**

Signature: **Date:**

Proposer: **Signature:**   **Date**

Seconder: **Signature:**   **Date**

                                       General Secretary

Name: **Yes I agree to be nominated**

Signature: Date:

Proposer: Signature: Date

Seconder: Signature: Date

                              Treasurer

Name: Yes I agree to be nominated

Signature: Date:

Proposer: Signature: Date

Seconder: Signature: Date

Board of Directors

Name: Yes I agree to be nominated

Signature: Date:

Proposer: Signature: Date

Seconder: Signature: Date

Board of Directors

Name: Yes I agree to be nominated

Signature: Date:

Proposer: Signature: Date

Seconder: Signature: Date

Board of Directors

Name: Yes I agree to be nominated

Signature: Date:

Proposer: Signature: Date

Seconder: Signature: Date

"Saskatchewan Muslim Voice on Public Affairs"

Ballot Paper

MPJ Board Election
President:
Vice-President:
Treasurer:
Secretary General:
B.Member:
B.Member:
B.Member:
President's & Secretary's Initial

MPJ Board Election
President:
Vice-President:
Treasurer:
Secretary General:
B.Member:
B.Member:
B.Member:
President's & Secretary's Initial

MPJ Board Election
President:
Vice-President:
Treasurer:
Secretary General:
B.Member:
B.Member:
B.Member:
President's & Secretary's Initial

MPJ Board Election
President:
Vice-President:
Treasurer:
Secretary General:

D.Member:
D.Member:
D.Member:
President's & Secretary's Initial

Membership

There are three Categories of Membership in MPJ. Details are noted in the Constitution of MPJ.

I. **TRUSTEE (Article III):** The persons listed in Appendix A (Signed by the President, the General Secretary on each page and by the Trustees against their names) of this Constitution document constitute the MPJ Trustees, referred to as the Trustees. The MPJ Trustees are those persons who attended the initial two formation meetings of MPJ, and who continued to support the purposes and objectives of MPJ. Also included are those who did not attend the two formation meetings, but supported the purposes and objectives of MPJ as well as participated in the activities of MPJ since the formation of the organization.

II. **General Member (Article1V Section 1):**
    a. Muslim citizens or Muslim immigrants of Canada residing in Saskatchewanmay become general members of MPJ by application using the membership application form
    c. At least two MPJ Trustees shall nominate a person for a General Membership
    d. A general member, who has paid all the fees and dues by March 1st of the year, shall be eligible to serve on the Board of Directors through election by the Trustees, and/or to be eligible to serve in another capacity as may be assigned by the Trustees and/or the Board

III. **Associate Members (Article1V Section 2):**
    Any person who is legally living in Canada, and supports the purpose, guiding principles and objectives of MPJ can become an associate member on approval by the Board

MEMBERSHIP FORMS
In the Name of Allah, the Compassionate, the Merciful

MPJ

Muslims for Peace & Justice
"The Saskatchewan Muslim Voice on Public Affairs"
MPJ Trusteeship Application Form
P.O. Box 28044
Regina, Saskatchewan S4N 7L1
Tel: 1 306 535 0155
Email: muslims4peace@yahoo.ca

I, _____, agree to become a Trustee of the Muslims for Peace & Justice (MPJ). I agree to abide by the MPJ Constitution and fulfill my responsibilities as an MPJ Trustee. I have read the Constitution. I am citizen of Canada (proof required). I have lived in Saskatchewan since _____

Name:_____

Address:_____

City:_____ Province:_____ Postal Code: _____

Telephone: _____ Email: _____

Signature: _____
Witness Name: _____Signature: _____
Dated: _____City of Regina, Province of Saskatchewan, Canada
Approved _____
President: _____Secretary:_____Date:_____

In the Name of Allah, the Compassionate, the Merciful

MPJ

Muslims for Peace & Justice
"The Saskatchewan Muslim Voice on Public Affairs"
MPJ General Membership Application Form
P.O. Box 28044
Regina, Saskatchewan S4N 7L1
Tel: 1-866-284-5910
Email: muslims4peace@yahoo.ca

I, with the particulars noted below agree to be a general member of MPJ. I am a citizen/Immigrant of Canada (Proof required). I have lived in Saskatchewan since _____

I shall abide by the constitution of MPJ which I have read, and any rules, regulation and guidelines developed by the MPJ from time to time.

Name: _____

Address: _____

City: _____ **Province:** _____ **Postal Code:** _____

Telephone: _____ **Email:** _____

Date: _____ **Signature:** _____

Name of 1ˢᵗ Nominator   Name of 2ⁿᵈ Nominator

Signature of 1st Nominator   Signature of 2nd Nominator

Approved_____President_____Secretary_____

Dated:_____City of Regina, Province of Saskatchewan.

In the Name of Allah, the Compassionate, the Merciful

MPJ

Muslims for Peace & Justice
"The Saskatchewan Muslim Voice on Public Affairs"
MPJ Associate Membership Application Form

P.O. Box 28044
Regina, Saskatchewan S4N 7L1
Tel: 1-306 – 535 0155
Email: muslims4peace@yahoo.ca

I, with the particulars noted below agree to be an Associate Member of MPJ. I am a legal resident of Canada (Proof required). I have lived in Saskatchewan since_____.

I shall abide by the constitution of MPJ, and any rules, regulation and guidelines developed by the MPJ from time to time.

Name: ....

Address: ....

City:................. **Province:**................. **Postal Code:** ....

Telephone: ....**Email:** ....

Date:.................................**Signature:** ....

Name of 1st Nominator   Name of 2nd Nominator

Signature of 1st Nominator   Signature of 2nd Nominator

Approved_____**President**_____**Secretary**_____

Dated: _____**City of Regina, Province of Saskatchewan.**

LIST OF LATEST TRUSTEES

LIST OF LATEST GENERAL MEMBERS

GENERAL MEMBERS 2005—FEB. 27, 2005					
Last Name	First Name	Paid	Signature	Telephone	Remark
Bouzertit	Khalid				
Darbi	Ashraf				
Fauzi	Ramadan				
Husain	Aijaz				
Leila	Makour				
Nazmia	Ramadan				
Taman (Fatima)	Beverly				
Moolla	Mohamed				Since 2005
Moolla	Faeeza				Since 2005
Surtie	Rubina				Since 2005
Surtie	Faizel				Since 2005
All Expires Jan 31st 2006					

Activities and Actions by Muslims for Peace & Justice

The reports cited here represent the activities and actions.

MUSLIMS FOR PEACE & JUSTICE (REGINA)

2001–2002 Annual Report

A. An overview of MPJ group activities: September 2001 – July 31, 2002

1. Initial informative meeting organized and chaired by Professor Ejaz Ahmed, October 2001 following a preliminary meeting among Dr. Ejaz Ahmed, Dr. Naiyer Habib and Dr. Abdul Jalil after the Leader-Post interview of Dr. Ejaz Ahmed and Dr. Naiyer Habib.

2. Press conference at University of Regina to explain the purpose of formation of this committee from matters arising of Sept 11 impact (a recorded tape version is available).

3. Informal group meetings held monthly to develop the objectives of the MPJ

4. MPJ organized a multi-faith, multi-cultural reception to inform non-Muslims about Eid al-Adha, March 10, 2002. About 10 faith and cultural organization representatives, two local MLAs, and six main media representatives attended the reception (CBC, Global, and CTV television, CBC and CKRM Radio)

5. On June 2, 2002 twenty four (24) members of the MPJ met under the chairmanship of Professor Ejaz Ahmed, to elect a Board of Directors - Dr. Habib (Chair), Dr. Mansoor Haq (V. Chair), Mrs. Zeba Hashmi (Secretary), Mr. Arif Sethi (Treasurer), and Mr. Riaz Ahmed (Community Liaison).

6. The new Board has now requested Dr. Anwarul Haque, and Mr. A. Qayyum to draft a constitution for the MPJ for presentation to and adoption by the general members. These members have accepted this responsibility.

7. MPJ supported and participated with the Regina Peace Council, and the Regina Council for Peace in Palestine in a Peace Rally held in Regina on April 20th, 2002. Dr. Habib spoke on behalf of the MPJ to support the Peace in Palestinian lands, and end of Israeli occupation of Palestinian lands since 1967.

8. The University of Regina organized the annual meeting of the Peace and Education Association of Canada on June 6-9, 2002. Riaz Ahmed spoke on the Palestinian – Israeli conflict as a source of instability in the world and lack of peace.

9. Bill C 36:
   1. A general information session was held for information to the community by hiring a lawyer.
   2. A letter to the Chair against the Bill was sent to the chair senate committee with copies to ministers.

10. Letter to Hon. Mr. Graham re Israel aggression on Ghaza dated July 26, '02.

B. To achieve the MPJ objective to cultivate friendly relations between Muslims and the larger Regina community, and to enhance the understanding of the main teachings of Islam among non-Muslims, the MPJ members have undertaken the following activities:

No.	Islamic Subject	Location	Name	Date	Attendance
1.	Basic Teachings and Beliefs Seminar	Sask. Environment Staff	Riaz Ahmed	Sept. 24 and 25, 2001	45 People
2.	Basic Teachings and Beliefs	Staff of Sask. Agriculture	Abdul Jalil	Sept. 25, 2001	60 People
3.	Basic Teachings, Concept of Jihad Salaat Observation	Regina Beach Interfaith Group	Ayman Aboguddah, Abdul Jalil Ejaz Ahmed Riaz Ahmed	Oct. 3, 2001	45-50 People
4.	Basic Teachings and Beliefs, and Concept Of Jihad	Sask. TV and Radio Writers Association, Regina	Riaz Ahmed	Oct. 10, 2001	40-45 Writers
5.	Basic Islamic Teachings, Concept of Jihad	Sask-Power Staff in Regina	Riaz Ahmed	Oct. 13, 2001	80+ People
6.	Basic Teachings, and Concept of Jihad	NDP Victoria Constituency Executive	Riaz Ahmed	Nov. 5, 2001	15 executive members + MLA
7.	Basic Teachings, Position of Women in Islam	Holy Rosary Cathedral, Regina	Riaz Ahmed, Zarqa Narwaz	Nov. 13, 2001 (p.m.)	200+ People
8.	Basic Teachings and Beliefs	Regina Rotary Club Members	Riaz Ahmed	Nov. 13, 2001 (noon)	19 Members

No.	Islamic Subject	Location	Name	Date	Attendance
9.	Basic Teachings	Antipoverty Group, Regina	Riaz Ahmed	Dec. 6, 2001	6 Board Members
10.	Sept. 11, 2001 Terrorist Attack Impact on the Regina Muslim Community	Community Human Justice Forum, Regina	Riaz Ahmed	Dec. 8, 2001	40-45 People and U of R students
11.	Basic Teachings, Positio of Women in Islam	Health Canada Staff, Regina	Riaz Ahmed, Zarqa Nawaz	Dec. 18, 2001	35-40 Staff Members
12	Basic Teachings and Beliefs, Jihad in Islam	SGI Staff, Regina	Riaz Ahmed	Dec. 20, 2001	15-20 Staff Members
13.	Basic Teachings and Belliefs, Concept of Jihad	Grace United Church, Weyburn	Riaz Ahmed, Abbas Hasnie	Jan. 20, 2002	100+ People
14.	Basic Teachings and Beliefs	Ressurection Catholic Church, Regina	Riaz Ahmed	Feb. 9 and 10, 2002	600-650 People
15.	Prophet Mohammad, Basic Teachings and Beliefs	United Heritage Church, Regina	Brenda Anderson of Luther College, Riaz & Samina Ahmed	Feb. 17, 2002	20 People
16.	Basic Teachings and Beliefs, Concept of Jihad	Christ the King Church, Regina	Riaz & Samina Ahmed	Feb. 27, 2002	30-35 People
17.	Concept of Jihad in Islam	Heritage United Church	Riaz Ahmed	Mar. 5, 2002	15 People
18.	Concept of Taqwa in Islam	Luther College Students, Regina	Riaz Ahmed	Mar. 14, 2002	30 Students

No.	Islamic Subject	Location	Name	Date	Attendance
19.	Basic Teachings and Beliefs	Luther High School Grade 9-10 students	Riaz Ahmed	Mar. 18, 2002	60 Students
20.	My Experience in Haj	Luther College Student Class	Zeba Hashmi	Mar. 26, 2002	24 Students
21.	Women in Islam	Know Your Muslim Neighbors, Luther College Distance Learning TV Series	Zarqa Nawaz	Apr. 11, 2002	Broadcast in 17 different learning centres in Sask
22.	Basic Teachings and Beliefs	Know Your Muslim Neighbors, Luther College Distance Learning TV Series	Dr. Samiul Haque	Apr. 18, 2002	Broadcast in 17 different learning centres in Sask
23.	Peace, Justice and Jihad	Know Your Muslim Neighbors, Luther College Distance Learning TV Series	Dr. Ayman Aboguddah and Riaz Ahmed	Apr. 25, 2002	Broadcast in 17 different learning centres in Sask
24.	Haj	Luther College	Zeba Hashmi or Zarqa Nawaz	Apr. 2002	
25.	Islam in General	Martin Leboldius	Ayman Aboguddah	Apr. 29, 2002	Grade 8-9
26.	Islam in General	Martin Leboldius	Naiyer Habib	Apr. 30, 2002	Grade 12
27.	Discover Islam	St. Francis	Naiyer Habib	May 13, 2002	75 Students
28.	Discover Islam	St. Michael Riffle High School	Naiyer Habib	May 24, 2002	50 Students
29.	Basic Teachings and Beliefs	Grace Mennonite Church, Regina	Riaz Ahmed	May 29, 2002	15 People
30.	Discover Islam	St. Andrews	Naiyer Habib	May 2002	100 Students

No.	Islamic Subject	Location	Name	Date	Attendance
31.	Development of Islamic Shariah and Fiqh	Regina Multi-Faith Forum board	Riaz Ahmed	Jun. 12, 2002	12 board Members
32.	Discover Islam	St. Josaphat	Naiyer Habib	Jun. 2002	50 Students
33.	Discover Islam	St. Michael	Naiyer Habib	Jun. 2002	30 Students
34.	Islam	Royal Bank	Riaz Ahmed	Sept. 2002	150 People
35.	My Life as a Muslim Canadian	Luther College	Zeba Hashmi	Oct. 16, 2002	

2003 Annual Report

Muslims for Peace & Justice

P.O. Box 28044 ~ Regina, SK ~ S4N 7L1 ~ Tel: 1.866.284.5910
In the Name of God, the Compassionate, the Merciful

President's Letter

Asalaamu'alaikum Wa Rahmatallahe Wa Barakatehu.

This has been a very eventful and fruitful year for MPJ. We have seen our fellow Canadian Muslims singled out for increased scrutiny at home and receiving insufficient protection by our government while abroad.

Yet, there has also been a positive face to these difficult times. In response to the challenges, Muslims have come together like never before. We have organized like we never thought we could. We have reached out to other Canadians like we never thought we would. Our response to these challenges has become a response to our chronic fragmentation, and has created a will for developing a space and a voice for Muslims that we never thought we could achieve.

Strength is emanating from our former weaknesses. Across Canada, Muslim institutions have been mobilizing and developing faster than ever. In Saskatchewan, Muslims for Peace & Justice (MPJ) has increased its support and membership, and I am confident the coming year will continue to see solid gains. There is ample momentum and a clear sense of direction that are seeing MPJ rise to unprecedented levels of performance and effectiveness. MPJ has been recognized in Saskatchewan by the government, media and other organizations as the voice of the Saskatchewan Muslim community on public affairs. Our activities have brought Muslims and their fellow citizens & elected officials, to a new level of understanding and cooperation. MPJ has been a consistent and reliable source to the Saskatchewan media & public on issues pertaining to Islam and issues that are important to the Muslim community. Every effort is being made to create a lasting, credible and viable institution with a clear sense of purpose and direction. Insha Allah, MPJ will be a dependable and solid base that will anchor our community for years to come. Clearly, across Canada, the Muslim community has embarked on an irreversible path of strengthening its institutions and enabling them to represent it more potently. It is time that our community is able to positively influence public opinion and have a voice on public affairs. The resources in terms of numbers and talent are abundant within our community. All we need is to organize them well. In Saskatchewan, MPJ has been doing just that. I thank the members of the MPJ executive board for their professional, timely and dedicated work. They have truly taken this organization to the next level. MPJ has sought to work in partnership with a variety of individuals and organizations in the pursuit of its goals. We have extended our hand to our fellow Muslims from all walks of life in defence of peace, justice, civil liberties, and human rights. To those whom we have not yet reached out to, consider this a standing invitation for you to join hands with us in working for the benefit of the Saskatchewan Muslim community and our beloved Canada.

Wa'alaikumsalaam.

Dr. Naiyer Habib
President
January 2004

MPJ 2003 Activity
Education & Conferences

- Between 2001 and 2003, MPJ has delivered over 40 presentations on Islam to a variety of institutions, including churches, government offices, schools, universities, and non-profit organizations. MPJ held its first Annual Convention on October 12, 2002, in which the keynote speaker was Sheikh Shabir Ally. The event was highly successful.

- MPJ held its 2nd Annual Convention on October 4, 2003, with over 300 participants. The keynote speaker was Dr.

Mohamed Elmasry, National President of the Canadian Islamic Congress. A variety of topics at the convention were aimed at educating and empowering the Muslim community. The convention was addressed by prominent Canadians like the former premier of Saskatchewan, the Honourable Allan Blakeney.

Community Relations

- MPJ sponsored a large rally against the invasion of Iraq on February 15, at Regina City Hall. MPJ President Dr. Naiyer Habib spoke at the rally. Over 1000 people attended the rally.

- On March 10, MPJ was successful in influencing city council to pass a resolution declaring that the city of Regina was against any attack on Iraq. MPJ executives contacted city councillors and Mayor Pat Fiacco, informing them that Saskatchewan Muslims were opposed to any attack on Iraq and asked them to vote in favor of the resolution. As a result of the MPJ lobbying efforts, city council overwhelmingly passed the resolution with 8 votes in favor versus 1 vote against. Mayor Pat Fiacco voted in favor of the resolution.

- MPJ officials appeared on the CBC Panel Talk Show *"What's it like being Muslim in Canada"* at the Central Library on March 11. President Dr. Naiyer Habib and Director of Communications Kashif Ahmed were guest panelists, as well as film-maker Zarqa Nawaz. The MPJ panelists voiced concerns about the 'Anti- Terrorism Legislation', treatment of Muslims and media stereotypes, but also affirmed that Canadian Muslims are treated quite fairly and are equal Canadians as everyone else. About 100 people attended the public forum.

- MPJ co-sponsored, along with the Peace Action Coalition, a rally against war in Iraq on March 15.

- On April 12, MPJ sponsored a large anti-war rally in downtown Regina. MPJ Director of Community Relations Riazuddin Ahmed addressed the rally.

- On April 27, MPJ organized a meeting with members of the Muslim community to discuss Muslim opinions and feelings about the attack against Iraq and hopes for the future of the Muslim community worldwide. Several Muslims attended the gathering and were able to discuss the situation and methods of dealing with and opposing such future wars.

- MPJ participated in the June 22 Centennial Celebrations of the Regina at the Multifaith Centennial Fair at the City Hall Forum. MPJ had a booth and table, displaying the history of the Muslim community, literature on Islam and Muslims, and information on MPJ and its work and mandate.

- MPJ sponsored two rallies in late October dealing with current issues important to the Canadian Muslim community. The first rally addressed the ongoing U.S. occupation of Iraq, on October 25, in downtown Regina. MPJ Director of Community Relations Riazuddin Ahmed coordinated the rally, and many members of the Muslim community came to show their solidarity with the Iraqi people. The second rally took place on October 31, amid growing concerns that Canada is holding secret trials on a variety of issues, including the trials of detained Muslims and Arabs under the new Anti-Terror Legislation of Bill C-36.

- On November 7, in a ceremony at 9:00 AM at the Hudson Bay store in the Cornwall Centre, Muslims for Peace & Justice (MPJ) recognized the Hudson Bay Company for its outstanding commitment to religious diversity through its Ramadan advertisements that were featured in flyers and posters across Canada. This was the first initiative by a mainstream Canadian company to promote and recognize the Canadian Muslim community and our religion of

Islam. MPJ President Dr. Naiyer Habib gave a Certificate of Appreciation to the Hudson Bay Company, while MPJ Director of Communications Kashif Ahmed spoke on the importance of diversity and understanding in Islam.

- On November 22, MPJ participated in a community seminar on Palestine at the Regina City Hall Forum. MPJ Director of Community Relations Riazuddin Ahmed gave a presentation on the Geneva Accords.

Media Relations

Press Releases

- On February 7, MPJ issued a press release about the annual Haj

- On March 20, MPJ sent out a press release praising Canada's decision not to join the illegal and unilateral attack on Iraq

- MPJ issued a press release on May 13 condemning the atrocious terrorist attacks in Saudi Arabia and called for the swift apprehension of the perpetrators

- MPJ sent out a press release on July 13 calling for an end to the use of 'security' certificates by Canadian law enforcement agencies

- MPJ issued a press release on August 30 demanding that the human rights of Pakistani detainees in Toronto be protected and guaranteed

- On September 10, MPJ released a statement in commemoration of the Sept. 11, 2001 terrorist attacks

- MPJ urged Saskatchewan Muslims to vote in the provincial and municipal elections, in a press release sent out on October 10

- On October 26, MPJ issued a press release about the beginning of the month of Ramadan

- On November 14, MPJ issues a statement condemning the vandalism of an Edmonton Mosque on November 11

- MPJ sent out a press release on November 16 condemning the terrorist attacks against a Jewish synagogue in Turkey

- MPJ released a statement on December 6 calling for a public inquiry into the case of Maher Arar

Interviews, Meetings & Major Articles

- MPJ responded with an article to an inflammatory headline in the February 8, issue of the Leader-Post. It was published in the Leader-Post on February 13

- On February 9, the Leader-Post and CTV interviewed MPJ about the beginning of the Haj

- On March 10, CBC Radio interviewed MPJ about the vote against war in Iraq by Regina City Council

- On March 11, MPJ was interviewed on CBC Radio about the misconceptions about Islam & Muslims

- On March 20, MPJ Director of Communications Kashif Ahmed appeared on a CBC Program debating Canada's decision not to join the invasion of Iraq

- On April 15, Global TV interviewed MPJ about the local anti-war effort

- On May 8, 2003, MPJ published an article in the Leader-Post in response to the smears made against Muslims by George Jonas's article in the April 23 issue

- On June 25, MPJ responded to a Leader-Post editorial with an article that clears up common misconceptions about Jihad and Islam

- On September 2, CJME Radio interviewed MPJ about the detained Muslim men in Toronto, Ontario

- On October 4, the Leader-Post and CTV News interviewed MPJ about the annual MPJ convention

- The Leader-Post, CTV, and CBC Radio interviewed MPJ about the Hudson Bay Company's Ramadan Ad Campaign

- On November 8 & 11, CJME Radio and CKRM Radio interviewed MPJ about Ramadan

- CJME Radio interviewed MPJ on November 19 about the situation of Canadian Muslims travelling abroad

- MPJ officials met with CTV News staff on December 17 to discuss the coverage of Islam and Muslims

Anti-Defamation

- On February 14, MPJ challenged the demonization of Muslims & Islamophobic statements of CJME Radio guest David Frum

- MPJ was successful on March 12, 2003 in forcing an Ontario-based website called "Christian Action for Israel" to remove anti-Islamic and anti-Muslim hate literature off its website. As a result of dozens of complaints sent to the web-host company Martin Business Services, the company sent a letter to MPJ apologizing for the hateful material and informed MPJ that it would be immediately removed

- On May 8, MPJ called the Leader-Post to express disdain over the publishing of a blatantly anti-Muslim article by George Jonas

- MPJ called CBC Radio on September 17 to express concern regarding the anti- Muslim comments made by a neo-conservative commentator

Government Relations

MPJ sent many letters and statements to our elected officials in the province and in Ottawa regarding issues of concern to the Muslim community.

Topics included:

- Invasion of Iraq
- Maher Arar case
- Status of Civil Liberties
- Canadian Islamic Congress (CIC) Position Papers

2003 Annual Report

Muslims for Peace & Justice

P.O. Box 28044 ~ Regina, SK ~ S4N 7L1 ~ Tel: 1.866.284.5910
In the Name of God, the Compassionate, the Merciful

President's Letter

Asalaamu'alaikum Wa Rahmatallahe Wa Barakatehu.

The year 2004 manifested new directions and challenges for Muslims for Peace & Justice (MPJ).

MPJ was able to solidify its cooperation with other organizations on issues of mutual interest. This year we continued to work with the Peace Coalition, Multifaith Forum and other organizations in promoting peace and justice. This work enhances the image of the Muslim community in mainstream society and provides our community with beneficial alliances for the future.

This year MPJ acquired a professionally designed website at www. mpjsask.org. This website contains information about the organization, our activities, press releases, articles, news briefs and statements. It also has information about Islam and the Muslim community.

One of our challenges is promoting MPJ within the Muslim community and attracting new members. MPJ took a number of initiatives in this regard. Along with an information meeting about the organization, we held educational workshops for the Muslim community. These workshops are designed to empower Saskatchewan Muslims with the necessary skills and knowledge about their legal rights, the media, and politics in Canada. Insha Allah, we will continue to hold these workshops in the 2005 year.

Alhamdulilah, MPJ increased the number of members in 2004 and saw growing support for our important work. This was clearly manifested in the MPJ 2004 Annual Conference, which saw an unprecedented number of Muslims attend. The conference was a huge success and was highly praised by Muslims and non-Muslims alike.

MPJ continues to be the most consistent and reliable source of information for the Saskatchewan media regarding Islam and the Muslim community. Our media relations work is the prime function of the organization and we were very successful in this field. This year, the Muslim community in Saskatchewan saw an increase in anti-Muslim rhetoric in the mainstream media, notably broadcast radio. With the help of our members, fellow Muslims and concerned citizens, MPJ was able to effectively challenge defamation against our community and offer accurate information about Islam and Muslims.

The members of the MPJ Board of Directors have been very dedicated and professional in their work for MPJ. Our new Board members have been invaluable in their contributions to the organization. I thank them for their hard work.

In administrative terms, MPJ applied for incorporation with the Province of Saskatchewan and we have been granted legal non-profit status. Alhamdulilah, this new development will solidify the organization and carry its work into the future.

This is my final term as the MPJ President. As you all are aware, I moved to British Columbia in November 2004. It has been my great pleasure and honour to serve this organization for the past few years. I am very confident that MPJ will prosper in its efforts to promote, articulate and defend the interests of the Saskatchewan Muslim community.

Finally, I ask you to help strengthen this institution for our community. Remember, it's your voice and your future.

Yours truly,

Dr. Naiyer Habib
President
January 2005

MPJ 2004 Activity
Conferences

MPJ held its 3rd Annual Conference on September 17 & 18 with over 200 participants. The theme of the conference was "Discovering Contemporary Muslim Religious Thought." The keynote speakers were Prof. Jamal Badawi of Saint Mary's University; Shaikh Ahmad Kutty of the Islamic Institute of Toronto; and Prof. Amir Hussain of California State University. A variety of important topics at the conference were aimed at educating and informing both Muslims and non-Muslims.

At the conference banquet, Zeba Hashmi was recognized for her community service with the MPJ President's Award of Excellence. Longtime Saskatchewan resident and founding president of the Islamic Association of Saskatchewan, Dr. M. Anwarul Haque, was given an award for his lifetime community service to the Muslim community.

Seminar to join Political Parties:

Community was asked to any join political party, to have a Muslim voice and guidelines were given about how to join and why.

Education & Community Relations

- MPJ held an information meeting on February 15 at Regina Huda School.

- MPJ held a workshop & seminar for the Muslim community on May 16 at Regina Huda School about knowing your rights in Canada, effective media relations, and joining a political party.

- The MPJ 2004 Annual Conference took place on September 17 & 18 at the University of Regina & Hotel Saskatchewan, with over 200 participants throughout the two days and featuring three keynote speakers from across North America.

- MPJ sponsored a presentation by the Palestinian Ambassador to Canada, Dr. Baker Abdul-Munem, at the University of Regina on October 9, about the Israeli Apartheid Wall.

- MPJ took part in Multifaith Series about faith & religion throughout the month of November; this gave an opportunity for us to highlight key Islamic concepts to a large non-Muslim gathering.

- MPJ took part in activities regarding the U.S. Missile Defence proposal in late November. This program highlighted the challenges to Canada and the threats to international peace & security.

Media Relations
Press Releases

- On January 12, MPJ issued a press release about the annual Haj.

- Issued a press release on January 29, praising the announcement of a public inquiry into the case of Maher Arar.

- Issued a press release on March 6 condemning the remarks of members of the Canadian Khadr family in Pakistan on a CBC program.

- Issued a press release on March 11 condemning the terrorist attacks in Madrid, Spain.

- Issued a press release on March 22 condemning the extra-judicial killing of Sheikh Ahmed Yassin by Israeli forces in Gaza.

- Issued a press release on March 24 condemning the vandalism of Jewish homes and a Jewish cemetery in the Toronto area.

- Issued a press release on March 26 denouncing the arson and vandalism of a *Masjid* in Pickering, Ontario.

- Issued a press release on April 18 condemning the extra-judicial assassination of Hamas leader Rantissi by Israeli forces in Gaza.

- Issued a press release on May 11 about the abuse of Iraqi prisoners by American soldiers.

- Issued a press release on May 12 condemning the brutal murder of an American civilian worker in Iraq by Al-Qaeda.

- Issued a press release on May 18 denouncing massacre of Palestinian civilians in Gaza.

- Issued a media advisory on September 10 about the MPJ Annual Conference.

- Issued a media advisory on October 1 about the upcoming public speech by the Palestinian Ambassador to Canada.

- Issued a press release on October 13 regarding the start of Ramadan.

- Issued a press release on November 11 offering condolences on the death of Yasser Arafat.

Interviews & Major Articles

- Article featuring MPJ was published in the January 5 issue of Leader-Post regarding the US-Visit program.

- Article featuring MPJ regarding the U.S. Missile Defence Shield was published in the January 12 issue of Leader-Post.

- CJME/CKOM Radio interviewed MPJ on January 29 about the launching of a public inquiry in the case of Maher Arar.

- CJME/CKOM Radio interviewed MPJ on March 3 about the terrorist attacks against Shia Muslims in Iraq & Pakistan.

- On March 17, CJME/CKOM Radio yielded under mounting pressure, and MPJ Vice-President Tracy (Abdou) Shier and Communications Director Kashif Ahmed spoke on CJME/ CKOM Radio with John Gormley Live for a 1 hour segment in response to a segment with Stewart Bell of the National Post newspaper.

- MPJ article published in the May 12 issue of Leader-Post about Iraqi prisoner abuse.

- MPJ article published in the May 12 issue of Leader-Post about the occupation of Iraq.

- MPJ article published in the June 30 issue of Leader-Post regarding Islam's view of violence.

- MPJ article condemning terror in Russia published in the September 10 issue of Leader-Post.

- MPJ 2004 Annual Conference covered by Leader-Post, CTV and other media outlets on September 18 & September 20.

- MPJ article published in the September 22 issue of Leader-Post responding to an anti-Muslim article.

- MPJ article published in October 6 issue of Leader-Post responding to hostile article against Muslims.

- MPJ interviewed by CJME/CKOM Radio about Ramadan on October 15.

- MPJ interviewed by CTV News about Ramadan on October 15.

- MPJ article about Ramadan published in the October 20 issue of Leader-Post.

- MPJ article about Ramadan published in October 22 issue of Star Phoenix.

- MPJ article about Muslim-Jewish relations published in the November 9 issue of Leader-Post.

- MPJ was interviewed on November 12 by the Leader-Post regarding the death of Yasser Arafat.

Anti-Defamation

- MPJ issued an 'Action Alert' on March 15 calling on Saskatchewan Muslims and concerned non-Muslims to contact CJME/CKOM Radio Host John Gormley to complain about his interview with anti-Muslim reporter Stewart Bell. This action was successful as hundreds of people e-mailed and phoned CJME/CKOM Radio, resulting in MPJ officials speaking on the show two days later.

- MPJ issued an 'Action Alert' on May 14 regarding anti-Muslim writer Shafer Parker being interviewed on the CJME/CKOM John Gormley Live Show. MPJ called the radio station to complain of outrageous remarks made by Parker. As a result of MPJ's previous success with the Stewart Bell issue, Parker's views were balanced by an interview with another guest rebutting Parker's allegations.

- Throughout 2004, MPJ consistently responded to anti-Muslim articles published in the Leader-Post.

- MPJ contacted the CRTC to complain about the anti-Muslim comments made by several people on CJME/CKOM radio.

Government Relations

MPJ sent many letters and statements to our elected officials in the province and in Ottawa regarding issues of concern to the Muslim community. Topics included:

- Security certificates
- Status of Civil Liberties
- Changes to Canadian Middle East Policy
- Muslim Arbitration Courts

MPJ in Media

We Asked the Media and the Media Asked Us

MPJ, being recognized by the media, received attention. Its cause was published.

Its personnel were invited and its news was published. Some letters on some issues were not published.

We issued multiple relevant press releases on various issues as they continued to be noticed.

They appear here in the following pages of this chapter. They are not according to dates.

Various matters related to Media can be seen in the section of "Activities and Actions by MPJ."

Note of thanks: We are especially grateful to *Leader-Post*, *Toronto Star*, CBC, and CTV, for allowing the content under their names for inclusion in this book.

Regina Leader-Post Publications

FAST IS A CHANCE FOR CANADIANS TO LEARN Regina Leader-Post, 7/11/02 See: http://www.canada.com/search/story. aspx?id=7b26f275-77fa-4451-8e24-9cab376bc9ad

Regina's Muslim community has started the annual Ramadan fast with the hope that other Canadians will be able to use this month-long event to focus on the religious traditions and values. "The Islamic month of Ramadan is an excellent time for our fellow Canadians to learn about Islam and the Regina Muslim community," Dr. Naiyer Habib, president of the Regina group Muslims for Peace & Justice (MPJ), said in a news release... "It is important for people of all walks of life to understand each other and further cultivate harmony between the different religious and ethnic groups in Regina and across Canada," Habib said in the news release... Ramadan, which started Wednesday, is the ninth month of the Islamic lunar calendar, with the precise starting and ending dates varying because it is linked with the sighting of the new moon.

canada.com **News**

The Leader-Post   **Ramadan Comes to an End**
Monday, December 16, 2002

Regina's Muslim community gathered on Sunday at the Neil Balkwill Civic Arts Centre to celebrate the end of the Islamic month-long religious celebration Ramadan.

Eid al-Fitr or the Festival of Fast-Breaking is a thanksgiving celebration marking the end of the holy month, when members of the Islamic faith observe a fast, which "includes refraining from food, drink and other sensual pleasures from the morning sunrise, until evening sunset," said Dr. Naiyer Habib, President of the Regina group Muslims for Peace & Justice.

Ramadan is a time when members of the Islamic faith focus on renewing their spirituality, he said.

"We invited non-Muslim members of the community to join with us in celebration so that they might learn a little more about our religion, our values and our traditions," said Habib, who explained the need to promote a greater understanding of Islam.

"This is an opportunity to interact with our family and neighbors, share our religious beliefs and values," he said.

Since the events of Sept. 11, 2001, the political climate has made it extremely important to dispel the suspicions and eliminate the misunderstandings, and promote harmony between the different religious and ethnic groups in Regina and across Canada, Habib said.

He explained with tensions building in the Middle East and talks of a military strike against Iraq it is important to let people know acts of terrorism are contrary to the teachings of the Islamic faith.

"We don't believe in violence and the killing of innocent people," Habib said, noting Muslims are against injustices anywhere in the world.

While there appears to be a great acceptance of Islam within the community, Habib, who has lived in Canada since 1973, said the ethnic profiling, intolerance, and treatment by some people south of the border, who have a bias against Muslims and the Islamic faith, is extremely disturbing.

"While some people are misbehaving at the border the majority of the people are very gentle," he said. That is why it is so important for people from all walks of life to understand each other.

© Copyright 2002 The Leader-Post (Regina)

A6 Leader-Post

PILGRIMAGE

Muslims unfazed by war talk

By SHERI BLOCK
Leader-Post

The possibility of war in Iraq will not affect the annual Muslim pilgrimage to Saudi Arabia, but it may force some people to come home early, says the president of Muslims for Peace and Justice in Regina.

Dr. Naiyer Habib, who travelled to Mecca for the Hajj in 1985 and again in 1987, said he hasn't heard of any concerns.

"Hopefully, things should go OK, not particularly related to Hajj. We hear that the war will begin in two weeks so some people who stay there for a month or so (will) have to leave early," said Habib.

He said many of the 600,000 Muslims in Canada are planning to make the journey, but will avoid travelling through the United States if they can. No one is going from Regina this year, but four Muslims from Saskatoon have already left.

"We really don't want to go through the U.S. unless we have to," said Habib, adding that people can be mistreated at the border due to their colour or religion.

The journey is a one-time obligation for Muslims who are physically and financially able to go. Habib said it is a chance to worship before God as equals with the entire body, mind and spirit.

Muslims face the cubicle structure in the centre of the Great Mosque in Mecca, called the Kaaba, to offer prayers to God. It is believed to be the first Mosque built by the Prophet Abraham and his son on the command of God.

"To see all the people of different race, places, colour, they are all doing the same thing, performing all the prayers and rituals together. It was a self-satisfaction to meet people and do the prayer, to visit this Kaaba, to face it right there and even touch it," Habib said of his own two journeys.

Everyone wears simple clothing so everyone is equal before God, he said. "Everybody is praying facing that cubicle so that's another uniformity that we are all one, one Muslim brotherhood."

The annual pilgrimage takes place during the Islamic lunar month of Dhul-Hijjah from Feb. 8 to 13, followed by congregational prayers for the first day of the Muslim holiday Eid ul-Adha.

'Don't go to the US': Islamic groups warn Saskatchewan Muslims
Leader-Post
Wednesday, January 7, 2004

Saskatchewan Muslims are being advised to avoid travel to the U.S. to protest what one group calls racial profiling at border crossings.

The Regina-based Muslims for Peace & Justice says new border control measures -- announced by the U.S. government this week -- are unfairly targeting people from the Middle East, Muslims in particular.

"Unless we really have something which we cannot avoid, we have said to our friends: 'Unless you are willing to go through this humiliation, don't go to the U.S.'," said a group's spokesman Riazuddin Ahmed.

A similar warning has been issued by the Canadian Islamic Congress.

Ahmed said too often Muslims are singled out at U.S. border crossings, and the launch of a tighter border-control policy Monday will only make it worse.

The U.S. launched a new security program, US-VISIT, which will mean travellers entering the U.S. will be randomly photographed and fingerprinted.

In Canada, landed immigrants from certain countries may be asked to submit to a personal interview with U.S. immigration officials -- for Saskatchewan people the nearest site is in Calgary -- and even then there is no guarantee they will be allowed to travel to the U.S.

Most Canadians, as well as residents of 28 other, mostly European countries, are exempt from the US-VISIT program because they don't need a visa to travel to the U.S.

But that's "not to say they won't take fingerprints or digital photos of you," said Doug Muskaluk, Saskatchewan's representative on the Association of Canadian Travel Agents.

"At any border crossing they could search your vehicle (or) they could not search your vehicle. A lot of it is discretionary."

The U.S. has said it will fingerprint and photograph anyone they believe is suspicious. It's that discretion that Ahmed said is singling out Muslims and non-Europeans.

Ahmed said he doesn't begrudge U.S. attempts to tighten its borders, especially in the aftermath of the Sept. 11 terrorist attacks.

But, he said, any border-security policy should apply equally to everyone.

Ahmed said there are several cases of Canadian Muslims who have been mistreated by the U.S. including Maher Arar, the Syrian-born engineer who was held and deported to Syria where he says he was tortured. Arar has since returned to Canada.

Ahmed also notes that last November, a Muslim Canadian professor decided to stay out of the U.S. after he was detained by U.S. officials.

"I, for one, have decided not to visit the States because of this treatment," said Ahmed, who has a brother and other family who live in the U.S.

"I don't want to face the mistreatment, unnecessary suspicion, at the border. This kind of racial profiling, religious profiling, is what I'm concerned about."

Ahmed said the official U.S. government line may be that no one will be unfairly targeted by the new border security policy, but "its implementation on the ground is discriminatory."

For his part, Muskaluk advises all of his clients travelling to the U.S. to carry a passport or -- at least -- government-issued identification and proof of citizenship.

Honoring Ramadan by
Ikea, Bay, Home Hardware, and Zellers

Naushaba Habib, Kashif Ahmed on behalf of MPJ
Nargis Bhimli and Samina Ahmed on behalf of
Canadian Council of Muslim Women

The stores mentioned honored Ramadan and Diwali across Canada with signs on doors and advertisement in the media.

This met with opposing views by Muslims. They did not repeat this since. Many supported it. We at MPJ, supported it and expressed our appreciation to the media— *Toronto Star* inteviewed Dr. Naiyer Habib, the president of MPJ. The president on behalf of the MPJ, presented a certificate of appreciation to the Bay in the mall. Sr. Nargis Bhimji, and Kashif Ahmed addressed the crowd.

Some Muslims criticized this initiative of the stores, indicating that they did not like the Muslim Holiday turn into Christmas festivities of business. This discouraged the stores. These Muslims apparently ignored the religious festivities and celebration of Muslim countries.

Publication of *Toronto Star* is Noted Here:
(Courtesy of *The Star* is greatly appreciated.)

TORONTO STAR
www.thestar.com

Nov. 17, 2003. 12:14 PM

Nod to Ramadan a trend in retailing
IKEA launches low-key campaign
Puts Muslims in the mainstream
LESLIE SCRIVENER
FAITH AND ETHICS REPORTER

When does a minority know it's become part of mainstream culture? When temples and Mosques are as much a part of the cityscape as churches? When Muslim women wear head coverings without attracting stares? When a home furnishings company recognizes that shoppers spend not only at Christmas, but also at Diwali, Ramadan and Chanukkah?

In a new public relations campaign, IKEA has highlighted Ramadan, the month-long Muslim fast that began Oct. 27. The campaign shows women wearing Hijabs and South Asian dress, photos of Mecca, sweet trays used for end-of-fast celebrations, and a text explaining the religious meaning of the holiday.

The series of photographs showing IKEA carpets, candles, table settings and gifts for children — ways of decorating the home for the holiday — is not a nationwide mail-out campaign but will be on the IKEA Canada Web site today.

It's a first for IKEA and part of a trend by retailers to acknowledge minority celebrations.

Hudson's Bay Company, for the first time this fall, included Ramadan greetings in flyers for The Bay, Zellers and Home Outfitters, plus posters and door signs. It will do the same for Chanukkah and other holidays.

"We realize that millions of Canadians are shopping in our stores, and we should be celebrating the cultures and diversity of all our customers," said spokesperson Hillary Stauth.

The company's efforts have already been recognized. The Multicultural Council of Regina and Muslims for Peace & Justice Saskatchewan sent the company a citation of thanks.

"We are a minority and these are especially bad times for us.

"We appreciate this first initiative to recognize Muslims as part of mainstream Canadian society," said Dr. Naiyer Habib, president of Muslims for Peace.

The IKEA campaign was created in the store's public relations department by Keka DasGupta, whose first project was home decorating for Diwali, the Hindu festival of lights, last month. She drew from her Bengali background to show how the festival is celebrated at home.

For Ramadan, she interviewed Muslim staff and was advised by Aneesa Razakazi, design consultant at the North York store.

"It's important to look at how people of all backgrounds live," DasGupta said. "It's not just about the products, it's about sharing what we've learned."

Muslims were generally appreciative, though wary that they will become another demographic group targeted by retailers. They don't want to see their holy month commercialized.

Ramadan ends Nov. 24, depending on the moon sighting, with Eid celebrations. With it comes cleaning and updating the home, buying new clothes or furnishings. ("Eid is a time for cleansing both the heart and the home," the IKEA copy reads.)

Showing ways to beautify the home and make it welcoming in a culturally sensitive way is valued, Muslims say.

"My first reaction was that this is good, that we're part of the mainstream, we have a voice, we are in large enough numbers to be recognized, but there's definitely a flip side," said Farheen Hasan, program manager for a Mississauga non-profit group.

"Islam isn't about consumerism. We don't come from a commercial, disposable culture. If Eid sales become part of a company's bottom line, I really don't like it. Eid is about spending time with family; it is a religious time, remembering people less fortunate, and comes at the end of the month of self-denial and prayer."

(IKEA's campaign includes charity references: "... one way to teach children these values: ask them to pick one gift they received for Eid and have them donate it to a family in need.")

While it's clear retailers are looking at Muslims as consumers, the overall message is welcome, said Riad Saloojee, executive-director of the Council on American-Islamic Relations Canada. "What I like is that Muslims are humanized, as are our cultures and traditions, and we are portrayed strictly as part of Canadian culture," he said. "It's not a foreign celebration."

IKEA is doing just what Muslim stores do, though on a bigger scale, said Imam Abdul Hai Patel, co-ordinator of the Islamic Council of Imams Canada.

"There is always a commercial side to every festival. At Eid we traditionally get something new. All in all, it doesn't diminish the spiritual aspect."

The Bay Honoring Ramadan

Sign at the door of The Bay

Naiyer Habib presented a Certificate of Appreciation to The Bay representative in the mall on behalf of MPJ

Nargis Bhimji addressing the crowd (Dr. Bhimji on her *left*)

Kashif Ahmed addresses on behalf of MPJ

The Crowd,* Samina Ahmed in the front on left, representing Canadian Council of Muslim Women

Learn at Lunch
March 11, 2003

What's it like being Muslim in Canada today? A Regina summit.

About 100 people brought their lunch to the Regina Public Library to hear from three prominent Saskatchewan Muslims. The discussion opened with **Dr. Naiyer Habib, President of Muslims for Peace & Justice.** He described his perceptions about portrayals of Muslims and misinformation about what Islamic believers feel

Second to speak was **Kashif Ahmed,** a University of Regina Student whose comments exposed the biases that exist in the media and how they serve to perpetuate stereotypes about Islamic people.

Finally, **filmmaker Zarqa Nawaz** presented her lighthearted approach to the painful and often absurd experiences of being a devout Muslim in a Judeo-Christian world.

The public discussion exposed a great desire for understanding between cultures. Stereotypes and media misrepresentations were exposed as tragic misunderstandings and xenophobia. The gathering ended with bridges being mended and a desire for understanding as the threat of war in the Middle East heightens our awareness of the complexities of eastern cultures.

- **Dr. Naiyer Habib** is president of Muslims for Peace & Justice, Regina. He arrived in Canada in 1973 from Purnea District, Bihir. He is former head of cardiology with the Regina Health District and has served as president of the Islamic Association of Saskatchewan.

- **Zarqa Nawaz** is a Regina-based filmmaker. Her most recent film, *"BBQ Muslims"*, is quickly becoming a cult classic, especially on university campuses in the United States. She takes a satirical approach to her films, calling them "terrodies" as in parodies. She is currently fine-tuning the script for a new film, *"Real Terrorists don't Belly Dance."*

- **Kashif Ahmed** is an 18-year-old University of Regina student, born and raised in Regina. He is very active in the Muslim community and is a member of Muslims for Peace & Justice. He has given several speeches concerning the current political climate.

Left to right: Zarqa Nawaz
Dr. Habib, Costa Maragos

Kashif Ahmed Zarqa Nawaz

CTV Television Inc.

216 - 1ˢᵗ Ave. N.
Saskatoon, Saskatchewan
Canada S7K 3W3

Tel 306.665.8600
Fax 306.665.0450

Thank you for attending our third Editorial Board Luncheon Meeting!

The meeting will focus on news issues affecting the Muslim community, and how these
issues are covered by the Regina CTV news cast. The following individuals have
planned to attend:

Dr. Ayman Aboguddah – Cardiologist ; President of Huda School (Public and
Islamic education)

Mr. Kashif Ahmed – University Student and Communication Director of Muslims
for Peace and Justice (MPJ)

Mr. Riaz Ahmed – City Planner / Director or Public Relations for MPJ

Dr. Naiyer Habib – Cardiologist; Former Head of Cardiology for Regina Health
District; Former President of the Islamic Association
of Saskatchewan (Regina); President of MPJ

Mrs. M. Naushaba Habib – MA (Political Science); President of Canadian
Council of Muslim Women (Regina Chapter)

Dr. Samiul Haque – Child Psychiatrist

Zeba Hashmi – Homemaker and Secretary of MPJ; Bilingual Medical Office
Administration Certification

Zarqa Nawaz – Journalist and Film Maker

Carl Worth - News Director - CTV Regina

Dale Neufeld - News Director - CTV Saskatoon / Prince Albert

Brian Zawacki - Director of Community Relations

Angela Loewen - Human Resources Specialist (Saskatchewan)

Geoff Bradley - Creative / Promotions Manager (Saskatchewan)

Wade Moffatt - Sales Manager - CTV Regina / Yorkton

Tara Robinson - News Anchor - CTV Regina

Manfred Joehnck - News Anchor - CTV Regina

Nelson Bird – Video Journalist; Host of Indigenous Circle

We want critical feedback on CTV Regina's news stories and interviews. We would like
you to consider the following discussion questions:

1.How do our news stories cover issues affecting the Muslim community?
Give specific examples.

2. Comment on how Muslim people are presented in the news.

3. What issues are being ignored? Give specific examples.

4. What news program do you watch all the time? If it's not CTV, explain why
you prefer it.

5. Describe what you like about our station's approach.

6. What suggestions do you have about how we could improve our ability to
serve your community?

A DIVISION OF
Bell Globemedia

Meeting with CTV

In the Name of Allah, Most Gracious, Most Merciful

MPJ OFFICIALS MEET WITH CTV NEWS GROUP

(December 17, 2003) Representatives from Muslims for Peace & Justice (MPJ), a Saskatchewan-based Muslim outreach & advocacy organization, met with the directors of the local CTV news station at a Monday luncheon meeting to discuss CTV's coverage of issues pertaining to Islam and Canadian Muslims.

MPJ was joined by representatives from the Regina Huda School and the Canadian Council of Muslim Women (CCMW) at the meeting. The meeting was aimed at opening up communication between the Saskatchewan Muslim community and CTV, and for Muslims to provide feedback on CTV news coverage.

MPJ officials expressed appreciation about the positive coverage of Muslim and Islamic events, yet raised concerns regarding misinformation and stereotypes that are still present in the mass media about Islam and Muslims. Aspects concerning how the coverage could be improved were also discussed. The CTV news officials were very receptive of the feedback, and encouraged Saskatchewan Muslims to keep them informed.

The meeting was a very fruitful and positive session, and MPJ looks forward to working with the Saskatchewan media in improving the image and coverage of Islam & Muslims in the public sphere.

--END--

Naiyer Habib & Mahlaqa Naushaba Habib

Muslims reach out to larger community

By Frank Flegel

REGINA — The Sept. 11, 2001, events in New York, Washington and Pennsylvania focused attention on the Muslim faith, but a Saskatchewan group is using that interest in a positive manner. Muslims for Peace and Justice (MPJ) in Saskatchewan began shortly after 9/11 to reach out to the general community and at the same time face internal changes. Its third annual conference, held Sept. 17 - 18 at the University of Regina, attracted some 200 people to hear Muslim speakers discuss their faith.

MPJ President Dr. Naiyer Habib said in an interview that some people blamed Islam because some Muslims took the name of Islam in the events of 9/11. That has led to new challenges for Muslims, he said, but the old challenges remain.

"There is a perception that Islam is a religion of war, particularly a war against non-believers, and that Islam considers everyone non-believers. That is not the case." The word jihad is often misinterpreted, Habib said. It allows Muslims to engage in war for lib-

eration and if being oppressed, but not otherwise. Christians, Jews and Muslims all come from one Abrahamic faith, he said, and Muslims respect the other faiths.

The old challenges are that different scholars have different views of what the Quran says, and their interpretations and comments have led to controversy. The same thing, he said, is happening to the tradition of the Prophet Mohammed and what he said and did.

The status of women within Islam has divided Muslims into two categories, according to Habib: conservatives who wish to exclude women from the mosque and active participation in virtually all areas of society outside the home (as the Taliban did in Afghanistan), and those who support women. Habib said excluding women is totally wrong: "That is not what it was like at the time of the Prophet."

Habib said there is a group of people who look at Islam in a different way. "They are saying that the presence of women creates evil desires. It is stupidity to make this kind of statement." Many Muslims are concerned that excluding women from the mosque has also

kept children away, and there is a fear that the younger generation will leave the faith.

Habib came to Canada from India more than 30 years ago. An American-trained heart specialist, he worked in Saskatoon for several years and then headed the cardiac unit at the old Plains Hospital until his retirement. He said that when he came to Saskatchewan, women and men interacted according to the tradi-

— MPJ, page 9

Flegel

Dr. Naiyer Habib

MPJ looking to Prophet

Continued from page 3

tions of the Prophet and the Quran, but that has since changed to the more conservative view. Habib said MPJ is trying to "rechange it to the time of the Prophet."

Riazuddin Ahmed, one of the founders of MPJ, said the organization has had success in

Saskatchewan changing some attitudes about Islam, but less success in the rest of Canada and the United States. "But the kind of speakers we have here are going to make a difference and are going to have an impact, and that's the purpose: to create better understanding between communities."

Acknowledgment: Courtesy of *Prairie Messenger*, Regina

MPJ Participates in Regina Centennial Celebration

It was a celebration of 100 years of the City of Regina. Various stalls by different groups of nationalities who acquired Canada as their motherland, contributing to make Canada what it is today, or who were already here. We were one of them. MPJ had a stall and representatives participated in the address from the podium.

City official

Naushaba Habib

Right to left: Mansoor Haq, Arif Sethi, and Naiyer Habib

Left to right: Ayman Aboguddah, Naiyer Habib

Left to right: Naiyer Habib, Abdul Qayyum, Arif Sethi, and Mansoor Haq

First row: Zeba Hashmi, her daughter,
Nargis Bhimji, and Tracy Abdou;
Second row: Sana Ahmed, Naushaba Habib,
Samina Ahmed, and Qudsia Qayyum

Left to right: Nargis Bhimji, Naushaba Habib, Zeba Hashmi, and Tracy Abdou

Nargis Bhimji (*left*) Samina Ahmed (*right*)

Left to right: Nusrat Jalil, Nargis Bhimji, Naushaba Habib

Nargis and Samina

Conferences

Annual conferences were arranged on important topics relevant to the objective of the Muslims for Peace & Justice. Speakers of high caliber were chosen for lectures and discussion. Conferences were held for the duration of two days each year 2002, 2003, 2004, and 2005.

It was open to public with special invitations to dignitaries and politicians.

The media was invited. Cable Regina recorded all proceedings. Highlights of the program with speakers are presented here. The recorded program on DVD is available with me (at my cost) till I am around.

Letters to Politicians
and
Their Responses

None of the politicians responded in any manner to our request of invitation or to send a representative to attend.
Lorne Nystrom attended on our personal invitation to him.
Mr. Spencer sent regrets to our personal invitation.

Letters to Politicians

Muslims for Peace & Justice
P.O. Box 28044
Regina, SK.
S4N 7L1
E-mail: muslims4peace@yahoo.ca

Naiyer Habib	M. Mansoor Haq	Zeba Hashmi	Arif Sethi	Riazuddin Ahmed
President	Vice-President	Secretary	Treasurer	Public Relations
(306)766-6999	(306)949-7165	(306)790-9787	(306)586-9049	(306)789-0416

Rt. Hon. Jean Chrétien
Prime Minister
Leader of the Canadian Liberal Party
House of Commons
Ottawa, Ontario, K1A 0A6

Dear Sir,

I have the pleasure of introducing to you the Muslims for Peace & Justice [MPJ] group in Regina, Saskatchewan, which was formed shortly after the September 11, 2001 terrorist attacks in the United States. The objectives of MPJ are to educate and inform the public about Islam and Muslims and to promote peace and justice in Canada and abroad.

The horrible event that took place on September 11th has affected the lives of North Americans, including Muslims in the United States and Canada. There is apprehension among the Muslim communities due to the talk of war with Iraq. In Canada, Muslims are proud of the country they live in, and want to lead peaceful, moral and productive lives as contributors to Canadian society as they have continued to do so.

As part of our activities to promote understanding of Islam, peace and justice, we are holding a one-day conference on October 12, 2002 at the University of Regina. Please find an attached poster announcing the program of the conference and the program

An important subject of discussion during the conference is a panel presentation on 'Waging War to Change Regimes in the Muslim World – Positions of the Federal Canadian Political Parties'. The war drums are resounding louder and louder in the United States. We as concerned Canadians would like to hear the positions of your government and Canadian politicians representing the federal political parties.

Therefore, we request your office to arrange for a speaker to represent the views of your government. Please advise the name of your representative by September 17, 2002 in order to finalize the conference program.

Yours truly,

Dr. Naiyer Habib, M.D;FRCPC
President, Muslims for Peace & Justice

Muslims for Peace & Justice
P.O. Box 28044
Regina, SK.
S4N 7L1
E-mail: muslims4peace@yahoo.ca

Naiyer Habib	M. Mansoor Haq	Zeba Hashmi	Arif Sethi	Riazuddin Ahmed
President	Vice-President	Secretary	Treasurer	Public Relations
(306)766-6999	(306)949-7165	(306)790-9787	(306)586-9049	(306)789-0416

Rt. Hon. Stephen Harper
Leader of the Canadian Alliance Party
House of Commons,
Ottawa, Ontario, K1A 0A6

Dear Sir,

I have the pleasure of introducing to you the Muslims for Peace & Justice [MPJ] group in Regina, Saskatchewan, which was formed shortly after the September 11, 2002 terrorist attacks in the United States. The objectives of MPJ are to educate and inform the public about Islam and Muslims and to promote peace and justice in Canada and abroad.

The horrible event that took place on September 11th has affected the lives of North Americans, including Muslims in the United States and Canada. There is apprehension among the Muslim communities due to the talk of war with Iraq. In Canada, Muslims are proud of the country they live in, and want to lead peaceful, moral and productive lives as contributors to Canadian society as they have continued to do so.

As part of our activities to promote understanding of Islam, peace and justice, we are holding a one-day conference on October 12, 2002 at the University of Regina. Please find an attached poster announcing the program of the conference.

An important subject of discussion during the conference is a panel presentation on 'Waging War to Change Regimes in the Muslim World – Positions of the Federal Canadian Political Parties'. The war drums are resounding louder and louder in the United

States. We as concerned Canadians would like to hear the positions of Canadian politicians representing the federal political parties.

Therefore, we request your office to arrange for a speaker to represent the views of your political party. Please advise the name of your representative by September 17, 2002 in order to finalize the conference program.

Yours truly,

Dr. Naiyer Habib, M.D.FRCPC.
President
Muslims for Peace & Justice

Muslims for Peace & Justice
P.O. Box 28044
Regina, SK.
S4N 7L1
E-mail: muslims4peace@yahoo.ca

Naiyer Habib	M. Mansoor Haq	Zeba Hashmi	Arif Sethi	Riazuddin Ahmed
President	Vice-President	Secretary	Treasurer	Public Relations
(306)766-6999	**(306)949-7165**	**(306)790-9787**	**(306)586-9049**	**(306)789-0416**

Rt. Hon. Mr. S. Day
Foreign Affairs Critic
Canadian Alliance
House of Commons
Ottawa, Ontario, K1A 0A6

Dear Sir,

I have the pleasure of introducing to you the Muslims for Peace & Justice [MPJ] group in Regina, Saskatchewan, which was formed shortly after the September 11, 2002 terrorist attacks in the United States. The objectives of MPJ are to educate and inform the public about Islam and Muslims and to promote peace and justice in Canada and abroad.

The horrible event that took place on September 11th has affected the lives of North Americans, including Muslims in the United States and Canada. There is apprehension among the Muslim communities due to the talk of war with Iraq. In Canada, Muslims are proud of the country they live in, and want to lead peaceful, moral and productive lives as contributors to Canadian society as they have continued to do so. As part of our activities to promote understanding of Islam, peace and justice, we are holding a one-day conference on October 12, 2002 at the University of Regina. Please find an attached poster announcing the program and the program of the conference. An important subject of discussion during the conference is a panel presentation on 'Waging War to Change Regimes in the Muslim World – Positions of the Federal Canadian Political Parties'. We as concerned Canadians would like to hear the positions of Canadian politicians representing the federal political parties. It is an irony that USA government is proceeding to attack Iraq but has completely ignored the Israeli and Palestinian conflicts other than passing in effective comments.

Therefore, we request your office to arrange for a speaker to represent the views of your political party. Please advise the name of your representative. We had written to Mr. Harper who sent his regret and asked I contact you. Considering the time factor I thought to contact Mr. Spencer, MP. with copy to you. He has some meeting in Ottawa that weekend and sent his regrets.

Therefore may I ask you for a favor to see that if any one perhaps an MP? From Saskatchewan can represent. I am attaching the program. The item is at 13:35 Hours on Saturday, Oct 12.

It is open conference for all to attend all or part as they wish.

Yours truly,

Dr. Naiyer Habib, M.D.FRCPC.
President, Muslims for Peace & Justice

Muslims for Peace & Justice
P.O. Box 28044
Regina, SK.
S4N 7L1
E-mail: muslims4peace@yahoo.ca

Naiyer Habib	M. Mansoor Haq	Zeba Hashmi	Arif Sethi	Riazuddin Ahmed
President	Vice-President	Secretary	Treasurer	Public Relations
(306)766-6999	(306)949-7165	(306)790-9787	(306)586-9049	(306)789-0416

Rt. Hon. Alexa McDonough
Leader of the National Democratic Party
House of Commons
Ottawa, Ontario, K1A 0A6

Dear Madam,

I have the pleasure of introducing to you the Muslims for Peace & Justice [MPJ] group in Regina, Saskatchewan, which was formed shortly after the September 11, 2002 terrorist attacks in the United States. The objectives of MPJ are to educate and inform the public about Islam and Muslims and to promote peace and justice in Canada and abroad.

The horrible event that took place on September 11th has affected the lives of North Americans, including Muslims in the United States and Canada. There is apprehension among the Muslim communities due to the talk of war with Iraq. In Canada, Muslims are proud of the country they live in, and want to lead peaceful, moral and productive lives as contributors to Canadian society as they have continued to do so.

As part of our activities to promote understanding of Islam, peace and justice, we are holding a one-day conference on October 12, 2002 at the University of Regina. Please find an attached poster announcing the program of the conference.

An important subject of discussion during the conference is a panel presentation on 'Waging War to Change Regimes in the Muslim World – Positions of the Federal Canadian Political Parties'. The war drums are resounding louder and louder in the United

States. We as concerned Canadians would like to hear the positions of Canadian politicians representing the federal political parties.

Therefore, we request your office to arrange for a speaker to represent the views of your political party. Please advise the name of your representative by September 17, 2002 in order to finalize the conference program.

Yours truly,

Dr. Naiyer Habib, M.D.; FRCPC.
President, Muslims for Peace & Justice

Muslims for Peace & Justice
P.O. Box28044
Regina, SK
S4N 7L1
E-mail: muslims4peace@yahoo.ca
In the Name of Allah, Most Kind, Most Merciful

October 3, 2002

Hon. Mr. Lorne Nystrom, MP-NDP
Regina-Qu'apelle, SK

Re: Conference on Islam and others October 12, 2002

We are so grateful to note that you will be presenting the views of your party Re Item in Section C of the finalized attached program.

I am attaching the letter addressed to Rt. Hon. Alexa McDonough, Leader of the NDP party who has so kindly agreed to send you. This is self-explanatory.

Please take your seat in the front row of the auditorium, which will have reserve sign along with your spouse who is more than welcome. Please ask for me or Mr. Riaz Ahmed. Please do not hesitate to call if you have any question.

Please attend all or part of the session as you please. It is open session for all. So any one can attend

Thank you so much.

Sincerely yours,

N Habib

Dr. Naiyer Habib, MD;FRCPC;FACC
President, Muslims for Peace & Justice

Muslims for Peace & Justice
P.O. Box 28044
Regina, SK S4N 7L1
E-Mail: muslims4peace@yahoo.ca

In the Name of God, Most Kind, Most Merciful

CBC TV Fax 347 9635 CBC Radio Fax 347 9635 Z99 – FM Fax 347 8557

CHAB Country 800 Fax 306 692 8880 CJME Radio Fax 347 8557

CKRM Radio/CHMX, Fax 781 7338, CTV Regina Fax 522 0991

Global Television Network Fax 721 8055 Leader-Post Fax 565 8812

Dear Sir / Madam:

Subject: Conference on Islam and Muslims Post 9/11 on October 12, Saturday '02

It gives me a great pleasure to announce that Muslims for Peace & Justice has arranged a Day-long conference on October 12 '02 on Islam and related subjects post Sept 11 incidence according to the attached program at the Main auditorium in the Education Building, University of Regina.

I have the pleasure of introducing to you the Muslims for Peace & Justice [MPJ] organization in Regina. MPJ is an organization formed by members of the Muslim community of Regina shortly after September 11, 2001 to educate and inform the general public about the religion of Islam and Muslims, to foster better relationship as well as communication on the basis of mutual understanding.

We invite you as Our Media in the city of Regina and for our province to send your representatives. We will appreciate any broad cast. There are political and religious discussions as it appears in the program. The Islamic Scholar is highly educated and knowledgeable person.

We request you to let all your department members and staff know. They may be interested to attend. Conference is open with no admission fee. I am faxing copy of poster and program with this letter.

Your contact person is ZebaHashmi, (306) 790-9787. Alternately you may contact me 766 6999 or any of the moderator on the program.

Hope to see you all.

Sincerely yours,

Dr. Naiyer Habib, M.D; FRCPC; FACC, President

Naiyer Habib & Mahlaqa Naushaba Habib

Muslims for Peace & Justice
P.O. Box 28044
Regina, SK
S4N 7L1
E-Mail: muslims4peace@yahoo.ca

TO SCHOOLS   September 7, 2002

Dear Sir/Madam,

I have the pleasure of introducing to you the Muslims for Peace & Justice [MPJ] group in Regina. MPJ is an organization formed by members of the Muslim community of Regina shortly after September 11, 2001 to educate and inform the general public about the religion of Islam and Muslims. We are having a conference entitled "Islam in Canada Post 9/11" on Saturday, October 12th, 2002 at the University of Regina. The conference will last from 9am to 4pm. Admission is free for all.

All staff and students from your collegiate are encouraged and welcome to attend all or part of the session. We look forward to seeing you at the conference. Please find an enclosed program and poster for further information and circulation at your institute.

Yours truly,

N Halil

Dr.Naiyer Habib
President
Muslims for Peace & Justice

Muslims for Peace & Justice
P.O. Box 28044
Regina, SK
S4N 7L1
E-mail: muslims4peace@yahoo.ca

Naiyer Habib	M. Mansoor Haq	Zeba Hashmi	Arif Sethi	Riazuddin Ahmed
President	Vice-President	Secretary	Treasurer	Public Relations
(306)766-6999	(306)949-7165	(306)790-9787	(306)586-9049	(306)789-0416

TO COMMUNITY
Dear Brothers and Sisters,

Assalamo Alaikum WRB,

Kindly find the attached program regarding the day-long conference on Saturday, October 12 '02 at the main Auditorium in the Education building on University Drive South - watch for the sign of the Education Building on your left as you drive East on entry from Wascana Parkway.

We urge your participation. Please spread the word to other Muslims whom you know. Some addresses I might not have. Please inform non-Muslims at work and others as well.

PLEASE BE ON TIME. ALL PROGRAMS WILL START ON TIME. IT IS OPEN CONFERENCE TO PUBLIC
Your attendance specially for the political program at 11 AM is of vital importance

We will appreciate any donation that you can give payable to Muslims for Peace & Justice. We will not be able to issue you any tax-deductible receipt as we are trying to look into tax exemption status for the organization. An advocacy group may not be able to get such privilege.

Wassalaam
Jazakallah Khair

Naiyer Habib & Mahlaqa Naushaba Habib

Thank you,

[signature]

Dr. Naiyer Habib,
President
306 766 6999

BABY SITTER HAS BEEN ARRANGED IN ROOM 114 near the auditorium. Please see the attached form. May contact Sr. Zeba Hashmi or Mrs. Habib for any assistance. Tele # below

---

Annual Conferences

The organization carried out annual conferences to fullfil its objective by selecting appropriate topics and speakers as it appears in its Program. Invitations went to the public, politicians, and organizations.

It was publicized by individual letters to them, Cable Regina community program, and news media.

Program

Master of Ceremony
Br. Omar Farooq, President, Muslim Student Association (U of R)

Morning Session

Session A: Moderator - Br. Omar Farooq

9:15 - 9:45 am — Opening Qur'an recitation - Br. Daoud Khalifa; Translation: Br. Kashif Ahmed
Observe one minute of silence for victims of violence and war in the world.
Welcome Address by MPJ President: Dr. N. Habib
Islam and Muslim Life in Canada Post 9/11- Opportunities and Challenges: Sr. Zarqa Nawaz

Session B: Moderator - Dr. N. Habib

9:45 - 10:30 am — Islam - the Misunderstood Religion, Key Note Address by Imam Shabir Ally (Toronto)

10:30 - 10:45 am — Questions & Answers

10:45 -11:00 am — Break

Session C: Moderator - Br. R. Ahmed

11:00 - 11:45 am — Canadian Political Perspectives on Waging War to Change Regimes in the Muslim World - Who is Next After Iraq?
Liberal
Mr. Roy Bailey (CA)
Honourable Lorne Nystrom (NDP)
Prof. S. Juyal (U of R)

11:45 - 12:00 am — Questions & Answers

12:00 - 1:30 pm — Lunch break - on your own (Zuhr Prayer - 1:15pm Stage of Auditorium)

Afternoon Session

Session D: Moderator - Dr. A. Aboguddah

1:30 - 2:15 pm — Peaceful Muslim Co-existence with Others: Let the Qur'an Speak by Imam Shabir Ally

2:15 - 2:30 pm — Questions & Answers

Session E: Moderator - Br. R. Ahmed

2:30 - 3:15 pm — Canadian Perceptions/Expectations of the Muslim Community Post 9/11
Presentation & Panel Discussion
Prof. F. V. Greifenhagen, Religious Studies, Luther College
Prof. Terry Marner, Chair, Regina Multi-faith Forum
Mr. Gerry Klein, University Editor, Saskatoon Star Phoenix

3:15 - 3:30 pm — Questions & Answers

Session F: Moderator: Dr. A. Aboguddah

3:30 - 4:00 pm — Place of Muslim Women in the Society - Home, Work, and the Mosque by Imam Shabir Ally

4:00 - 4:15 pm — Questions & Answers

4:15 - 4:30 pm — Closing remarks by Dr. N. Habib, supplication by Dr. M. Haq

---

In the name of Allah, most Gracious, most Merciful
Muslims for Peace and Justice presents
a 2002 conference on

Islam and Muslim Life in Canada Post 9/11- Challenges and Opportunities

Saturday, October 12, 2002

Education Building, Main Auditorium,
University Drive South
University of Regina
Free Admission

Key Note Speaker:
Imam Shabir Ally

For more information, please contact:
N. Habib 766-6999; M. Haq 949-7165;
Z. Hashmi 790-9789; A. Sethi 586-9049;
R. Ahmed 789-0416

P

Free Parking
East of Education Building, Lot 3 Middle
Section University Drive East, Lot 14,
University Drive South. With sign
"Authorized M permit holder area and
Lot 17 University Drive East.
Metered Parking is free on the weekend.

The lectures are available on DVD discs

Elaborating about the Conference to the Media

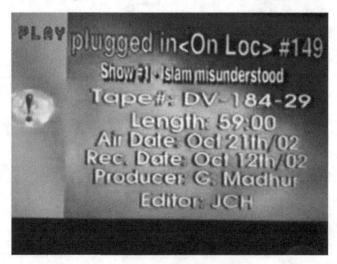

President's Welcome Address at MPJ Conference 2002

Peace and Blessings of Allah be on all of us.

I will like to welcome you all on behalf of the Muslims for Peace & Justice organization. This organization was formed soon after the incidence of 09/11 to deal with this impact and to foster mutual relationships and understanding between Muslims and others. We have chosen some of the topics that will reflect the matters that we are going to discuss.

I will like to add a few comments. There is a great deal of growing apprehension in the Muslim population in the West and suffering in the United States at the government's hands. A case of Mr. Baloch is well known. Mr. Baloch was a Pakistani Canadian waiting for some extension of his visa in the USA, and was put in confinement in a 5 x 7 cell with no windows and a flashing light from the door for six months. He was later released with no fault found and there are many who are suffering right now. Canadian government did object, but it was not listened to. He was released when the USA wanted to.

Muslims left their homes with no return. There is no plan of return. They live peacefully and are contributing to the nation as anybody else. It was never expected, the treatment of Muslims after 09/11 as of Japanese loyal citizens at the time of Pearl Harbor. So far, Canada has not followed and we hope it does not. We have to stand for Canada as for its protection. Things are likely to worsen as the situation in the Middle East escalates. There is light in the tunnel because the majority of Westerners and especially Canadians are standing by the side of the Muslims. It will be up to the Muslims to explore it, co-operate and co-ordinate with them.

As to Islam, it has been a misrepresented and misunderstood religion in the West. It will not only be misunderstood and misrepresented by non-Muslims, but also by Muslims themselves. Many non-Muslim and Muslim authors admirably and truthfully have authored Islam, which nullify these misrepresentations. There will always be Franklin Graham describing Islam as an evil religion as well as Pat Robertson and lately Falwell calling the Prophet Muhammad (PBUH) a terrorist.

Another topic, the topic of Muslim women in Islam, seems always to attract the most attention of all. On one side, women are to be covered from head to toe, confined in their home and even eliminated from some Mosques. On the other side, women scholars are emerging. They indicate that Islam has been interpreted by men, who have interpreted to suit themselves. We have a topic to discuss that.

Neglected Palestinian issue and pretext to go to Baghdad and even beyond as it is reflected in an article that I have put outside by Pat Buchanan. It reflects the morality or immorality of nations, who are joining one by one siding with one another. I hope Canada as we understand it or as we understood it when we decided to make it our home, will stand on justice and morality. As I said at the peace rally, when nations derail from the path of humanity and honesty, it ignites hatred; the flame of hatred engulfs nations to burn. There has never been a superpower everlasting, but the power of God and when things have gone extreme, God has replaced them and I quote you from Sura 6, Ayah 6 of Qur'an, "*See they not how many of those before them We did destroy?- generations We had established on the earth, in strength such as We have not given to you - for whom We poured out rain from the skies in abundance, and gave (fertile) streams flowing beneath their (feet): yet for their sins We destroyed them, and raised in their wake fresh generations (to succeed them)."*

God bless us all. God bless you all.
Thank you.
Dr. Naiyer Habib
FACP, FRCPC, FACC

Moderator

Guest speaker Imam Shabir Ally

Post Speech Media Interview

Speakers

Moderator

Speakers

Add-on Program

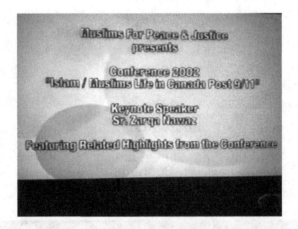

Audience

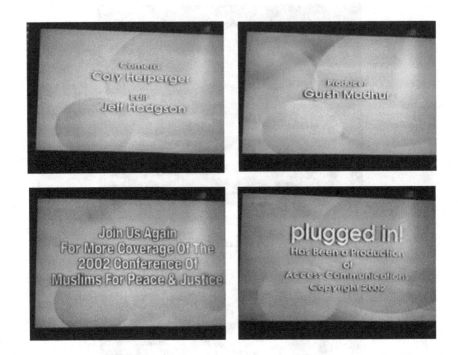

Annual Conference 2003:
Letters of Invitation

MPJ Saskatchewan Muslim Voice on Public Affairs
Muslims for Peace & Justice

P.O. Box 28044
Regina, SK
S4N 7L1
E-mail: muslims4peace@yahoo.ca
Tel: 1-866-284-5910 URL: mpjregina.tripod.com

September 4, 2003

In the Name of God, Most Kind, Most Merciful

Dear Friends

Subject: Second Annual MPJ Conference on Saturday October 4th 2003

It gives me a great pleasure to invite you to attend the above conference. Muslims for Peace & Justice has arranged a day-long conference on Saturday October 4th '03 with the theme of "Breaking Barriers & Building Bridges." I have attached the program to be held in the main auditorium in the Education Building, University of Regina. Day program is open to public.

MPJ is an organization formed by members of the Muslim community of Regina shortly after September 11, 2001 to educate and inform the general public about the religion of Islam and Muslims, to foster better relationships as well as communication on the basis of mutual understanding among all. We provide speakers and material on Islam if asked for.

The topic of Canadian Muslims and Media is an award winning research project of Canadian Islamic Congress primarily by Dr. Elmasry. The topic of "Spiritual Fitness for life", a book authored by Dr. Elmasry, is of special interest drawing widespread publicity and commentaries from media and others. There are other notable speakers such as Mr. Blakeney, the banquet topic for which seats are limited. "Breaking Barriers and Building Bridges" is such that we all have to work as Canadians.

We are enclosing the program, registration form (not needed if not attending the banquet), and bio data of the keynote speaker, Dr. Elmasry.

We invite you to attend with your family and staff. You may extend invitations to others.

Please call us if you have any questions.

Sincerely yours,

Dr. Naiyer Habib,
President, MPJ, Regional Director Canadian Islamic Congress

MPJ Saskatchewan Muslim Voice on Public Affairs
Muslims for Peace & Justice

P.O. Box 28044
Regina, SK
S4N 7L1
Email: muslims4peace@yahoo.ca
Tel: 1-866-284-5910
URL: mpjregina.tripod.com

In the Name of God, Most Kind, Most Merciful

September 4, 2003

Respected Reverend, Members of the Church

Dear Sirs and Madams

Subject: MPJ Conference on Saturday October 4th 2003

It gives me a great pleasure to invite you to attend the above conference. Muslims for Peace & Justice has arranged a day-long conference on Saturday October 4th '03 with the theme of "Breaking Barriers & Building Bridges." I have attached the program to be held in the main auditorium in the Education Building, University of Regina. I have also attached a registration form, which is only required if anyone wishes to attend the evening banquet.

MPJ is an organization formed by members of the Muslim community of Regina shortly after September 11, 2001 to educate and inform the general public about the religion of Islam and Muslims, to foster better relationships as well as communication on the basis of mutual understanding among public and interfaith groups. We provide speakers if asked for.

The topic of *"Spiritual Fitness for Life"* will be of special interest to your church group. Dr. Elmasry has authored this book. It has received attention and commentary of media and others. Summary of commentary is enclosed.

We request you to kindly distribute copies to all your church groups and congregations and extend our invitation to them. You may make copies for distribution or contact us to send you.

If you cannot open the program if emailed to you, please let us know. Please call us if you have any questions.

Sincerely yours,

Dr. Naiyer Habib,
President, MPJ & Regional Director, CIC

MPJ Saskatchewan Muslim Voice on Public Affairs
Muslims for Peace & Justice

P.O. Box 28044
Regina, SK
S4N 7L1
Email: muslims4peace@yahoo.ca
Tel: 1-866-284-5910 URL: mpjregina.tripod.com

In the Name of God, Most Kind, Most Merciful

September 4, 2003

Respected Members of the Council, City of Regina

Dear Sir/ Madam

Subject: MPJ 3rd Annual Conference on Saturday September 18th, 2004

It gives me a great pleasure to invite you to attend the above conference. Muslims for Peace & Justice has arranged a day-long conference on Saturday **September 18th 2004** with the theme of **"Islam in the 21st Century: Discovering Contemporary Muslim Religious Thought."** to be held in the main auditorium in the Education Building, University of Regina. **There is an evening banquet at the Hotel Saskatchewan as well.** I have attached the day program, which is open to the public.

We are enclosing a flyer, the program, and the registration form. Registration may be done on site on the day of the conference. If you intend to have lunch or/& attend the banquet, you are required to register in advance.

MPJ is an organization formed by members of the Muslim community of Regina shortly after September 11, 2001 to educate and inform the general public about the religion of Islam and Muslims, to foster better relationships as well as communication on the basis of mutual understanding among all. We provide speakers and material on Islam if asked for.

We invite you to attend with your family and staff. You may extend this invitation to others.

If you cannot open the program emailed to you please let us know. Please call us if you have any questions.

Sincerely yours,

Dr. Naiyer Habib, President

Naiyer Habib, President 766 6999

Tracey Abdou, Vice-President 525 9173

Zeba Hashmi, Secretary 790 9789

M. K. Arif Sethi, Treasurer 586 9049

Riazuddin Ahmed, Public Relations 789 0416

Kashif Ahmed, Communications Director 789 0416

MPJ Saskatchewan Muslim Voice on Public Affairs
Muslims for Peace & Justice

P.O. Box 28044
Regina, SK
S4N 7L1
Email: muslims4peace@yahoo.ca
Tel: 1-866-284-5910
URL: mpjregina.tripod.com

In the Name of God, Most Kind, Most Merciful

September 4, 2003

To the Members of the Muslim Community

Dear Brothers and Sisters in Islam,

Assalamo Alaikum Wa Rahmatullahe Wa Berkatahu,

I request you to join the Muslims for Peace & Justice or at least participate in its activities. MPJ has entered into its 3rd year of establishment. During this, it Alhamdulillah has achieved much more than its resources. Thanks to Allah SWT under whose blessing the untiring effort of the board of directors and ongoing efforts of a few members of the community have allowed MPJ to achieve its goal. It can do more. Insha Allah.

MPJ does not belong to individuals. It belongs to you. By joining in its effort you will be participating in building the Mosaic of Islam and Muslim component of Canadian Society. The strong efforts of our national advocacy organizations, such as Canadian Islamic Congress (CIC) and Council on American Relations - Canada (CAIR-CAN) are worthy of note.

You may help these organizations and your home organization, MPJ. You can assist by being a member, giving a donation, even a small amount, and in participating in its activities. Your ongoing suggestions will be of great value. Please let us know if you have found a negative aspect of MPJ that has kept you away from it. We will do our best to honor your suggestion. You ought to consider serving on the board. We are always looking for active and intuitive people to serve on the board.

You can donate whatever you can. We ask for a membership fee of $100 and donation of $50 once a year to allow MPJ to keep up the momentum of its activities. Since the organization is an advocacy group, it does not have tax exempt status.

We ask you to attend the second annual conference hosted by MPJ on Saturday October 4th '03 with your family, friends, and neighbors. May we request you to copy the program and distribute it in your neighborhood in the mailboxes and at your places of work. The program and registration form is self explanatory. They'll be forwarded to you shortly.

We have planned the conference according to the present situation. Dr. M. Elmasry is a professional engineer and very knowledgeable about Islam and politics. His curriculum vitae is enclosed for your perusal. He authored the book, *"Spiritual Fitness for Life"*. It received widespread praise and publicity. Canadian Islamic Congress is an award winner for "How Muslims were Represented in Media". This was a researched primarily by Dr. Elmasry. Both are the topics of the conference. You will also note other guests of high caliber and topics of interest.

Please make sure to participate in all elections actively. Muslims are the least participating group in political activities. According to statistics in USA, Muslims participated 10 to 15% where as Jews 60 to 70% in elections. It is now time for us to come out and get involved in the community and national affairs in order for us to make a difference.
Wassalaam,

Yours truly in Islam,

Dr. Naiyer Habib, President MPJ & Regional Director, Canadian Islamic Congress

MPJ Saskatchewan Muslim Voice on Public Affairs
Muslims for Peace & Justice

P.O. Box28044
Regina, SK
S4N 7L1
Email: muslims4peace@yahoo.ca
Tel: 1-866-284-5910 URL: mpjregina.tripod.com

In the Name of God, Most Kind, Most Merciful

September 4, 2003

Hon. Ralph Goodale
Minister of Public Works
M.P., Regina Wascana
310 University Park Drive
Regina, Saskatchewan
S4V 0Y8

Dear Sir:

I would like to extend an invitation to you requesting your attendance and participation at the Muslims for Peace & Justice (MPJ) 2003 Convention taking place on Saturday, October 4, 2003.

Muslims for Peace & Justice (MPJ) is a Saskatchewan-based Muslim outreach & advocacy organization, dedicated to developing a more vibrant and mainstream Muslim community. Moreover, MPJ is committed to presenting an Islamic perspective on important issues within Canadian public affairs.

This year's convention theme is *"Breaking Barriers & Building Bridges."* As part of the proceedings, we will be having a panel session on the topic of *"Canada's Relationship with the Muslim World: Present & Future"*. MPJ is requesting members of parliament from different political backgrounds to offer their perspectives on this important subject. The session will run from 11:30 AM to 12:15 Noon. In addition, MPJ will be having an evening banquet dinner at the Regina Delta Hotel from 5:30 PM to 8:30 PM.

It would be our pleasure if you could attend both of these proceedings. MPJ strongly believes in fostering a healthy and strong relationship between Muslims and non-Muslims in this great nation of Canada.

I await your positive response so that we can discuss your participation in detail. You can contact me directly at (306) 766-6999 or call MPJ at the number listed above.

Sincerely,

Dr. Naiyer Habib
President

Registration and Child Care
Muslims for Peace & Justice
2003 CONVENTION
"Breaking Barriers & Building Bridges"
Saturday, October 4, 2003
10:00 AM – 3:30 PM & 5:30 PM – 8:30 PM
University of Regina & Delta Hotel

REGISTRATION FORM

- **Day Program Fees: $5/person** - Under the age of 12 and Students with proper ID are FREE – the payment of $5/person can also be paid at the Convention Auditorium on the morning of Saturday, October 4, 2003. (*** *Note - Lunch will be provided by MPJ **at cost** to the Convention participants – choice of Vegetarian or Tuna Sandwiches***)*

- Childcare/Babysitting provided during Day at $5/child per session (Morning or Afternoon)

- **Evening Banquet Fees: $25/person** (Limited Seating – 150 people **Deadline: September 25, 2003** – FREE Parking at Delta Hotel - Halal Chicken will be served as the Main Course for everyone – Otherwise, please indicate below the alternate choice of the Salmon Main Course)

- **You will receive your Banquet/Registration ticket at the Reception Desk**

- **Full Convention Discount: $25/person** (includes Day Program & Banquet)

PLEASE PRINT CLEARLY

Name(s):
    1) _____
    2) _____
    3) _____
    4) _____
Address: _____
City: _____ **Province:** _____ **Postal Code:** _____
Phone: () _____ **Email:** _____
Method of Payment: **Cheque** _____ **Cash** _____
Attending: (Please mark an X below, beside only one choice)
Only the Day Program _____ **Only the Banquet**
Full Convention _____
Banquet Dinner: (Please mark an X below **only if you do not** want Chicken as your Main Course)
Salmon Main Course _____ For how many people? (please circle) 1 2 3 4

Please send cash or make your cheque payable to "Muslims for Peace & Justice" *and mail it with your registration form to the address:* Muslims for Peace & Justice P.O. Box 28044 ~ Regina, Saskatchewan S4N7L1. If you have any questions or concerns, please call MPJ at 1-866-284-5910

Muslims for Peace & Justice
2003 CONVENTION

Child Care Registration Form

Saturday, October 4, 2003 10:00 AM–3:30 PM
University of Regina Room # Posted, near Auditorium

Name of Child: _____

Age: _____

Name of Child: _____

Age: _____

Name of Child: _____

Age: _____

Name of Child: _____

Age: _____

University of Regina

Muslim Students' Association (MSA)
****

September 12, 2003
Dr. Naiyer Habib
President
Muslims for Peace & Justice
P.O. Box 28044
Regina, Saskatchewan
S4N-7L1

Dear Dr. Habib,

Asalaamu'alaikum Wa Rahmatullahe Wa Barakatehu.
I am pleased to inform you and Muslims for Peace & Justice (MPJ) that the University of Regina Muslim Students' Association (MSA) has approved the sponsoring of the MPJ 2003 Convention taking place on Saturday, October 4, 2003 at the Education Building, University Regina.

The MSA looks forward to working with MPJ in making this year's convention a vibrant event. MSA members will be helping to administer the day's proceedings to ensure a smooth convention.

Yours in Islam,

Shahryar Khan
MSA Interim President

Annual Conference 2003

Program

In the name of Allah, Most Gracious, Most Merciful

**Muslims for Peace & Justice
2003 CONVENTION**

Co-sponsors:
Canadian Islamic Congress (CIC)
Muslim Students' Association (MSA)

"Breaking Barriers & Building Bridges"
Saturday, October 4, 2003

University of Regina & Delta Hotel
10:00 AM – 3:30 PM & 5:30 PM – 8:30 PM

Admission
Day Program: $5.00 / person
(may be paid at the Convention entrance)

Evening Banquet Fees: $25.00 / person
(Register in Advance by September 20, 2003)

Full Convention Discount : $25.00 / person

Under age of 12 & Students with proper ID are FREE for the Day Program Only

KEY NOTE SPEAKER

DR. MOHAMED ELMASRY
National President of
Canadian Islamic Congress

FREE PARKING
East of Education Building, Lot 3 Middle Section University Drive East, Lot 14, University Drive South, With sign *Authorized M permit holder area and Lot 17 University Drive East Metered Parking is free on the weekend.
Free Parking at the Regina Delta Hotel

Morning Session	Main Auditorium, Education Building, University of Regina Master of Ceremony Dr. Samiul Haque	
10:00	Registration	
10:30 – 10:45	Opening & Prayer – Fatih Hamad Welcome: Dr. Naiyer Habib – MPJ President & CIC Regional Director	
10: 45 – 11:15	**Session A: Moderator - Riazuddin Ahmed – MPJ Community Relations Director** *Canadian Muslims & the Media – Award Winning CIC Research* Dr.Mohamed Elmasry	
11:15 – 11:30	Question & Answer	
11:30 – 12:00	**Session B: Moderator – Hamid Javed – Muslim Civil Rights Activist** Panel Session – *Anti-Terror Law & Canadian Civil Liberties* Speakers: Prof. Allan Blakeney, Canadian Civil Liberties Association Representative from Justice Canada	
12:00 – 12:15	Question & Answer	
12:15 PM	Lunch – *Provided by MPJ at a cost to Convention participants*	
Afternoon Session	Master of Ceremony Zeba Hashmi – MPJ Secretary	
1:30 – 2:15	**Session C: - Moderator – Tracy Abdou – MPJ Vice President** Keynote Address: Dr. Mohamed Elmasry *Spiritual Fitness for Life*	
2:15 – 2:30	Question & Answer	
2:30 – 3:15	**Session D – Moderator Dr. Ayman Aboguddah – President, Regina Huda School** Panel Session - *Canada's Relationship with the Muslim World* Speakers: Lorne Nystrom, Member of Parliament, NDP Larry Spencer, Member of Parliament, CA *Foreign Policy & International Trade* - David Orchard, Former PC Party Leadership Candidate	
3:15 – 3:30	Question & Answer	
3:30	Closing Remarks: Dr. Naiyer Habib	
	MPJ Evening Banquet – Regina Delta Hotel Master of Ceremony – Zarqa Nawaz	
5:30	Reception	
6:00	Welcome: Dr. Naiyer Habib – MPJ President & CIC Regional Director	
6:10	Greetings from the Government of Canada	
6:15	Greetings from the Government of Saskatchewan	
6:20	Greetings from the City of Regina	
6:30 – 7:30	Banquet Dinner (7:15 Maghrib Prayer – Led by Dr. Mohamed Elmasry)	
7:40	**Keynote Address: Dr. Mohamed Elmasry** *Breaking Barriers, Building Bridges* **Moderator: Kashif Ahmed – MPJ Communications Director**	
8:15	Closing Remarks: Dr. Naiyer Habib - MPJ President & CIC Regional Director	

If you have any questions or concerns, please contact MPJ at 1-866-284-5910

Presidential address

2nd Annual Muslims for Peace & Justice Convention, Presidential Welcome Address

October 4, 2003

In the name of God, Most Kind, Most Merciful. I greet you with the Islamic greetings of Assalamo Alaikum. WRB, that is, peace be upon you and the mercy of God be on you.

I would like to extend our welcome to all our audience—the general public, speakers, political leaders, and members of Churches, Synagogues and Hindu Temples to whom all we have extended our invitation.

We welcome the representatives of the press, police force and intelligence services.

We thank all our speakers, the majority of whom have traveled from far away. They will be introduced in detail by their moderators in their sessions.

I am very much disappointed with our governing party who ignored us despite advanced notice and a request to send even an alternative or a simple regret by phone call from the office, or even a letter to be read here. They did the same last year. Minister of of Justice's office was also unable to send a speaker on anti-terror law.

This tells the Muslims to get involved in politics vigorously. However, you all are here. It is a great pleasure, sense of honor and encouragement to have you with us. Our mutual understanding of the Canadian Mosaic will help us co-exist peacefully with prosperity. It will make our new home Canada, which we all cherish, a more unique country from economy to morality.

I will give you a brief background of Muslims for Peace & Justice. This was formed after the incidence of 9/11 to remove the misunderstanding about Islam and Muslims and to deal with any injustice. 9/11 was one of the most recent acts of horror, not the only one in human history. This occurred at our next door. This reminds us other horrors of the past. There were approximately 1500 Muslims killed in this horror but we did not hear this in the media. This act of terror was launched by a group of Muslims misquoting Qur'an out of context to justify terror. Similarly other religious books can be misquoted out of context. 9/11 brought terror to

Muslims and Arabs and to the people who resembled them, namely Sikhs and Hindus in USA as well as in Canada, by the government and by the people.

Many Muslim organizations stood for the challenge, namely Canadian Islamic Congress, Council of American Islamic Relationships and Muslims for Peace & Justice. We limit our activity to Saskatchewan. There are many other organizations in the USA and some in Canada.

The public has started to understand. We do not see much positive response from the government. They have started to realize our presence. Muslims are primarily professionals and workers. They are working, minding their business and serving the country and society.

They are not much of a people of media know-how. The media also ignored their contribution to the country and society. You will hear more of this from Dr. Elmasry. Things have started to improve. Saskatchewan media have been cooperative with us all along.

Muslims are here to stay. The majority of them came here to enjoy democracy. Democracy has received a dent for them because of recent incidences and their treatment by the government and by the public, to some extent in Canada but much more in the United States of America.

We need the support of public and justice from government. We all should remember that it was Japanese and Italian then and now Muslims – who next?

We must build society and elect a government that must stand above all of what we see happening today.

Dialogue by all and with all, especially with Muslims now, will create a healthy and just society and establish appropriate government.

Now regarding the conference, last year we had topics of important aspects of Islam. These have been shown by Cable Regina throughout the year. Thanks to Cable Regina for this community service.

This year we have parted from it. Next year, we will bring a mixture of topics, God willing! This year we are focusing on important topics according to the program.

Muslims in Canada and media will reflect - who and what about Muslims and how media reported on Islam and Muslims. It is improving. Saskatchewan media have been fair to us.

We must know anti-terror law and how it affects civil liberties. We need protection but is it the way to do that?

The Patriot Act of USA and Anti-terror Law in Canada have terrorized Muslims and Arabs. These have turned USA as well as Canada into almost a police state. According to a recent New York Times article, the Patriot Act is being used for many other crimes.

It seems the anti-terror law and the Patriot Act were made by a majority group of people, which will not affect their group, but the minority Muslims and Arabs. Their representation was heard but was not taken into account.

The topic of Spiritual Fitness for Life will be self-explanatory in the words of our renowned speaker and national Muslim leader, Dr. Elmasry.

As to Canada's relationship with the Muslim world, I will leave this question to the speakers. Is it the Muslim world of the Muslim mass or the world of the Muslim mass ruled by kings and dictators that are appointed or supported by the West, out of which some are turning into terrorists? Should we attempt to bring democracy to these countries?

As to international trade, we must look up to the Third World and East Europe, rather than have dependency on our neighbor. Various incidents and the most recent example of Mad Cow Disease teach this. Our neighbor's best friend is our neighbor itself, and rightly so. We must take this into our lesson-learning experience.

Our foreign policy must be Canadian, based on justice, honesty, caring attitude and dignity. I think our Iraq experience seems to point in the right direction of our government.

However, we have to do more. The world is a global village. Justice, honesty, caring attitude and dignity are respected. They last for ever.

Riazuddin Ahmed
Moderator

Hamid Javed
Moderator

Allan Blakeney

Merv Phillips

Spiritual Fitness for Life

Master of Ceremonies Zeba Hashmi

Moderator Tracy Abdou
(the nameplate of Zeba Hashmi was left on the podium)

Dr. Elmasry

Ayman Aboguddah
Moderator

Lorne Nystrom

David Orchard

Moderator

Breaking Barriers, Building Bridges

MPJ 3rd Annual Conference 2004

Islam in the 21st Century:
Discovering Contemporary Muslim Thought

Form for letter of invitation sent out to dignitaries, organizations, the media, and Muslim communities:

MPJ Saskatchewan Muslim Voice on Public Affairs
Muslims for Peace & Justice

P.O. Box 28044
Regina, SK S4N 7L1
Email:info@mpjsask.org
306 535 0155
www.mpjsask.org

In the Name of God, Most Kind, Most Merciful

Dear Sir/Madam

Subject: MPJ 3rd Annual Conference
on Saturday September 18th 2004

It gives me a great pleasure to invite you to attend the above conference. Muslims for Peace & Justice have arranged a day-long conference on Saturday **September 18th 2004** with the theme of **"Islam in the 21st Century: Discovering Contemporary Muslim Religious Thought"** to be held in the main auditorium in the Education Building, University of Regina. **There is an evening banquet at the Hotel Saskatchewan as well.**

I have attached the program. I have also attached a registration form, which is only required in advance if anyone wishes to attend the evening banquet and/or takes lunch; otherwise they can register on site on the day of the conference. A flyer is also attached for general circulation and posting. Please visit our website: www. mpjsask.org

MPJ is an organization formed by members of the Muslim community of Regina shortly after September 11, 2001 to educate and inform the general public about the religion of Islam and Muslims, to foster better relationships as well as communication on the basis of mutual understanding among public, intercultural and interfaith groups. We provide speakers if asked for.

We request you to kindly distribute copies to all staff, members, friends, relatives, organizational groups, churches and congregations and extend our invitation to them. You may make copies for distribution or contact us to send you. If you cannot open the program, if emailed to you please let us know. Adobe reader is required which can be downloaded free from: http://www.adobe. com/products/acrobat/readstep2.html).

Please call us if you have any questions. We are looking forward to your participation in this event with speakers of high caliber.

Sincerely yours,

N Habib

Dr. Naiyer Habib, M.D; FRCPC; FACC
President, MPJ & Regional Director, CIC

MPJ

Saskatchewan Muslim Voice on Public Affairs
Muslims for Peace & Justice

P.O. Box 28044
Regina, SK S4N 7L1
Email:info@mpjsask.org
306 535 0155
www.mpjsask.org

In the Name of God, Most Kind, Most Merciful

Assalamo Alaikum wa Rahmatullahe wa barkatehu

Subject: MPJ 3rd Annual Conference
on
Saturday September 18, 2004

It gives me a great pleasure to invite you to attend the above conference. Muslims for Peace & Justice have arranged a day-long conference on Saturday **September 18th 2004** with the theme of **"Islam in the 21st Century: Discovering Contemporary Muslim Religious Thought"** to be held in the main auditorium in the Education Building, University of Regina. **There is an evening Banquet at the Hotel Saskatchewan as well.**

I have attached the program. I have also attached a registration form, which is only required in advance if any one wishes to attend the evening banquet and/or takes lunch; otherwise they can register on site on the day of the conference. A flyer is also attached for general circulation and posting. Please visit our website: www. mpjsask.org

MPJ is an organization formed by members of the Muslim community of Regina shortly after September 11, 2001 to educate and inform the general public about the religion of Islam and Muslims, to foster better relationships as well as communication on the basis of mutual understanding among public, intercultural and interfaith groups. We provide speakers if asked for.

We request you to kindly distribute copies to all brothers, sisters, staff, members, friends, relatives, organizational groups, and extend our invitation to them. You may make copies for distribution or contact us to send you. **If you cannot open the program, if emailed to you please let us know. Adobe reader is required which can be downloaded free from the internet (copy and paste in the Address of internet:** http://www.adobe.com/products/acrobat/readstep2.html**).**

Please call us if you have any question. We are looking forward to your participation in this event with speakers of high caliber.

Wassalaam

Sincerely yours,

N. Halil

President, MPJ & Regional Director, CI

Registration and Seating for Ladies (Optional)
REGISTRATION MPJ 2004 CONFERENCE

- **Conference Fees: $10/person or $15/family** – Under the age of 12 and students with proper ID are FREE. Register at the reception desk on the day of the Conference (*** *Note: Lunch will be provided by MPJ **at cost** to the Conference participants – This requires advanced registration by September 5th, 2004*)

- **Childcare (at cost)** provided during Conference & Banquet. Register in advance by August 31, 2004. Please contact the MPJ General Secretary Zeba Hashmi at (306) 790-9789 to register your child

- **Banquet Fees: $35/person** (Limited Seating: 200 people – **Deadline: September 5th 2004** – Halal Chicken will be served as the Main Course for everyone. Otherwise, please indicate below the alternate choice of the Fish/Vegetarian Main Course

- **Conference & Banquet: $35/person** – Register in advance by August 31, 2004

- You will receive your **Registration & Banquet ticket at the reception desk** on the day of the Conference

- **Conference Donors: 1.** $100 donation – Entitles free Conference registration for one (1) person, but Banquet ticket is extra **2.** $200 donation – Entitles free Conference registration & Banquet ticket for one (1) person **3.** $250 or more donation – Entitles free Conference registration & Banquet tickets for two (2) persons

<u>PLEASE PRINT CLEARLY (Attach extra sheet if more than 4)</u>

Name(s):
      1) _____
      2) _____
      3) _____
      4) _____

Address: _____
City: _____ **Province:** _____ **Postal Code:** _____
Phone: (__)_____ Email: _____
Method of Payment: **Cheque** _____   **Cash** _____

Attending: **(Please mark an X below beside only one choice)**

Only the Conference _____ Only the Banquet _____ Both _____

Lunch: I would like to have lunch at the Conference:
YES _____ NO _____ for how many
Egg Salad Sandwich, Soft drink and Salad $7.50/Person

Banquet Dinner Choice:
(Please mark an X beside "Fish" or "Vegetarian" ONLY if you do not want Chicken as your Main Course)
Fish ____ # of People (Please circle) 1 2 3 4 Vegetarian ____ # of People (Please circle) 1 2 3 4

Please send cash or make your cheque payable to "Muslims for Peace & Justice" and mail it with your registration form to the MPJ P.O. Box 28044 Regina, Saskatchewan S4N 7L1give it to an MPJ Board Member Muslims for Peace & Justice (MPJ). For questions or concerns, call MPJ at **(306) 535-0155** or e-mail us at info@mpjsask.org

Sign on Chairs:
"OPTIONAL RESERVED
Seats for Ladies"

Note: It was optional for ladies to sit as they pleased but provision was made for those who wished to sit separate from men (An example of leadership to accommodate the wishes within Islamic parameters).

MUSLIMS FOR PEACE & JUSTICE

In the Name of Allah, Most Gracious, Most Merciful

3rd Annual MPJ Conference

Islam in the 21st Century: Discovering Contemporary Muslim Religious Thought

Speakers

Prof. Jamal Badawi

Prof Jamal Badawi, PhD is the Director of the Islamic Information Foundation and is a professor of Management at Saint Mary University, Halifax. He has authored many books and articles on Islam and produced 350 half hour segments TV shows on Islam. He lectures extensively on Islam in North America and abroad

Shaikh Ahmad Kutty

Doctorate degree from McGill University, He is specializing in Shariah. Imam and lecturer at the Islamic Institute of Toronto and non-Resident Imam of various Islamic Centers

Prof. Amir Hussain

Is a member of the Department of Religious Studies at the California State University. He is an Islamic Scholar, Author, Researcher and Award winner.

Registration

Conference: $10/person or $15 Per family

(may be paid at the Conference entrance)

Students with ID—Free for Conference

Discount : Conference & Banquet: $35/person

Evening Banquet Fees: $35/person

(Register in Advance by September 5, 2004)

University of Regina & Hotel Saskatchewan
September 18th, 2004
9:00 AM – 5:00 PM & 6:30 PM – 9:00 PM

MUSLIMS FOR PEACE & JUSTICE

P.O. Box 28044
Regina, SK S4N 7L1
Tel: 306.535.0155
E-mail: info@mpjsask.org
Website: www.mpjsask.org

Please contact us for more information.

Meet the Speakers Reception – Regina Huda School

7:00 PM	Opening – Recitation of Quran
7:05 PM	Welcome: Tracy Shier, MPJ Vice President
7:05 – 7:30 PM	Meet the Speakers Reception
7:30 – 7:45 PM	Isha Prayers
7:45 – 9:00 PM	**Moderator: Riazuddin Ahmed, MPJ Member**
	The Currents in the Contemporary Muslim Religious Thought In the West and East
	Panel Discussion by all invited guest speakers
	Closing Dua

In the Name of Allah, Most Gracious, Most Merciful

**Muslims for Peace & Justice
2004 CONFERENCE**

**ISLAM IN THE 21ST
CENTURY:
DISCOVERING
CONTEMPORARY MUSLIM
RELIGIOUS THOUGHT**

Friday,
September 17, 2004

Regina Huda School
40 Sheppard Street
Regina, Saskatchewan

Speakers

Prof. Jamal Badawi
Prof. Jamal Badawi is the director of the Islamic Information Foundation, Halifax, Canada. Prof. Badawi is a professor of Management at Saint Mary University in Halifax.
He has authored several books and articles on Islam and designed and participated in the production of nearly 350 half-hour segments of a TV series on Islam.
He has lectured extensively in North America and abroad, and is an excellent speaker on a variety of topics including Islam & Christianity. He is expert in Christian-Muslim Dialogues. Prof. Badawi is also a member of the Islamic Society of North America (ISNA) Fiqh Council. An Egyptian by birth, he obtained his Ph.D. in Business Administration.
Active in journalism and broadcasting he has had a series of programs concerning Islamic belief and practices shown on Canadian television throughout the world.
In Canada, he is the author of a number of books and articles on Islam.

Shaikh Ahmad Kutty
Educational background
- 1975-1980: McGill University, Montreal: Doctoral Studies; Specialized in Shari'ah Thought.
- 1972-1973: University of Toronto: Masters in Islamic Studies.
- 1968-1972: Islamic University of Madinah, Saudi Arabia: Licentiate in Usul al-Ddeen (first rank).
- 1957-1967: Islamiyya College: Graduated in the Traditional Islamic Sciences and received the 'Ijazah (title) of al-Faqih fi al-ddeen (first rank).
Career/experience
1. Presently: Senior Lecturer/Imam at the Islamic Institute of Toronto & and a non-resident Imam/Khatib (orator) at the following centers/mosques in Toronto: Islamic Center of Canada, Islamic Center of Canada, Bosnian Islamic Center, and Ansar Mosque
2. 1984-1994: Director/Imam Islamic Foundation of Toronto
3. 1979-1982: Director/Imam: Islamic Center of Toronto
4. 1973-1975: Assistant Director: Islamic Center of Toronto

Prof. Amir Hussain
Prof. Amir Hussain is a member of the Department of Religious Studies at California State University, Northridge, where he teaches courses in world religions. His own particular specialty is the study of Islam, focusing on contemporary Muslim societies, specifically those in North America. His academic degrees (BSc, MA, PhD) are all from the University of Toronto where he received a number of awards, including the university's highest award for alumni service. Amir's PhD dissertation was on Muslim communities in Toronto. Amir taught courses in religious studies at several universities in Canada. He is active in academic groups such as the American Academy of Religion (where he is co-chair of the Religion, Film and Visual Culture group, and serves on the steering committees of the Study of Islam section) and the Canadian Society for the Study of Religion, publishing and presenting his work at conferences. Amir is also interested in areas such as religion and music, religion and literature, religion and film and religion and popular culture Amir has won a number of awards at CSUN, both for his teaching and research. In 2001 he was selected for the outstanding faculty award by the National Center on Deafness. For the academic year 2003-04, he was selected as the Jerome Richfield Memorial Scholar. Amir will be on sabbatical in the Fall semester of 2004, working on a textbook entitled Muslims: Islam in the 21st Century.

In the Name of Allah, Most Gracious, Most Merciful

Muslims for Peace & Justice
2004 CONFERENCE

ISLAM IN THE 21ST CENTURY: DISCOVERING CONTEMPORARY MUSLIM RELIGIOUS THOUGHT

University of Regina & Hotel Sask
Saturday, September 18, 2004
9:00 AM – 5:00 PM & 6:30 PM – 9:00 PM

Admission
Conference: $10/person or $15/family
(may be paid at the Conference entrance)

Banquet Fee: $35/person
(Register in Advance by September 5, 2004)

Under age of 12 & Students with proper ID are FREE for Conference only

A BLOCK OF SEATS ARE AVAILABLE FOR LADIES WISHING TO SIT SEPARATELY

P
FREE PARKING

East of Education Building, Lot 3 Middle Section University Drive East, Lot 14, University Drive South, With sign "Authorized M permit holder area and Lot 17 University Drive East Metered Parking is free on the weekend.

Main Auditorium, Education Building, University of Regina
Master of Ceremony: Tracy Shier – MPJ Vice President

9:00 – 9:05 AM	Opening Prayers
9:05-9:15 AM	Welcome Address by Dr. Naiyer Habib, MPJ President
9:15 – 10:00 AM	**Session A - Moderator: Dr. Naiyer Habib, MPJ President** *Normative Muslim Beliefs and Practices in the Interfaith Context (Areas of Commonality and Particularity)* **Speaker: Prof. Jamal Badawi**
10:00 – 10:15 AM	Question & Answer
10:15 – 11:00 AM	**Session B - Moderator: Kashif Ahmed, MPJ Communications Director** *Concept of Jihad and Traditional Practices– Do Ends Justify Means in Islam?* **Speaker: Shaikh Ahmad Kutty**
11:00-11:15 PM	Question & Answer
11:15-12:00 PM	**Session C - Moderator: Prof. F. Greifenhagen, Religious Studies, U of R** *Human Rights and Responsibilities in Islam – Current Practices and Challenges for the 21st Century* **Speaker: Prof. Amir Hussain**
12:00-12:15 PM	Question & Answer
12:15 - 1:25 PM	Lunch on your own (available for advanced requester $7.50/person) Zuhr Prayer
	Master of Ceremony **Dr. Samiul Haque, MPJ Community Relations Director**
1:30-2:15 PM	**Session D – Moderator: Zeba Hashmi, MPJ General Secretary** *Gender Equity in Islam – Scripture VS Culture* **Speaker: Prof. Jamal Badawi**
2:15-2:30 PM	Question & Answer
2:30-3:15 PM	**Session E – Moderator: Dr. Ayman Aboguddah, President, Huda School** *Traditional Islamic Fiqh (Laws) –Its Development and Implementation* **Speaker: Shaikh Ahmad Kutty**
3:15-3:30 PM	Question & Answer
3:30-3:45 PM	**Coffee break**
3:45-4:30 PM	**Session F – Moderator: Riazuddin Ahmed, MPJ Member** *The Impacts of Contemporary Muslim Religious Thought* **Panel Discussions by All Guest Speakers**
4:30-4:50 PM	Question & Answer
4:50-5:00 PM	Closing Remarks: Riazuddin Ahmed, Vote of Thanks: Dr. N Habib **Closing Dua: Dr. Samiul Haque, MPJ Community Relations Director**
	MPJ Evening Banquet – Hotel Saskatchewan
6:30-7:00 PM	Reception Quranic Recitation – Prof Amr Henni & Welcome by Tracy Shier
7:00-8:00 PM	Banquet Dinner
8:00-9:00 PM	**Moderator: Riazuddin Ahmed, MPJ Member** *A Clash or Dialogue of Civilizations?* **Prof. Amir Hussain**
9:00 PM	Closing Remarks: **Riazuddin Ahmed, MPJ Member** **Closing Dua: Prof. Amr Henni, MPJ Director**

Muslims for Peace and Justice
2004 Conference

Islam in the 21st Century:
Discovering
Contemporary
Muslim Religious
Thought

On Location #315
Muslims for Peace & Justice '04 - Part 1
Tape#: DV184-117
Length: 59:30
Rec. Date: Sept. 20/04
Producer: Dr. Naiyer Habib
Editor: GC

Opening By Amr Henni –Qur'an Recitation

Tracy Abdou, Vice-President MPJ
Master of Ceremonies

Presidential Address

President's welcome address at the third annual conference of Muslims for Peace & Justice at Regina on September 18, 2004—Dr. Naiyer Habib.

In the name of God, the Compassionate, the Merciful. Praise is to God the Lord of the universe and peace and prayers are upon all of the prophets and His final prophet and messenger Ahmed Mujtaba Mohammed Mustafa (SAWS). The peace and blessings of God be with you all. I welcome you all to our third annual conference.

My special welcome to our guest speakers alphabetically:

Dr. Gamal Badawi of St. Mary University, Halifax
Professor Amir Hussain, California State University
Sheikh Ahmed Kutty, Islamic Institute of Toronto.

They will be introduced in detail in their sessions. Our sincere thanks to them for sparing the time for us from their ever busy schedules. God bless them.

This conference would not have been successful without your participation and financial support. We thank you for that. We hold such conferences to highlight some aspects of Islam that are relevant to the time. Muslims for Peace & Justice was formed by us immediately after the 9/11 incident to remove misunderstandings about Islam and Muslims and to defend Muslims who were maligned or victimized. They are still facing problems today on an ongoing basis, not as much in Canada but certainly in Canada and almost regularly in the U.S.A.

Some of the remarks that follow are in no way for our audience or the majority of the citizens of the world but for an aggressive minority who are able to drive their agenda very dominantly against us. These are the feelings which some or many of us have. I remain apprehensive that some Muslim enemies be it a nation, a group or an individual, may create terrorism in Canada to malign Muslims to show "Look what is happening" and compel them to act against us. Canada has remained peaceful. It has not participated in mistreating Muslims and Arabs as fully as expected by the neo conservatives. I was not expecting that Arabs would be victimized in the West—the modern and civilized world of today. A friend of mine present in the audience remarked with a grim face during ethnic cleansing that was occurring in Bosnia, "I hope this does not happen to us here." I told him with a smile, "No! It will not happen here in the West. They are civilized people. There is repentance for what happened with the Japanese." Lo and behold, what is happening in the civilized society of the West? Who is the worst violator of human rights? Please note this statement "Muslims are lucky that their properties have not been confiscated and they have not been interned." Do you know whose words these are? These are the words of Ashcroft, one of the very few high ranking and very close members of the Bush administration who are driving the agenda of our friend country and the world. We are here to stay. We have burned our boat. We are loyal to our new land as second to none yet doubts are perceived about our loyalty. There are demands of condemnation of events occurring elsewhere. There is criticism of the degree of condemnation done by us to do more. Some of the talk show audiences reflect poisonous views about Muslims. Some talk show moderators and some news media choose topics that target Muslims. No doubt it is not the majority but the minority. The biased minority has an aggressive personality to dominate their thoughts and acts.

I am apprehensive. The worst is still to come. The second win of Bush will give a mandate to go further unless it learns by its mistake and rolls back. Of course, if it considers its policy to be a mistaken policy.

Problems occur elsewhere. The impact is here. People in Chechnya, Palestine and Kashmir or elsewhere are fighting their battles for their causes in the manner they can and by the means they have. It so happens that they are Muslims—down trodden by the British Empire and ruled by kings and dictators appointed or supported by the West.

What do we have to do with them in this regard?

Islam is a religion of peace but war is permissible to maintain peace if required. It is permissible in Islam to fight the aggressor who drives people from their home or confiscates their property. Such permission is reasonable and practical. This may be interpreted differently by different groups. This is like using pretext in some circumstances. Pretext has been and is being used by nations to wage war against innocent nations for self gain. History tells that. The use of pretext must be condemned.

Oklahoma bombers, fighters in Ireland are not different from these people who happen to be Muslims.

Let us understand one another, be just, not lose civility or practice double standards. These are important for ever lasting peace.

It will not be out of place for me to pass some comments on the situation of women and Muslim leadership.

As Muslims are targets of various elements, the Muslim women are targets of Muslims and non-Muslims. Their status in society is yet to be defined. They are being banned or put behind curtains or placed in the most rejected room of the Mosque. Their children are abandoning Mosques. Their men—fathers, brothers and husbands have taken back seats as obedient disciples of some *Imams* from the pulpit. This was not the case at the time of the prophets or in the early '60s or '70s when we came here. A change is to be brought and it will be, God willing. The majority of Muslim women in the West feel threatened by Islamic law, not Qur'an. Over the course of centuries Qur'an and prophetic traditions have been interpreted and I say interpreted differently by scholars or sub-scholars or non-scholars. By the latter, non-scholars. I mean people of the least knowledge but claiming the most. This has created confusion and controversies all through. This needs to be looked at.

The women scholars of Islam, although few, based on their research, claim that Islamic law, not Qur'an has biases and prejudices against women as they were made or interpreted by men.

This needs our attention jointly with open and cool minds by men and women.

Hijab or head scarf is one of the greatest targets. Muslim women with a Hijab are discriminated against. Yes, many non-Muslims do respect them. It is considered to be a sign of opression as well as a sign of breeder of terrorism. France banned it. Others are looking at it. Canadians did not approve a ban by majority, but a fair number were in favor of it. Thanks to our prime minister for reassuring Muslims. I wonder whether such comments and steps might have been taken if our respectable nuns had continued to wear their respectable attire. The majority of the Muslim women do not wear a Hijab for these reasons, although some have reacted against Mullahs. I like to see the Muslim women wearing Hijabs and sitting in the parliament. This was the case at the time of the Prophet where women used to interact. I would like them to get back into Hijabs to support those who are battling to keep Hijabs, including the non-Muslim girls supporting their Muslim girlfriends by wearing Hijabs at the time of 9/11.

Lastly, it is my appeal to Muslim leaders and to you to ask your Muslim leaders to join hands to sit together to deal with problems jointly in a concentrated effort to have credibility for the governments, the media and the public. No doubt each leader with his or her organization is doing a marvelous job but it is like blowing their own trumpets in different directions.

With these words I urge the Muslims and other citizens to be just, sincere, not follow a double standard and make efforts to co-exist together with respect, justice and honesty and also help others to do the same. Let us make our land, the world, a better place for all to live.

My friends, this is my last address to you all as the President of the Muslims for Peace & Justice as I leave Saskatchewan after 31 years of stay to begin a new chapter of our life in the next few weeks. God bless you. God bless Saskatchewan and Canada. Amen.

Moderator: Dr. Naiyer Habib

Moderator

Moderator: Prof. F. Griefenhagen

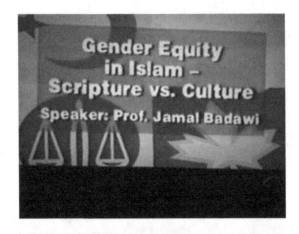

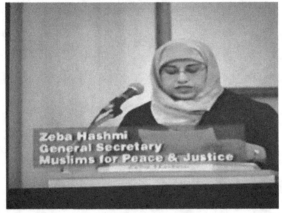

Moderator

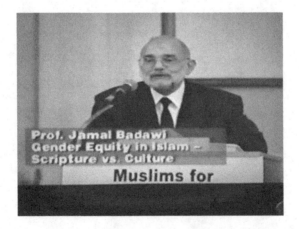

Moderator

Moderator

Forum

Audience

MPJ Evening
Dinner at Hotel Saskatchewan

Welcome by President Naiyer Habib

Award and recognition of Dr. M. Anwarul Haque as founding
president of the Islamic Association of Saskatchewan by
the founding president of MPJ on behalf of MPJ

Award of Excellence to Zeba Hashmi for MPJ

Recognition of the founding and outgoing president of MPJ by
Tracy (Abdou) Shier, Vice-President and Riazuddin Ahmed, Director of MPJ

Riazuddin Ahmed
Moderator

Guests

Left to right: Naiyer Habib, Ahmed Kutty, Samiul Haque, Ayman Aboguddah, Jamal Badawi, Qudsia Qayyum, Tracy (Abdou) Shier, Zeba Hashmi; *Back*: Amir Hussain, Amr Henni

Sitting, left to right: Anwarul Haque, Aijaz Hussain, Alex Marion, Samiul Haque

Regina Interfaith-Intergroup Peace Committee

The Regina Interfaith-Intergroup Peace Committee was formed in 1990 just before the First Gulf War started to prepare the Muslim and the Regina community to engage in a dialogue on issues of war and peace and its impact on the Regina community at large and the Muslim community in particular. This was initiated by the Islamic Association of Saskatchewan while I was the president. The idea was produced by Riazuddin Ahmed. Riazuddin Ahmed was elected the chair. I continued to represent the Islamic Association.

First informative meeting was held in the Masjid on Montague Street. All subsequent press conferences against the war also occurred in the Masjid. Later, the group transformed into the current Regina Multi-Faith Forum from 1993–1994. Father Nichols of the Roman Catholic Church was the chair. Riazuddin Ahmed served as the chair of this forum from 1994–1996. From 1996-1998, Reverend Ken Power of the United Church was the chair.

It was incredible to note the support of this cause to avert war, aiming for negotiated settlements by this group. A Christian faith group asked to help protect the Muslims and Masjid if such situation arises, seeing some onslaught of this event on Muslims elsewhere because of Iraq's declaration that it would be holy war. See further detail in the chapter on *Iraq War I*.

World Peace Day Observed by Multi-Faith Group in Pictures at Synagogue in Regina in January 2004

Riazuddin Ahmed in Multi-Faith group in Synagogue in Regina

Riazuddin Ahmed addressing as MPJ Representative

Reverend Ken Powers addressing

Standing: Dr. Raza Bhimji with cap behind Riazuddin Ahmed

MPJ Successful Award Nominations

➤ Kashif Ahmed for Youth Community Service Award of Excellence by Canadian Islamic Congress 2003 with success

➤ Ayman Aboguddah for Award of Excellence for service to the community by Canadian Islamic Congress for establishing Regina Huda School

➤ Riazuddin Ahmed for Round Table Secretariat, Public Safety, and Emergency Preparedness Canada with success

Dr. Naiyer Habib, MB.BS; MD; FRCPC; FCCP; FACP; FACC
Clinical Professor of Medicine
INTERVENTIONAL CARDIOLOGY

Regina General Hospital
3rd Floor – Medical Office Wing
1440 14th Avenue   **Fax: (306) 766-6990**
Regina, SK S4P 0W5   **Tele: (306) 766-6999**

6 July, 2003

Prof. Mohamed Elmasry, FRSC, FCAE, FIEEE
National President
The Canadian Islamic Congress
np@canadianislamiccongress.com
420 Erb St. W.
Suite 424 Waterloo, Ontario
N2L 6K6

Re: The Canadian Islamic Congress 2003 Prophet Muhammad (PBUH) **Youth** Community Service Award or **any other**.

Dear Professor Elmasry,

Assalamo Alaikum Warahmatullahe Wabarkatehu,

I like to nominate **Kashif Ahmed of 2254 Mahony Cr. E. Regina. SK S4V 1B5, 306 789 0416,** kahmed@accesscomm.ca
for the above award (or any other). Kashif is 18 years of age, a practicing, very active, innovative Muslim student. He is very mature. He is very responsible individual. He has no hesitation in taking up assigned tasks or volunteering to do tasks on his own

He is communication Director of Muslims for Peace & Justice. We appointed him on that position noting his interest and ability.

A. **He participated in the talk show on CBC:**
   1. "What's it like to be Muslim in Canada?" Recorded tapes as well as a copy of Learn at Lunch session where this topic was discussed are enclosed.
   2. Iraq war—a debate. Transcript is not available. Please note the following

The date of the Debate was Thursday March 20, 2003 at 4:00 pm on CBC Saskatchewan News. The host was Costa Maragos and the participants were:

1) **Kashif Ahmed—Muslims for Peace & Justice**
2) **Janice Goodman— Saskatoon Peace Coalition**
3) **A Student—Law School of Saskatchewan**

The debate revolved around "Did Canada make the right decision not to join the U.S. in the war against Iraq?"

In summary he said that MPJ supports Canada's decision not to join because 1) Illegal and unilateral war 2) loss of innocent human life 3) bad precedent for the future and other countries

B. **He is prompt in defense of Islam and Muslims. He wrote many such defensive articles in our local Newspaper— Leader Post as follows:**
   1. Islam not to blame for Terrorism June 12 '02
   2. Israel Stole Palestinian land Sept 24 '02
   3. Muslims must speak out Jan 9 '03
   4. Muslims unjustly maligned May 8 '03
   5. 'Atrocious' actions of Hamas contravene Islamic teaching. 25 June '03
   6. Hostile Arab States and Israel myth July 5 '03

He was instrumental in having an Islamophobic Website removed. Martin Business Services [MBS] regarding their hosting of the website **"Christian Action for Israel"** located at www.cdn-friends-icej.ca

C. **He constructed and maintains our Web page in timely fashion:**
    http://mpjregina.tripod.com

I nominate him for the award without any reservation. We wish him the best in all his endeavor and devotion. May Allah accept his services and make him a successful individual in this world and the world here after.

If you have any question, please do not hesitate to contact me.

Wassalaam,
Yours in Islam,

Dr. Naiyer Habib
Regional Director CIC, Regina
President, Muslims for Peace & Justice
drnhabib@yahoo.ca

Kashif receiving award from Dr. Elmasry, President,
Canadian Islamic Congress at the
Annual Dinner Function in Parliament Dining Hall

Ayman Aboguddah receiving award from Dr. Elmasry,
President of Canadian Islamic Congress at the
Annual Dinner Function in Parliament Dining Hall

Riazuddin Ahmed for Round Table Secretariat, Public Safety, and Emergency Preparedness

MPJ Saskatchewan Muslim Voice on Public Affairs
Muslims for Peace & Justice
P.O. Box28044
Regina, SK S4N 7L1
Email:info@mpjsask.org
306 535 0155
www.mpjsask.org

In the Name of God, Most Kind, Most Merciful

September 14, 2004

Round Table Secretariat
Public Safety and Emergency Preparedness Canada
340 Laurier Ave. West
Ottawa, Ontario K1A 0P8

I, Dr. Naiyer Habib, President, Muslims for Peace & Justice Regina, and past-president (multiple terms) of Islamic Association of Saskatchewan, Regina, have the pleasure of nominating Mr. Riazuddin Ahmed, MCIP as a member of the proposed Cross-Cultural Roundtable on National Security reporting to the Minister of Public Safety and Emergency Preparedness Canada.

I have known Mr. Riazuddin Ahmed since he arrived in Regina in 1978. Mr. Ahmed has been an energetic community activist member of the Muslim community in particular and of the larger Regina community in general.

In 1991, when the First Gulf War was looming on the horizon, he initiated and formed the Regina Interfaith-Intergroup Peace Committee to prepare the Muslim and the Regina communities to engage in a dialogue on issues of war and peace and their impacts on the Regina community at large and the Muslim community in particular. He chaired this committee for two years, and after the gulf war, he led the transformation of this committee into the present Regina Multi-Faith Forum. Since the terrorist attacks of September 11, 2001, Mr. Ahmed has played a leading role in the formation and current functions of the Regina Muslims for Peace & Justice group, and the Regina Peace Action Coalition.

Mr. Ahmed is a prolific speaker on Islamic topics and holds progressive views on contemporary issues facing Muslims in Canada and the world. Since 9/11 he has organized and delivered many workshops on Islamic topics from fundamentals of Islam to the concept of Jihad, and gender equity issues. He has shown a very good grasp of the anti-terrorism issues, the Canadian laws to fight terrorism, and the enhanced need for ensuring national security of Canada from internal and external sources.

Since the Iraq war he has strongly supported the Canadian government's policy of not sending any forces to fight in Iraq, and the need to maintain diplomatic Canadian influence on the US in respect to war and international peace issues.

Mr. Ahmed possesses excellent communication and interpersonal skills, and is experienced in working harmoniously with diverse groups, and cultures.

On behalf of the Regina Muslims for Peace & Justice, I highly recommend Mr. Riazuddin Ahmed for appointment as a member of the Cross-Cultural Roundtable on National Security.

Sincerely yours,

Dr. Naiyer Habib, M.D; FRCPC; FACC
President, MPJ & Regional Director, CIC
306 766 6999

Leader-Post Publishes:

Reginan Named to Roundtable
Ryan Ellis
The Leader-Post

Thursday, February 10, 2005

A Regina man named to a new federal government roundtable to discuss national security matters says he hopes that the new group can play a role in "(bridging) the gap between the Muslim community and the security work going on at the hands of Canada's security agencies."

Riazuddin Ahmed was one of 15 members appointed Monday to the Cross-Cultural Roundtable on Security that has been established as a forum for the discussion of emerging trends and developments in national security matters. The group will work with the federal government by providing insights on how national security policies may impact Canada's diverse ethnic communities.

"I think some (recent) news items have created sort of a misunderstanding among the Muslim community of the purpose and the intent of the government," Ahmed said in an interview, citing the government's handling of the Maher Arar case as an example.

"I felt that there is a need to bridge this gap and approach the national security issues from the Muslim perspective in a positive way," he added.

The group was created following the release of the federal government's National Security Policy in April of last year. The policy committed itself to the creation of a group that would engage Canada's ethno-cultural and religious communities in ongoing security-related issues.

"Their collective experience, broad range of perspectives, and willingness to contribute to the development of security policy will be tremendous assets to the roundtable," said Justice Minister Irwin Cotler in a press release.

"It's going to be some interesting work," said Ahmed of his appointment, adding that the main function of the group will be to "develop communication between the government and the various segments of society, including the Muslim community."

Ahmed is actively involved in a number of local organizations, and is a founding member of both the Regina Multi-Faith Forum and the Regina Muslims for Peace & Justice.

"I have been involved with the Muslim community since 1978 when I came here (to Regina)," said Ahmed. "I understand the nature and some of the inner dynamics of the Muslim community and also some of the thinking of the Muslim community around the issue of Canadian relations. I feel that if I can contribute anything in this regard it will be a service to the country and the community."

The roundtable will convene in Ottawa for the first time in early March, working in conjunction with both the minister of justice and the minister of public safety and emergency preparedness.

Published courtesy of *Leader-Post*, Regina—Marion Marshal

MPJ Gives Award of Excellence to Individuals

- ➤ Tracy Abdou
- ➤ Dr. M. Anwarul Haque
- ➤ Zeba Hashmi
- ➤ Riazuddin Ahmed and Mrs. Samina Ahmed
- ➤ Dr. Naiyer Habib
- ➤ Dr. Mohamed Elmasry for founding Canadian Islamic Congress and representing the Muslims, Islam, and others in a dignified manner at the national level—political and media by Ayman Aboguddah*, President of Huda School, in a welcome meeting to Dr. Elmasry by MPJ

Award of Excellence to Tracy Abdou, Vice-President of MPJ
Presented by the president in 2003

Dr. M. Anwarul Haque was recognized as the founding president of the
Islamic Association in 1971 and serving in this position from 1971–1977. (2004)

Zeba Hashmi received the Award of Excellence for serving the MPJ in exemplary manner since its founding (2004).

Zeba Hasmi was an asset not only to the MPJ since its founding, but also to the community at large with her exemplary contribution, be it as an example in raising the family, being on the board of the association or Muslims for Peace & Justice. Zeba's contributions to engage in society at large, extra curricular activities, the media, and Huda School are immense and admirable, being a mother of three children by the grace of God.

Dr. Naiyer Habib received an award as Outgoing Founding President and for serving from 2002 to 2004, by MPJ, represented by Tracy Abdou, Vice-President and Riazuddin Ahmed, Communications Director of MPJ

Raizuddin Ahmed received an Award of Excellence from MPJ for his longtime service to the community in MPJ and the Islamic Association of Saskatchewan in exemplary manner.

He assumed the responsibility of presidency of MPJ after the departure of Dr. Naiyer Habib in 2004.

Dr. Mohamed Elmasry receives award as founder of Canadian Islamic Congress by Dr. Ayman Aboguddah, President of Huda School* in a meeting of MPJ while visiting as a guest speaker for MPJ conference.

End of Habib Era with Muslims for Peace & Justice

Naiyer Habib initiated and joined MPJ as one of the original three. He was elected as founding president.

Now, he decided to wind up and move from Regina with his family to Abbotsford, British Columbia.

There was provision for the Habibs to continue as trustees, but they felt not to continue as trustees of the organization, as they would not be able to contribute anything to it, living far away. Their e-mail is noted below as well.

In preparation for this, he felt, along with the trustees, the need to finalize the constitution and wind up various matters related to Muslims for Peace & Justice. A meeting was held on February 15, 2004, at Regina Huda School at 40 Sheppard Street. The following trustees were present: Ayman Aboguddah, Kashif Ahmed, Riaz Ahmed, Samina Ahmed, Sheela Ahmed, Raza Bhimji, Kheliefa Daud, Naiyer Habib, Naushaba Habib, Abbas Hasanie, Zeba Hashmi, Anwarul Haque, Samiul Haque, Raabia Hatcher, Amr Henni, Abdul Jalil, Nusrat Jalil, Zarqa Nawaz, Abdul Qayyum, Qudsia Qayyum, Shahedur Rahman, and Tracy (Abdou) Shier.

Chairman: Naiyer Habib

The meeting was opened with Surah Fatiha recited by Kashif Ahmed.

This meeting was called to finalize the constitution. It was discussed in detail and that the constitution was finalized.

Election for the Term February 2004:

Anwarul Haque and Abdul Qayyum volunteered to be election officers. Abdul Qayyum explained the seven positions that were available, which were for president, vice-president, secretary, treasurer, and three directors.

The following directors were elected:

President—Naiyer Habib

Vice-President—Tracy (Abdou) Shier

Secretary—Zeba Hashmi

Treasurer —Qudsia Qayyum

Director 1—Amr Henni

Director 2—Samiul Haque

Director 3—Kashif Ahmed

The meeting was adjourned with supplication.

Final Meeting and Election Prior to Departure of Naiyer Habib

A meeting was held at the residence of Amr Henni at 4243 Wascana Ridge, on Saturday, February 26, 2005. The meeting was primarily to prepare for the meeting of February 27, 2005. The following points were discussed and were to be dealt with in the meeting of the MPJ on February 27, 2005:

1. Opening with Qur'an recitation.
2. Review of the minutes of the general body of February 15, 2004.
3. Matters arising out of that meeting.
4. Review of the minutes of the previous board meeting—time permitting
5. Matters arising out of the minutes of the board meeting— time permitting
6. Conduction of election for all positions.
7. Review of the nomination papers and ballot papers.
8. Membership fee collection and ID card.

9. Safe keeping of the constitution.
10. Various items belonging to MPJ. Others—time permitting as advised by the board members
11. Invitation for Brother Ahmed Aboudheir

Annual General Body Meeting, Sunday, February 27, 2005, at Regina Huda School, 40 Sheppard Street

The following trustees were present: Samina Ahmed, Riazuddin Ahmed, Amr Henni, Khalid Berzoutit, Ayman Aboguddah, Fasahat Wasty, Samiul Haque, Fateh Hammad, Sheela Ahmed, Shahid Rehman, Abdul Jaleel, Khalifa Daudi, Raabia Lacher, Tracy (Abdou) Shier, Naiyer Habib, Kashif Ahmed, Ejaz Hussain, Abbas Hasanie, Arif Sethi, Raza Bhimji, Nargis Bhimji, Zarka Nawaz, Zeba Hashmi.

Ahmed Aboudheir (Guest—President, Islamic Association of Saskatchewan, Regina)

> Chairman: Naiyer Habib
> Opening recitation of Surah-Fateha by Amr Henni
> Welcome address—Tracy (Abdou) Shier

The agenda was adopted and moved by Ayman Aboguddah, seconded by Fateh Hammad, and carried unanimously.

The minutes of the meeting of February 15, 2004, were reviewed and had been recirculated. This was accepted by all.

The chair indicated that the constitution will be submitted to the corporation branch for incorporating the MPJ in the province, and subsequently, MPJ will apply to Revenue Canada for tax exemption for donors. If the incorporation branch recommends any modification in the constitution, it will require the approval of the trustees. It was accepted by all.

Note: This responsibility was to be dealt with by the elected board of this meeting.

Safe keeping of the constitution: The chair spoke about the importance of retaining an original copy of the constitution. He stated that two original copies, which are signed and initialed on every page by the president and secretary (completed) would remain with the president and secretary and any new amendment will be signed and initialled on the pages of the amendment by the current secretary and the president on an ongoing basis.

Membership card: A membership card was issued and it was pointed out that future renewal may require placement of the year of renewal for members that are trustees.

Invited guest: Ahmed Aboudheir, President of Islamic Association of Saskatchewan:

He was invited by the MPJ. He showed appreciation to the founders, members, and volunteers whose accumulative work went into forming the Islamic Association. He further stated that the Islamic Association of Saskatchewan's constitution was a great achievement, and that he will work toward maintaining it. He expressed about his vision to activate every article and protect the rights of every community member. He further mentioned that different committees have been formed. He would like to see people become members in good standing of the Islamic Association of Saskatchewan.

Elections were held and the following candidates were elected:

Riazuddin Ahmed—president for two years
Tracy (Abdou) Shier—vice-president for one year
Zeba Hashmi—general secretary for two years
Sheela Ahmed—treasurer for one year
Kashif Ahmed—director for one year
Samiul Haque—director for two years
Amr Henni—director for two years

Note: This election was according to the newly finalized constitution.

Before adjournment, Riazuddin Ahmed thanked everyone for their confidence in him and stated that he will try to build on the success of Naiyer Habib's achievements. The chair acknowledged Riazuddin Ahmed's contributions.

Riazuddin Ahmed spoke about the security roundtable objectives and mandate. He spoke of other Muslims on the roundtable. He emphasized that it was important for the Muslim community to involve itself in national level discussions and make aware to them the concerns of Muslims.

Note: For detail about the Cross-Cultural National Security Roundtable, you can go to the Government of Canada's website or look up on the Internet. Naiyer Habib had recommended Riazuddin Ahmed to be on the roundtable. He was successfully placed on the roundtable board.

Finally, the chair and president thanked all board members for their extraordinary and sincere help in the work of MPJ over the years and wished them well. He thanked all members of MPJ for their cooperation.

The meeting was adjourned with recitation from Qur'an by Amr Henni.

Trustees No More

Date:	Fri, 24 Jun 2005 12:20:41 -0400 (EDT)
From:	"Naiyer Habib"
Subject:	Trustees
To:	"Kashif Ahmed", "Riaz Ahmed", "Sheela Ahmed", "Samiul Haque", "Zeba Hashmi", "Amr Henni", "Tracy S"

Assalamo Alaikum WRB,

We pray to find you all in good health and happiness.

After considerable deliberation we decided not to continue as trustees of MPJ.

We are leaving here. We will not be active participants to contribute anything to MPJ. It is best that the seats are vacated to bring in new trustees. This will further the progress of MPJ with participation of new members.

We highly appreciate your cooperation in the work of MPJ. We appreciate much more the love and affection of our community in Regina over the years and in particular in giving us such a farewell.

We will always remember everyone,

Your Brother and Sister in Islam,

Naiyer Habib

Mahlaqa Naushaba Habib

Glossary

Logo on book cover - Bismillah hir Rahman nir Raheem Arabib: In the Name of God, Most kind, Most merciful

Ablution: Prewashing of body parts for prayers

Amen/Ameen: Seeking God's approval for supplication

Assalam o Alaikum Wa RahmatullahiWa Bara kataho: Peace be unto you and so may the Mercy of Allah and His blessing

As-salamu alaikum: Peace be upon you

Deen: Path of religion to comply with Divine law

Eid Milad un Nabi: Rejoicing the birth of the Prophet

Eid al Adha: Festival of remembering the Sacrifice offered by Ibrahim

Eid al Fitr: Festival of completion of Ramadan

Fajr: Muslim Prayer in the morning before sunrise

Fatwa: Islamic religious ruling

Hadith or Hadeeth: Saying, Deed of the Prophet

Ibn: Son of

Imam: A religious leader of knowledge

Insha Allah: God willing

Jazakallah khair: May Allah reward you with the best

Juma or Jummuah Prayer: Weekly Muslim Prayer in congregation

Karim: Generous

La illaha illallah: There is no god, but God

Masha Allah: Expression of appreciation to Allah

Masjid: Mosque

Mehndi: Decoration of hands/feet of bride with coloring leaves of henna

PBUH: Peace be upon him

Qur'an: According to Islam words of God for all mankind revealed to the Prophet Mohammad

Qur'an Karim: Karim, meaning generous, is added to Qur'an with respect

Ramadan: A month of sincere observation of religious duty, along with daily fasting dawn to dusk

Rasool or Rasul: The prophet who is declared officially to be the messenger by Allah

Sahaaba: Companion of the Prophet Mohammad (PBUH)

Sallalah-O-Alayehe Wassalam (SAW, SAWS): May Allah send blessings and peace upon him

Sharia or Shariah: Muslim religious law

Sunnah: Deed and words of the Prophet Mohammad (PBUH)

SW or or SWT or Subhanahu wa ta'ala: Glory be to Him the Most High

Tabien: A Muslim who had seen the companion of the Prophet Mohammad (PBUH)

Taqwa: Believing in God in terms of protecting self from God's displeasure

Ummah: Community

Wassalam: Peace be with you

Zuhr: Noon Prayer, when sun is just off the meridian

Printed in the United States
By Bookmasters